Arbitration Act 1996:

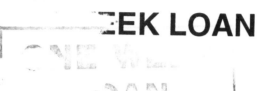

Margaret Rutherford dedicates this book to her beloved family—Michael, Marcus, Pearl, Alexander, David and Mzigi

Arbitration Act 1996: A Practical Guide

Margaret Rutherford QC, LLB, FCI Arb
A Past Chairman of the Chartered Institute of Arbitrators

John H M Sims FRICS, FCI Arb, MAE, FRSA
*A Past Chairman of the Chartered Institute of
Arbitrators and Past President of the Society of
Construction Arbitrators*

Foreword by
Rt Hon Lord Ackner PC

LAW & TAX

© Pearson Professional 1996

Margaret Rutherford and John Sims have asserted their right under the Copyright, Designs and Patents Act 1988 to be identified as the authors of this work

ISBN 085121 9829

Published by
FT Law & Tax
21–27 Lamb's Conduit Street
London WC1N 3NJ

A Division of Pearson Professional Limited

Associated offices
Australia, Belgium, Canada, Hong Kong, India, Japan, Luxembourg, Singapore, Spain, USA

First published 1996

Reprinted 1997

A CIP catalogue record for this book is available from the British Library

Printed in Great Britain by Bell and Bain, Glasgow

Contents

Contents

Contents

Introduction

The Arbitration Act is an exciting vehicle to take us boldly into the third millenium. During its prolonged gestation there was wide-ranging and comprehensive consultation of a kind rarely seen before with users of all descriptions, from judges and arbitrators to professional experts and academics, contributing suggestions, criticisms and comments. Everyone who was interested, both individuals and committees specially constituted for the purpose, like that of the Law Society, had the opportunity to 'put in their pennyworth'. All suggestions, however revolutionary, were most courteously and seriously taken on board by the Departmental Advisory Committee (DAC) of the Department of Trade and Industry (DTI) on Arbitration Law. (John Sims has been a member of the DAC since 1990.) As research and practical suggestions for improvement were tested and incorporated into various drafts, and as refinements in drafting resolved ambiguities, simplified and clarified, so the exciting and matchless Bill emerged, butterfly-like, from the dead chrysalis of the past confusion/disillusion of the law on arbitration. The writers are unashamedly enthusiastic about the new Act and, practising arbitrators both, have actively participated in encouraging its development. They will attempt in what follows to describe its innovative and far-reaching provisions.

In order fully to understand the fundamental changes which this Act has brought about, it is necessary, in the authors' view, to appreciate why those changes were in any event necessary, sometimes essential. This was in order to revitalise, indeed transform, the process of arbitration and bring back to it the commercial practicality it once had. What is set down next then, is a history of events that led to the

Arbitration Act 1996. It is most important, in the authors' view, to see the Act in the context of its conception, gestation and birth.

Following that is a brief introduction to arbitration. This is provided in the interests of completeness and in particular for any readers who may be new to arbitration and wish to get an introductory overview of the process. There may be readers who wish to skip this part of the book.

The main section of the book, starting at page 39 deals with the statutory provisions. The sections are generally set out in words which are close to, on occasions exactly the same as, those used in the statute. The previous law is considered, and changes made by the new provisions clearly spelled out. Various comments of a practical or explanatory nature, follow. Mindful of *Hedley Byrne & Co Ltd v Heller & Partners Ltd* [1964] AC 465, the writers offer no advice, but from time to time offer suggestions. For ease of reference and in order to aid memory, this part of the book is numbered to accord with the sections of the Act. Readers will note that some sections have been commented on very fully. This may be because, in the authors' view, they represent key matters, or because they introduce totally new concepts, or because the changes which they make have altered the previous law to a significant degree and therefore need to be particularly highlighted. It might be simply that the authors, in the idiosyncratic way in which writers create their work, preferred certain areas to others! Some sections, however, have much shorter commentaries, and this may be because, such is the immaculate clarity with which so much of this beautifully produced Act is written, they are self-explanatory. The writers have also, quite deliberately, repeated points from time to time. This (and similarly the setting out of the substance-matter of each section as it is referred to) is again in order to assist the reader more easily to familiarise himself with the Act and/or to commit provisions to memory. Readers will also note that the authors have interchangeably used the word 'arbitrator' for 'tribunal', as has the Act, eg references to payment of 'arbitrators' fees'. The Act mainly relies on the use of the word 'tribunal'. However, where it refers to an individual, for instance relating to immunity (s 29), it refers to 'arbitrator'. There is no significance in the authors'

choice of word, although as they are both practising arbitrators they favour that term. Politically correct readers will
frown at the emphasis throughout on maleness, in particular, genders which indicate that arbitrators are exclusively
men. Margaret Rutherford feels that if she, as an arbitrator,
is content to be 'embraced' by males, as is traditional in our
legislative interpretation, then readers will be similarly generously disposed to recognise that 'he', 'him' and 'his' refer
also, of course, to 'she', 'her' and 'hers'. The use of the one
gender rather than the other is hopefully to keep the text as
lucid and clear as the Act.

Acknowledgements

The authors are very much indebted to the DAC and for the help and guidance which they have received from the various consultation papers they have produced and generously shared. In particular the DTI Consultation Paper on Draft Clauses and Schedules of an Arbitration Bill, February 1994; DTI Consultation Paper on the Arbitration Bill, July 1995; DTI House of Lords Arbitration Bill—Notes on Clauses, January 1996; DAC (under the chairmanship of Lord Justice Saville) of DTI Report on Arbitration Bill, February 1996. They have gratefully drawn on this material and express their thanks. Any mistakes in this text, however, are entirely those of the authors alone.

Other help gratefully received by the authors came from the attendance at numerous seminars, for example that organised by Norton Rose under the chairmanship of Sir Michael Kerr (28 March 1994) on the DTI's Consultation Paper, and the Arbitration Bill Working Conference at King's College (14 July 1995), organised so efficiently by Professor John Uff and Dr Julian Lew. The authors also acknowledge with gratitude knowledge gleaned from various lectures which they attended, or Papers which they read, for example, 'Arbitration Law Reform' (the Ronald Bernstein Lecture 1990) by Mr Justice Steyn (as he then was) and Arthur Marriott; the Denning Lecture 1995, 'Arbitration and the Courts', delivered in May at Lincoln's Inn by Lord Justice Saville. There are other acknowledgements, for example to a paper by Stewart Boyd QC in *Arbitration International*, which are incorporated in the text.

Many books and journals have been studied and their authors are gratefully acknowledged. These include the

Handbook of Arbitration Practice by Bernstein and Wood, 2nd edn (*Bernstein's Handbook*); *Mustill and Boyd Commercial Arbitration,* 2nd edn (*Mustill & Boyd*); *The Law and Practice Relating to Appeals from Arbitration Awards* by Professor D. Rhidian Thomas; all recent volumes of *Arbitration,* the journal of the Chartered Institute of Arbitrators and in particular numerous thought-provoking leaders by Alan Shilston, Honorary Editor; *A Guide to the UNCITRAL Model Law on International Commercial Arbitration* by Howard M Holtzman and Joseph E Neuhaus; *International Commodity Arbitration* by Derek Kirby Johnson; *Law and Practice of International Commercial Arbitration* by Redfern and Hunter, 2nd edn; *International Commercial Arbitration* by Huleatt-James and Gould. In addition the Woolf Report, *Access to Justice,* has been most helpful, as have all editions of *Hansard,* in particular those volumes which dealt with the passage of the Arbitration Bill. All help is most gratefully acknowledged but again the authors must make it clear that all mistakes or misconceptions are theirs alone.

The authors would also particularly like to thank the College of Law, Jill (McMahon) Thomas, Mark Cato and Lord Hacking for their generous practical help. Of course, they are also deeply grateful to Lord Ackner for so kindly writing the Foreword.

Foreword

The Arbitration Act 1996 is a vital part of our commercial law. It has been ten years in the making and is a product of extensive consultation and great industry by many and particularly Lord Mustill, Lord Steyn, Lord Justice Saville, Professor Uff QC, Mr Arthur Marriott, Dr Julian Lew and Mr Geoffrey Sellers, the Parliamentary draftsman. It is unusual for its outstanding clarity, a feature of very great importance since the majority of arbitrators are not lawyers but laymen—architects, surveyors, valuers etc.

The Act provides in a comprehensive and coherent form a restatement of the current statutory law with the codification of the more important principles of arbitration law developed through cases, together with significant innovative and far-reaching reforms. As far as possible, it reflects the format and provisions of the Model Law on Commercial Arbitration developed by the United Nations Commission on International Trade Law which is well-known by its acronym of UNCITRAL.

If arbitration is to be a preferred alternative to litigation it must not only be final and fair but it must strive to be speedier and more cost effective. At the heart of the legislation lies the principle of party autonomy. Section 34(1) states, 'It shall be for the tribunal to decide all procedural and evidential matters, subject to the right of the parties to agree any matter'.

The survival of arbitration thus depends upon the good sense of the parties and their advisers, or if they agree, then upon the arbitrator to tailor-make the procedures to the particular dispute in order to achieve its fair resolution with the minimum of delay and expense. The Act confines judicial intervention to the minimum and the resort to delaying tactics by unnecessary applications to the courts should be a thing of the past.

Margaret Rutherford QC and John H M Sims, both past chairmen of the Chartered Institute of Arbitrators, are to be congratulated on their painstaking explanation of the historical background to the legislation and the purpose and practical operation of each of the many sections of the Act. This practical guide should prove invaluable to all manner of arbitrators, both the lay arbitrator and the legally qualified arbitrator, to all existing and potential users and students of arbitrations, and in particular to foreigners who use English arbitration for the resolution of international commercials disputes; together with those who appear before such arbitrators, whatever may be their particular qualifications.

Rt Hon Lord Ackner PC

Table of Cases

Table of Cases

Table of Statutes

Table of Statutes

Table of Statutes

Table of Statutory Instruments

I

Background

Chapter 1

The History of the Arbitration Act 1996

Arbitration law—general

Arbitration has an extremely long history. It was known of in Egyptian times. References are made to arbiters by Horace, Ovid and Tacitus in their writings. In the Middle Ages merchants plied their trades all over the world, and in particular travelled across Europe buying and selling merchandise at fairs. When disputes arose they had need for speedy justice with simplicity of procedure, particularly since the courts were increasingly constrained by procedural formalities. Customs of these merchants developed into legal rules. England, and in particular London, became the centre of merchants' courts for the resolution of disputes in international trade between traders from all over the world. The common law absorbed much of this mercantile law. The earliest English statute on the subject of arbitration was in 1698.

The previous statutory framework was developed principally from the Arbitration Act 1889, and that related back to earlier statutes, common law and equitable rules. By the twentieth century there was a mosaic of law, scattered in a diffuse body of cases, and with relevant statutory provisions spread across several Acts. The previous law tended to be reactive, that is to say there were statutory responses to specific perceived shortcomings in the common law which arose from time to time. However, this meant that if there were no such shortcomings the statute would be silent on that/those points and therefore some legislation lacked sufficient substance to make it comprehensible without more.

3

In short, to understand the law it was not possible simply to read existing statutes alone since they were only comprehensible when interpreted in conjunction with a huge body of case law. This was fine for those who were familiar with the law. Laymen and foreigners were considerably disadvantaged.

However, the creation, and the successful improvements in the trial procedures, of the Commercial Court helped to establish and develop principles in arbitration law and practice. They dealt mainly with shipping disputes. Together with Official Referees, a highly specialised tribunal tackling most difficult areas of building and engineering disputes, they were also largely responsible for creating the high reputation of independence, specialist expertise and fair dealing in arbitration in the United Kingdom. They adopted various fast-track procedures which led by example to a radical improvement in arbitration procedures. In certain fields, for example construction, rent review, shipping, international trade, commodities and insurance, arbitration has become the normal way of resolving disputes. London is still the leading world centre for arbitration.

Arbitration Act 1950

Until now this has been the cornerstone of arbitration law, containing some 44 sections and two schedules. However, its structure was indefensibly illogical and caused confusion and difficulty to those trying to comprehend it. For example, s 1, instead of 'beginning at the beginning', say with the appointment, somewhat surprisingly dealt with the irrevocability of authority of arbitrators. Section 2 dealt with the death of a party, and s 3 covered bankruptcy. The various powers of the court to deal with challenges of arbitrators were spread out illogically in four different places (ss 1, 10(1), 13(3) and 23(1)). Drafting and language were obscure. The Act was difficult to read. There were no rules for the detailed conduct of arbitration. It spelled out no features of party autonomy. It was largely preoccupied with the relationship between arbitration and the courts. It dealt with general matters, eg staying proceedings, appointment of arbitrators, costs, fees and interest, but was far from user-friendly.

It was subject to various amendments, for example s 19A was added by s 15 of the Administration of Justice Act 1982, and s 12(6) modified, and s 13A added, by s 103 of the Courts and Legal Services Act 1990. It used the drafting technique of 'deeming' provisions, ie 'unless a contrary intention is expressed therein, every arbitration agreement shall be deemed to include a provision that ...'. This was confusing to foreign users not used to the concept of 'deeming' provisions in contracts and even rendered agreements for arbitration in England in some foreign contracts unenforceable.

Section 21 entitled the arbitrator (or he could be ordered by the court) to state any question of law arising during the reference, or from his award, in the form of a special case for the opinion of the High Court. This procedure (Common Law Procedure Act 1854, subsequently re-enacted in the Arbitration Act 1889; in 1934 the special case and consultative case procedures were consolidated under the Arbitration Act 1950) was originally of great value, enabling the arbitrator to obtain the view of the court on difficult points of law before he made his award. The law was able to develop, to change with different circumstances and grow, and this was good.

However, after about a hundred years or so the procedure was increasingly abused. Deliberate delaying tactics by a party, possibly even taking a legal point as far as the Court of Appeal, could postpone the day of reckoning. It was even possible that the other party, finally worn down by the endless delay, might, because of the mounting costs, settle. If he did, it was invariably unfavourable. Many very experienced users of arbitration will have anecdotes which echo this deplorable situation, as have the writers. English arbitration was viewed less favourably. London's pre-eminence as a world's arbitration centre began to be challenged. Foreign users were dissatisfied with such delays and high costs. They wanted less delay, less cost. They wanted their disputes resolved with certainty. The law was ripe for reform.

Arbitration Act 1975

This Act contained important provisions relating to international arbitrations, for example staying court proceedings where a party proved an arbitration agreement, and to the ratification of the New York Convention of 1958, concerning enforcement of Convention awards. It contained eight sections. (As will be seen, the provisions in the current Act on the enforcement of Geneva Convention awards and the recognition and enforcement of New York Convention awards, have been restated.)

Arbitration Act 1979

Change was in the air. The 1980s in particular saw attempts by other countries to attract arbitration business. Many international arbitration centres were created abroad. Foreign legislation was passed to encourage international arbitration users to choose their country rather than others as places in which to hold arbitrations. The Netherlands, France, Sweden and the Far East tried to seize a share of the multimilllion-pound industry. London as an arbitration centre began to look less attractive, particularly in view of the daunting delays and expense engendered as a consequence of the 'case stated' procedure. There was a feeling abroad that English courts were too ready to intervene. This meant delay, increased cost and uncertainty.

The 1979 Act was enacted to redress some of these problems. It was largely concerned with appeals and limits placed thereon. It materially reduced the opportunities open to the parties to frustrate an award on an alleged error of law or to raise for the opinion of the court a question of law (the consultative case procedure). The Act abolished the special case procedure thus cutting down delays with which arbitration had become plagued and brought into disrepute. It established a new process for the judicial review of awards. A unitary appeal procedure was introduced based on reasoned awards. Such appeals were confined to questions of law and there was a two-stage process, ie for leave to appeal and, once leave had been given, the substantive appeal itself.

It was a short Act of only eight sections, and s 1, concerning judicial review of arbitration awards and the right of appeal on questions of law, seemed to suggest that the courts would hear an appeal on virtually any question of law which might conceivably arise from an award, no matter how remote and unlikely to succeed. This view was at first supported by a number of court decisions, not least by Robert Goff J (now

Lord Goff of Chievely), one of the outstanding legal minds of our time, who clearly read the Act as having that effect. To foreigners, this meant that arbitration would be likely to be lengthy and expensive, with large numbers of awards passing inexorably on appeal through the Commercial Court, the Court of Appeal and even the House of Lords, effectively cancelling out the benefit of the repeal of the special case procedure. The House of Lords recognised the danger. Unlike Lord Goff in his then relatively lowly position, it had the power to do something about it. The Law Lords imposed substantial conditions on the right of appeal principally through what became known as the 'Nema guidelines' (from *Pioneer Shipping Ltd v BTP Tioxide Ltd (The Nema)* [1982] AC 724; see also *Antaios Compania Naviera SA v Salen (The Antaios)* [1985] AC 191), on the grounds that the 1979 Act was intended 'to promote speedy finality in arbitral awards' (per Lord Diplock in *The Antaios*) and should be construed accordingly. These restrictions, which could only be found by perusal of the law reports and text books, while correcting an abuse, also added to the inaccessibility and complication of our arbitration law. This was now spread across three major Acts and numerous minor ones, and in substantial case law, and was seen as a major disincentive to the use of England as a forum by some foreign parties discussed below.

The most radical parts of the 1979 Act were embodied in ss 3 and 4. These permitted exclusion agreements, subject to certain rules, under which the parties could exclude the right to apply for leave to appeal, to seek an order for reasons or to apply to the court to determine a preliminary point of law. However, parties to marine, commodity and insurance contracts were regarded as a 'special category'. They were not free to exclude the right of appeal to the courts (even with leave of the court) in their contracts. Many users failed to appreciate why this distinction was necessary.

The 1979 Act also provided that while, subject to the 'special categories', parties to international arbitrations could enter into exclusion agreements at any time, parties to domestic arbitrations could only do so after a dispute had arisen. (This distinction is preserved in the present Act but provision is made for its removal in the future. It is hoped that it soon will be).

Some have criticised the 1979 Act for having been rushed through the legislative process with indecent haste, some say that it was ill-prepared, made in response to pressure from the international arbitration community. It was certainly not particularly well drafted; no one, apparently, has succeeded in fathoming the meaning of s 5 (interlocutory orders). Many cases began to build up, causing uncertainty and delay and a further loss of confidence in England as a centre for international arbitration.

Others see the Act as having occupied 'a dominant position in the contemporary law and practice of arbitration, not simply because of its precise area of concern but, more widely, because of its impact on the entire jurisprudential landscape of arbitration' (per Professor Rhidian Thomas, *Appeals from Arbitration Awards*). And of course it is undeniably true that the law which emerged from cases decided under the 1979 Act considerably enriched and developed our law. This is why the current Act largely retains the substance of the 1979 Act but additionally incorporates the restrictions imposed by case law.

Miscellaneous Acts concerning arbitration

Miscellaneous Acts also contained law relating to arbitration, for example, the Supreme Court Act 1981, and the Administration of Justice Acts 1970, 1982 and 1985. The Consumer Arbitration Agreements Act 1988, for example, provided that where a person entered into an agreement as a 'consumer' (and this was defined), an agreement that future differences between him and a businessman (ie one who is not a consumer) would be resolved by arbitration could not be enforced against him, subject to certain conditions. It was a classic example of consumer protection. No one should be deprived of his right to go to the courts for redress, and often the terms of a contract (for example, those contained in the brochure of a tour operator) contained arbitration clauses which would provide for unsettled disputes to be resolved by arbitration, a fact perhaps unappreciated by the disappointed holiday-maker when he made his initial booking. The law simply clarified the position, so that *after* the dispute arose (for example, following a disastrous holiday), the aggrieved person could then decide whether or not to litigate instead. Once having decided upon arbitration, however, and having given his written consent, he was bound by his choice.

The Courts and Legal Services Act 1990, also inserted various provisions into the 1950 Act, for example, s 13A gave an arbitrator the power, subject to certain conditions, to dismiss a claim for want of prosecution (the statutory reversal of *Bremer Vulcan v South India Shipping* [1981] AC 909 and *The Hannah Blumenthal* [1982] AC 858).

There are also numerous bodies of rules which govern the conduct of arbitrations, eg UNCITRAL Arbitration Rules, the International Chamber of Commerce Rules, a code of international arbitration rules designed for any country and under any legal system produced by the London Court of International Arbitration, those of the Chartered Institute of Arbitrators etc.

Finally, there is a huge body of case law which has built up over the years and which is to be found in the law reports. Concerns were felt that users, and in particular foreigners, found the mass of legislative provisions and precedents, set out briefly *above*, hard to find, let alone follow.

> 'We have highly developed rules and principles governing all aspects of arbitration, which is one of the main reasons why this country has been and still is a world centre for arbitration. But there is a major defect in that it is very difficult, without expert legal knowledge, to find even the most basic of the rules and principles governing arbitration' (Lord Justice Saville).

The need for change

Change was again in the air, not only in arbitration but in litigation and the development of other means by which disputes could be resolved. The Civil Justice Review in 1988, and Lord Woolf's diagnosis in 1995 of the ills at the heart of our civil justice system, revealed that excessive cost, delay and complexity were bedevilling it.

> 'It is doubtful within living memory, if ever there has been a time when such a head of steam has built up in the civil justice system in England and Wales to push through procedural reform in how disputes are judicially decided, either

through the public court or private arbitration tribunal av-
enues' (per Alan Shilston, *Arbitration*, November 1995).

Arbitration, particularly following the 1979 Act and the decision that was taken that England should not adopt the
Model Law (see below), was especially ripe for reform. It
needed 'a complete spring clean' (Lord Mustill). There was a
strong feeling that our arbitral system should take account
of the needs and wishes of the commercial and trading community. There was also increasing concern that the major
problems which affected arbitration—not only in England
but elsewhere, and not only in international circles but in
domestic arbitration as well—were excessive cost, complexity and delay. Arbitration seemed to have lost its way as a
practical, quick, and economic procedure for the resolution
of commercial disputes. For example, the construction industry was long notorious for the excessive cost and ineffi-
ciency of its dispute resolution procedures. Apparently only
in America have arbitration procedures been devised (excluding pre-trial discovery of witnesses and documents, a
feature of American litigation and much abused) which work
efficiently, quickly and comparatively cheaply.

Concerns had been felt for some time that users were increasingly unable to find their way through the inpenetrable
thicket of law and practice. They needed to know that certain principles relating to arbitration law were only to be
found in the law reports—such decisions being 'so voluminous as to be almost impenetrable to anyone except the specialist English lawyer' (Lord Mustill). There was a need for a
comprehensive and coherent statement of the principles and
practice of arbitration law, for it was becoming inaccessible
and incomprehensible to foreign and domestic users. (During the second reading of the Bill Lord Hacking told of a
comment he received from an American lawyer colleague,
that it was deemed to be an act of professional negligence in
New York, and certainly in his practice, to include into a
contract an English arbitration clause!) Of widespread concern to the commercial community was the fact that existing procedures were too time consuming and costly,
particularly in small claims, when possibly an adversarial
procedure was inappropriate. Arbitrations were aping all the
worst features of the courts. It was in the national interest

that England returned to being/remaining the centre of international arbitration as it had been for some 200 years. Commercial disputes are part of business life and something needed to be done to return English arbitration law to the position of pre-eminence it had once held.

'Without (the Act) the present unsatisfactory situation could ... have had serious repercussions for the future of London as a world centre for the arbitration of international commercial disputes' (Lord Fraser of Carmyllie).

UNCITRAL Model Law

One of the most remarkable achievements by the United Nations Commission on International Trade Law (UNCITRAL) was the publication of the Model Law in 1985. It is devoted exclusively to international commercial arbitration. Very briefly, this provides a ready-made and internationally recognised package of arbitration law which could be adopted in full or in part by those countries which, unlike England, did not have a developed and comprehensive arbitration system of their own. It is laid out in a beautifully logical order, starting at the beginning of the arbitration process and following it through to its end. It is written in plain language. This makes it both accessible and intelligible to all users. It provides 'a pragmatic and sensible consensus of what is feasible in the field of international arbitration' (Lord Steyn). In addition to the text there are *travaux preparatoires*, providing 'a rich storehouse of knowledge and insights into the working of international commercial arbitration', all available to the public. The advantages of such a Model Law are self-evident and many countries have adopted it as a more or less self-contained package.

Rejection of the UNCITRAL Model Law

A report of the Department of Trade and Industry's Departmental Advisory Committee on Arbitration Law (DAC) under the chairmanship of Lord Justice Mustill (now Lord Mustill) who had played a leading role in the formulation of the Model Law proposed by UNCITRAL, was published in 1989. After the most rigorous and detailed enquiry and extensive consultation, it was the recommendation of the DAC that

UNCITRAL should *not* be adopted by the United Kingdom (but it was adopted for Scotland). It was suggested that its effect would be detrimental. The refusal to adopt it, however, did not mean that it would be ignored. Both the structure and text provide a valuable guide or comparison against which to measure standards of legislation. In general terms it was rejected because it was felt that England, unlike many countries (eg Australia, Bulgaria, Canada, Cyprus, Nigeria, Scotland etc), had a developed and comprehensive body of arbitration laws and thus had no need for such a package (rather like, by analogy, the failure of England to 'receive' Roman law because it did not need to, already having its own common law). It is interesting to note that The Netherlands, France and Switzerland also rejected the adoption of the Model Law. It will be seen later that it was the rejection of the Model Law which contributed towards the urgently felt, and growing, need for reform.

Lord Mustill, in making this recommendation, however, considered that English statute law on arbitration was unsatisfactory in that it was widely dispersed and fragmentary. Thus the Report concluded (para 100) that only the specialist knew where the law was to be found. The Committee recommended (para 108 of the Report) that, as an intermediate solution, there should be a new and improved Arbitration Act. This should not simply consolidate existing arbitration law, but be a statement in statutory form of the more important principles of the English law of arbitration, both statutory and, to the extent that this was practicable, common law principles:

- it should be uncontroversial;
- it should be set out in a logical order in clear, non-technical language so that it was readily understandable by lay persons;
- it should generally apply to domestic and international arbitrations;
- it should not be limited to the subject matter of the Model Law;
- it should embody such proposals for legislation as have by then been enacted; and
- it should have, so far as possible, the same structure and language as the Model Law, thus enhancing its accessibility.

The wheels which had started to turn in the 1980s were gathering momentum.

Private initiative—the Marriott Group

Much valuable work was carried out by a private sector working group under the chairmanship of Arthur Marriott, himself a well-known and distinguished lawyer and arbitrator. This group, all interested in arbitration law reform, represented law firms, barristers' chambers, arbitration institutions and others. A Bill drafted by Basil Eckersley (one of the leading maritime arbitrators and a lawyer of great experience and learning), was produced by the Marriott Group and circulated for discussion and comment in May 1991. Many considered it to be a masterly achievement and it provoked great interest which spread infectiously.

The Department of Trade and Industry Departmental Advisory Committee on Arbitration Law (DAC)

The DAC, under the chairmanship of Lord Justice Steyn, (now Lord Steyn) advised from time to time on the drafting of an Arbitration Bill. In April 1992 it recommended that the DTI should take over the responsibility for the work on the Bill from the Marriott Group. In June 1992, the President of the Board of Trade said that the Bill was to be taken forward by government as a public project under the supervision of the DTI with advice and assistance of the DAC. It was proposed that the Bill should be introduced in the House of Lords. In February 1994 a draft was produced by the DAC, together with a consultation paper. It was a disappointment, particularly after the excitement engendered by the Eckersley draft. Widespread dissatisfaction was expressed during the consultation process, and masses of critical comment was received by the DAC. 'To say it was not well received would be something of an understatement' (Lord Justice Saville). Subsequently there was total abandonment of the 1994 draft. While skilfully drafted in its own terms, it simply failed to meet the basic criteria which all considered to be essential.

Consultation with users

An extraordinary amount of interest was generated among arbitration users as the development of the legislation progressed. This was unusual, and compared favourably with the response to the Mustill Committee Report. For example, bodies such as the Bar and the Law Society set up working parties to discuss and report on proposals. Firms such as Norton Rose set up seminars on the consultation paper, under the chairmanship of Sir Michael Kerr (March 1994). Working conferences were set up, for example (thanks to enormous and enthusiastic efforts of Professor John Uff QC and Dr Julian Lew) at King's College London (in July 1994 and July 1995) under the chairmanship of Lord Mustill. Various branches of the Chartered Institute of Arbitrators held meetings and submitted papers etc. Architects, surveyors, engineers, valuers, maritime, consumer and insurance experts—all were consulted or provided with opportunities for discussion. There was vigorous and informed input at every stage. There was an unprecented degree of public consultation. A very wide range of comments, suggestions, criticisms and views came from a large cross-section of arbitration users. Michael Heseltine, in answer to a parliamentary question (6 February 1995) said, *inter alia:*

'... some 158 often extremely detailed submissions were received during the period that followed the publication in 1994 of the consultation document on the draft Arbitration Bill. They are currently being considered.'

And many more followed the 1995 consultation document.

Draft Bill July 1995

Lord Justice Saville took over from (now) Lord Steyn as Chairman of the DAC in 1994. He and his team (and in particular Geoffrey Sellers, the parliamentary draftsman) worked prodigiously hard to produce the new draft Bill. Particular tribute should be paid to a young and highly gifted barrister, Toby Landau, who produced a masterly analysis of the vast bulk of responses and comment which undoubtedly helped the DAC enormously in its work. The DAC wanted

'to make the format and language of the Bill more user-friendly ... to restate the major aspects of the current law on arbitra-

tion in a clear and accessible way so that it is readily understandable to all those who are considering using arbitration
... at the same time to introduce changes which will help
[achieve] speedy and cost effective dispute resolution.'

It proposed to explain the main provisions of arbitration law
in non-legalistic English 'so that those contemplating arbitration in this country and those engaged in such arbitration will know what this entails without the need, which
exists at present, to consult experts in the subject' (consultative paper which accompanied the draft Bill). Particular importance was attached to the objective of easy comprehensi-
bility, freedom from technicality and accessibility to laymen.

Further consultation ensued and the Bill was finally introduced in the House of Lords in December 1995. There were
several matters which might have been included and were
not (for example on the question of confidentiality). Several
matters caused some problems (for example, the inclusion
of the Consumer Arbitration Agreements Act 1988 and
whether it should be re-enacted in full) and there were several areas where more radical reforms might have been incorporated, but were not, (for example, whether or not to abolish
the procedural distinction between domestic and international
arbitrations). A parliamentary slot, however, had been won
after a prolonged period of discussion and debate. The time
was right for action. The tide was at the flood. As was stated in
the Conclusion of the Final Report of the DAC (February 1996):

'... many people have stated to us that for this reason [the
need for new legislation] they were not disposed to delay
progress by stubbornly insisting on their point of view on
particular points; and have demonstrated that this is the case
by being ready and willing to reach compromise solutions.
We are convinced (as all are) that further delay will do grave
and probably irretrievable damage to the cause of arbitration
in this country, thus damaging our valuable international
reputation as well as the promotion here of this form of dispute resolution.'

It was enacted and given the Royal Assent on 17 June 1996
and comes into force on 1 January 1997. Interestingly, its
long title which was originally 'To consolidate with amendments the Arbitration Acts 1950, 1975 and 1979 and related enactments' became 'An Act to restate and improve

15

the law relating to arbitration pursuant to an arbitration agreement; to make other provision relating to arbitration and arbitration awards; and for connected purposes.'

Chapter 2

What the New Act is

The new Act is innovative and beautifully structured—'A joy to read,' said Lords Hacker and Donaldson; 'a masterpiece of drafting clarity and a model for future draftsmen,' said Lord Roskill; 'it is, I think everyone agrees, a quite exceptionally good [Bill],' said Lord Byron. Lord Mustill said 'It is a quite outstanding piece of draftsmanship and an outstanding work of scholarship'. He also said, ' True, it is long, but it is ambitious and all-embracing, in marked contrast to the meagre and inadequate legislation which it (is) designed to supplant; and also in contrast to the Model Law which, for all its merits, covers only some of the legal aspects of arbitration'. Lord Ackner spoke of 'the near unanimity on a Bill whose clarity has been praised to the rooftops'. These were just a few of the laudatory comments which greeted the second reading of the Bill in the House of Lords. It has been universally acclaimed and huge enthusiasm has been engendered.

What the Act does

By way of an overview only (as the commentaries on the sections in Chapters 5, 6 and 7 will describe the provisions in detail), this lengthier version of the 1995 draft can be summarised as follows. It is proactive, rather than reactive, with many of the deficiencies or gaps in the previous law conveniently filled in. It recasts in a clear logical fashion, in simple 'user-friendly' language, existing legislation on arbitration by consolidating the principal Acts. It uses particular and most carefully considered drafting devices (for example, it employs bracketed cross-references between sections), which make it so much easier to read than other legislation. It has also replaced 'deeming' provisions (such as 'unless a contrary intention is expressed therein, every arbitration agreement shall be deemed to include a provision that ...', a device which is legalistic and unclear to some users) by substituting a much simpler drafting technique of prescriptive statements, sometimes mandatory, such as 'unless the parties otherwise agree' or 'as the parties otherwise agree'. This follows the Model Law and the result is a much more readily understandable document. To have produced a statute where the intention of the legislature was inadequately communicated to the user would have been disastrous. This has not happened. It can be read, understood and even implemented by foreign and/or lay users.

The Act reflects the format and provisions of the Model Law in many other respects, for example competence of the arbitral tribunal to rule on its own jurisdiction (Article 16). Although the Act applies to England, Wales and Northern Ireland, and will probably be used predominantly in relation to domestic arbitrations, yet there is concern, which the Act by implication addresses, to safeguard and promote the position of England as an international commercial arbitration centre. It is 'based on the proposition that arbitration is a valid alternative to litigation as a means of resolving those disputes which inevitably arise in trade and business' (Lord Fraser of Carmyllie).

The Arbitration Act codifies important, established principles, for example, the Nema Guidelines are now incorporated into an updated version of s 1 of the 1979 Act (now repealed), thus neatly arranging the relevant law relating to appeals in a coherent and comprehensible fashion. The Act introduces changes in the law, for example, the immunity of arbitrators.

The objective of the legislation, set out—properly—right at the beginning, is to provide for the fair, speedy and cost-effective resolution of disputes by an impartial tribunal. To achieve this end a double-stranded golden thread runs through the Act: *the autonomy of the parties and the corresponding supporting role of the courts.* The parties are free to adopt whatever procedure is the most appropriate for their particular kind of dispute. This is radical and far-reaching. In the absence of such agreement default procedures in the form of model sets of rules for the conduct of the arbitration, which the parties can use, modify or exclude—whichever is preferred—are available which encourage and enable more effective management of the arbitration. Such rules include the sort of matters which might be considered, for example, when and where the proceedings will take place, the language which will be used, what sort of statements should be exchanged, whether or not to apply the strict rules of evidence etc. Parties may agree to consolidate arbitral proceedings or to hold concurrent proceedings. They may even require the arbitrator to decide the dispute not according to law but on equitable grounds.

The court's role is to support the arbitration process, rather than to interfere, which can frustrate it. Sometimes such support is necessary, for example if the machinery of appointment breaks down, or where it becomes necessary to remove an arbitrator. The critical balance between the autonomy of the parties and the intervention of the courts is addressed. The freedom of the parties to decide how the dispute is to be resolved is not absolute, however, since there are a few mandatory provisions which, on the grounds of public policy, cannot be overridden. The autonomy of the parties is strengthened by limiting judicial review. As to appeals, the courts will not interfere unless a tribunal gets it badly wrong. They would not tolerate, for example, questions of fact dressed up as questions of law.

There are innovations. For example, while there has been an established rule that an arbitrator acting in a judicial capacity is immune from liability in negligence, a new provision in the Act makes his status clear. Immunity is conferred not only on members of a tribunal, their employees and agents for anything done or omitted to be done in the discharge of their functions, save when an act or omission is in bad faith, but also (albeit a limited immunity) on arbitral institutions, extending to appointing bodies.

An important provision concerns the competence of the tribunal to rule on its own substantive jurisdiction. This is both sensible and fair. Any objection to the jurisdiction can still be challenged in the courts by a discontented party either by way of a preliminary ruling or otherwise. The part of the Act devoted to proceedings is most interestingly

19

prefaced by the general duty of the tribunal, which is to act fairly and impartially as between the parties, giving each a reasonable opportunity to put his case and deal with that of his opponent. The common law rules as to natural justice are thus restated. 'Fair' or 'fairness' is a novel innovation in an arbitration statute and this concept of reasonableness and justice permeates the Act.

Arbitrators are given enhanced powers. They can appoint lawyers or others to assist them. They are mandatorily obliged to adopt procedures which are suitable to the particular case, avoiding unnecessary delay or expense so as to provide a fair means for the resolution of disputes. A mandatory duty is also imposed on the parties to do all things necessary for the proper and expeditious conduct of the hearing and correspondingly wide powers are given to the tribunal in case of a party's default or refusal to co-operate. The tribunal may order a party to provide security for costs, give directions in relation to any property the subject of the proceedings and make property preservation orders. An arbitrator may award compound as well as simple interest, at rates other than the judgment debt rate. The court has far-reaching powers for the enforcement of peremptory orders which have not been complied with.

The Act is divided into mandatory provisions and the much more important non-mandatory provisions. Mandatory provisions are set out in Sched 1 and are effective notwithstanding any agreement by the parties to the contrary. They include such matters as stay of legal proceedings, power of the court to extend agreed time limits, application of the Limitation Acts etc. The non-mandatory provisions are those which encourage the parties to make their own rules and provisions regarding proceedings, but in so far as they fail or deliberately choose not to do this a model set of rules for the conduct of the arbitration can be used. The parties may include, exclude or modify these rules: it is their choice.

Has the Act succeeded in its aims?

Lord Steyn, in the Ronald Bernstein Lecture 1990 on 'Arbitration Law Reform', spoke of Sir Mackenzie Chalmers. He was a superb draftsman who was responsible for drafting the Bills of Exchange Act 1882, the Sale of Goods Act 1893 and the Marine Insurance Act 1906. He has the reputation of having attained a simplicity and precision which was always a desired aim. He always strove to adhere closely to what he saw as the ideal, which was to state the law as he thought it was. Thus he considered that any reform of the law should first incorporate existing common law in statutory form. The authors would most respectfully add that the age of superb draftsmen is not dead. The Arbitration Act is lucidly drafted with great skill, making it user-friendly and comprehensible. No longer do we need to look back for perfection.

The Act incorporates existing common law, in particular relating to the appeal structure. It consolidates the principal Acts. It is the authors' view that it achieves a logicality of structure, a clarity of expression, a gratifying simplicity of language and explanation which will be readily understood by all users, which will result in the Act ranking among the best of our statutes. 'It is truly an (Act) designed to take English arbitration into the twenty-first century' (Lord Lester).

Criticisms can of course always be made. However, there can be little doubt that, properly understood and applied, the Act bids fair to revolutionise the practice of arbitration in England and Wales and Northern Ireland. Under previous legislation and practice, arbitrators were almost entirely in the hands of the parties, or more likely, their legal advisers. There was very little arbitrators could do to drive the proceedings forward and to enforce their orders and directions without the co-operation and agreement of the parties. This has now been completely reversed, so that where the Act confers certain powers on the arbitrator, he will only *not* have those powers if there is unanimous agreement between the parties that he should *not* have them. If there is not unanimous agreement he *has* the powers and may exercise them—for which see particularly ss 34 (procedural and evidential matters) and 41 (powers of the tribunal in case of party's default). At last arbitrators have teeth! While the principle of party autonomy does prevail so that the parties can have overall control of the proceedings if they so wish, if there is not unanimous agreement between them the arbitrator is in the driving seat. While of course he must always have regard to each individual party's wishes, and must not do what none of them want him to do, he will be in control of

21

the proceedings and has power to apply sanctions if one or other party does not comply with his directions.

Further, the attitude of the courts to arbitration is revolutionised. Section 1(c) spells it out in words which the authors do not believe appear in any other statute: 'the court should not intervene' except as provided in the Act that it may or, in some circumstances, must. The concept of there being an overriding power of the court to intervene whenever and wherever it thinks fit, no longer exists. The function of the court is primarily to support the arbitral process and to assist where necessary (see ss 42–44 which set out the court's powers to enforce an arbitrator's peremptory orders, to secure the attendance of witnesses and to support the arbitral proceedings by exercising powers which an arbitrator cannot have since he is a private individual and not an arm of the state). The court may also assist by determining important issues of law during the course of the arbitration where this would help the proceedings, and it will enforce arbitration agreements and awards except in circumstances where it would clearly be wrong to do so. The supervisory powers of the court are kept to a minimum, restricted only to intervening on the application of a party to the arbitration proceedings where things have, or may have, gone badly wrong, or to hear appeals on a strictly limited basis, on important issues of law arising from an award.

In short, the philosophy of the Act may roughly be stated as: 'if the parties have chosen arbitration, arbitration they will have'. For the good of arbitration the court is given powers to assist the process and to exercise the minimum of supervision—and that is all.

What the Act does not do

There is nothing in the Act about confidentiality or privacy, both having been assumed as a general principle in English commercial arbitrations for many years. It is axiomatic that privacy is one of the advantages which arbitration offers over litigation. There are many occasions, for example, concerning disputes over share deals, when such privacy is vital. Concern is felt by some about these matters ('an extremely serious omission' said Lord Roskill). For example, has a party the right to divulge details of the award, who were the parties to an arbitration etc? Attendance at hearings is restricted and the existence of an arbitration is private—but word sometimes gets out. The award itself may have to be revealed, for example, if there is an appeal. Can evidence and documents be released? There seems to be no clear certainty although the Court of Appeal has implied that there is confidentiality. Is it an essential element in arbitration? And should the Act have dealt with this? Should the Act have protected the confidentiality of communications between a party and his non-legal advisers or representative by extending the concept of 'legal privilege' to them? 'It would have been difficult to conceive of any greater threat to the success of English arbitration than the removal of the general principles of confidentiality and privacy' (Sir Patrick Neill, Bernstein Lecture). Should an appropriate statement of the principle that unless the parties agree, confidentiality should apply to all arbitrations to which the Act applies, have been added to the statement of general principles? After very detailed consideration of all the arguments the DAC was of the view that 'no attempt should be made to codify English law on the privacy and confidentiality of English arbitration'.

Potential problem areas

Concern has been voiced by some as to the ability of the arbitrator to handle the extensive powers with which he is now armed. Is it going too far, for example, to allow him to make declarations about a person's rights? Is this not something which should be reserved for judges? For example, Tony Bingham, a barrister and construction arbitrator, writing in *Building* (March 1996) said:

> 'It is all very well for retired law lord judges to cope with extensive new arbitral powers and to make binding unappealable awards. They are used to handling such power. But the lads and lasses who are not judges are going to need help—the architect, surveyor, engineer and technical arbitrator ... Come summer 1996, the arbitrator will be a very powerful person. In the wrong head, that power will ruin rather than revive the reputation of arbitration.'

It was Mr Bingham who likened the arbitrator to 'a biker who, having been accustomed to a 150cc BSA Bantam, now had to control a 1,000cc monster'. While the authors are regrettably ignorant of the machines to which he refers, yet they can appreciate the thrust of the analogy and accept that arbitrators should be, and will have to be, highly skilled professionals. That is not to say that arbitrators should necessarily be legally qualified, a suggestion they have heard on several occasions. But arbitrators should be experts in their primary professions with developed management skills, and with the authority and confidence to use such powers effectively. Since they are using rules they must be very familiar with them, and of paramount importance, they must possess that indefinable quality of judicial capacity. It has been suggested, for example, that the Act, and in particular s 33 (general duty of the tribunal) 'will cause the demise of the amateur arbitrator', a matter which is discussed in the commentary to that provision.

The authors have also heard concern expressed by members of the judiciary about the 'average' arbitrator's ability to deal with the complex and difficult area of costs. However, that concern is believed to be misconceived. So far as allocation of the responsibility for costs between the parties is concerned, arbitrators have always dealt with this and, inevitably with some exceptions, have done so reasonably successfully. So far as determining the amount of costs is concerned, there is an assumption that costs in arbitration should be treated in exactly the same way, and be exactly the same costs, as are 'taxed' in court in litigation. It is believed that the Act does not make that assumption and does not intend that it should be made. A clear indication is given in s 63 (the recoverable costs of the arbitration) of the principles by which costs should be determined. While the authors have sought in the commentary on the relevant sections to give some further guidance on both these aspects, they consider that the principles are perfectly clearly set out and should present no problems to the reasonably intelligent arbitrator.

Some see the Act as 'one of the most prescriptive Acts of any on the world scene' (a comment made to one of the authors by a very eminent arbitrator). The authors do not agree. The Act has enormous potential for freeing arbitration and arbitrators from the restrictions imposed by the very lack of specific procedures and powers in previous legislation and the openings that gave for the imposition of fetters on arbitration and arbitrators through the common law. As the reader will probably have gathered by now, both authors are enormously excited by this Act and the possibilities it opens for arbitration in the future to be what it ought always to have been, and once was: a quick, effective, economical method of dispute resolution having some disadvantages but many more advantages over litigation when properly applied to disputes for which it is inherently the better method of resolution. They hope that, in its small way, this book will help to achieve this.

Summary of the Act

- Objective set out
- User-friendly, easy to understand
- Autonomy of parties
- Support of the court
- Strengthening of tribunal's powers
- Restatement of existing legislation
- Codification of recent case law
- Changes in the law to improve the arbitration process
- Reflects format and provisions of the Model Law.

Chapter 3

What Arbitration is

Arbitration is a judicial process by which the parties to a dispute agree to have it settled by a person of their choice and to be bound by the decision he makes. This agreement may arise after a dispute has arisen and the parties then agree to have the matter dealt with by an arbitrator, or it may arise out of a contract which, among its various clauses, also contains a clause referring a future dispute which might arise out of that contract to arbitration. Lord Donaldson once described arbitrators and judges as 'partners in the business of dispensing justice, the judge in the public sector, the arbitrator in the private sector'. There are, however, fundamental differences between litigation and arbitration (see *below*).

The three essential elements of arbitration are:

- the existence of a dispute between the parties;
- an agreement between them, whether in the original contract or made subsequently when the dispute arose, to refer it to arbitration; and
- a decision by one or more impartial persons acting in a judicial manner by which both parties agree to be legally bound.

Users will have selected arbitration as the most appropriate process for them for the following commercial/professional reasons, because:

- they consider their dispute needs to be resolved by someone who is familiar with their field (eg an experienced surveyor in a construction dispute);
- they require the privacy which arbitration provides;

27

- in using an expert as arbitrator, the dispute can be resolved more expeditiously (and thus more economically);
- the long delays in court listings make arbitration a better option;
- or for any other reason which to them makes commercial good sense.

The arbitrator (or arbitrators—there can be more than one— and in the following text the word 'arbitrator' will be used interchangeably with 'tribunal', which is the description generally adopted by the draftsmen), is not a judge sitting in a court provided and financed by the state. He is sometimes a lawyer but often an independent, often self-employed, experienced expert in some particular field, either specifically chosen by the parties themselves (or their legal representatives), or chosen by someone to whom they have given the power as a term in their contract, for example, by the President of the Chartered Institute of Arbitrators (see below). Areas where arbitration is common include commodity transactions, financial services such as insurance and banking, maritime contracts, the construction industry and consumer contracts, such as travel, financial agreements, household appliances etc. Hundreds of thousands of arbitrations take place all over the world, but London has a reputation as a world centre, and millions of pounds-worth of international commercial work is generated there.

Differences between arbitration and litigation

By its very nature arbitration is a wholly different method of dispute resolution from litigation. It requires a different approach from the very outset. Neither is 'better' than the other, and the expression 'horses for courses' most appropriately reflects this. 'The plain fact is that each sector requires the other', as Lord Donaldson said during the second reading of the Bill, pointing out that the limited capacity of the courts means that if all disputes were resolved there they would grind to a halt. On the other hand, sometimes arbitrators need the assistance of the courts. 'The administration of civil justice in this country is in the hands of a partnership between the public ... and private sector' (Lord Donaldson).

The obvious differences are that in litigation the services of the judge, secretariat facilities and the premises are provided by the state. An arbitrator requires fees, as do other persons whose services he uses, for example stenographers, translators, interpreters, lawyers whose advice he might require to take, etc, and costly aids to expedition, such as computer-aided instantaneous transcripts, and the venue, must be paid for. Litigation is governed by established court rules, in particular the *White Book*. It is adversarial and sometimes, consequently, ' ... as a way of resolving disputes is often unfair, very slow and cost-ineffective' (Lord Noel-Buxton).

Arbitrators have fewer powers than judges (although the Act has given them more and encourages them to use such powers robustly). Legal aid for litigation, available subject to certain stringent financial requirements, is not available for parties to arbitration. The main difference, however, remains in the approach. The infinite variety of procedures which arbitration can adopt because of the boundless flexibility of the process gives advantages which litigation cannot match— take the example of dispensing entirely with an oral hearing and dealing with the dispute on documents alone, something which the courts are unable to do. This is best dealt with in looking at the specific advantages which arbitration can offer over other forms of dispute resolution (see below).

Differences between arbitration and mediation/ conciliation

Because of the infinite diversity of the types of dispute which require to be resolved (see Arthur Marriott's classification below), it is clear that not all will be amenable to resolution in the more conventional ways, ie through the courts or by arbitration. Some, such as those concerned with the construction industry, which traditionally have been dealt with in this way, have resulted in enormous cost, after prolonged and unsatisfactory hearings, sometimes with inconclusive results (because, for example, one or both parties can no longer continue and is forced into a settlement).

Conflict is, alas, a growth industry, and a large majority of disputes never get to trial because of the spectre of uncontrollable costs, wasted time and unwanted publicity. An ever increasing number of disputes are settled by negotiation. However, this often fails, and conciliation or mediation is used instead. Conciliation and mediation are procedures whereby an independent, impartial person assists the parties to reach an agreed settlement of their dispute, the difference being that in the former the conciliator (or 'neutral') may suggest a solution which the parties are free to accept or reject. The process is extra-judicial and voluntary. However, if the parties do reach such a settlement and the settlement is embodied in written form, it is a contract which is enforceable between them.

It appears that more and more cases are being dealt with in America by way of mediation. Canada, too, is active in the field. In Australia there is widespread use of mediation in family disputes. There is also an upsurge in Hong Kong, and a mediation clause is standard in all Hong Kong construction contracts of a particular kind. The use of mediation is well settled. It is considered by many construction arbitrators/other users that in time mediation will become the principal method by which such disputes are settled. This is as much due to the advantages which mediation offers as to perceived disadvantages with arbitration, hopefully now largely removed by the Act.

The obvious disadvantage of mediation/conciliation is that it is unenforceable, and that failure will inevitably mean resorting to either litigation or arbitration in order to achieve a binding, legally enforceable decision, with all the consequent additional expenditure of money and time. However, it may be that arbitration/mediation will be used within the same procedures as a means of dispute resolution. The Chartered Institute of Arbitrators recently published a Consumer Dispute Resolution Scheme, the novel feature of which is the introduction of a formalised conciliation stage prior to arbitration, and in Hong Kong there is legislation which permits an arbitrator to become a conciliator during the arbitration, resuming his role if the conciliation fails. For a binding, enforceable award, however, the only two procedures to guarantee this remain arbitration and litigation.

Advantages of arbitration over other forms of dispute resolution

It was stated above that litigation and arbitration are totally different processes. The most important characteristic of arbitration in the authors' view is its flexibility. Different disputes require different means of resolution. Arthur Marriott has suggested that disputes fall into six broad categories:

- those concerned with commodity and maritime contracts;
- consumer contracts;
- construction contracts;
- contracts for high technology and involving intellectual property;
- those concerned with economic development agreements between third-world governments and multinational companies intended to develop some natural or other resource over many years; and
- those dealing with partnerships, joint ventures and other long-term relationships.

Each of these requires a different approach. Consumer arbitrations, for example (and it is important to remember that there are some 360 million consumers in the European Market) generally require very quick, low cost procedures. The various Codes of Practice schemes developed and administered by the Chartered Institute of Arbitrators in consultation with, and the approval of, the Department of Fair Trading, are usually on documents alone, or with site visits plus documentary evidence etc. This cuts down cost, is effective and speedy. As to long-term economic development disputes, procedures are needed, and can be devised, which adapt and preserve contracts rather than end them. Similarly partnership disputes need to be resolved in ways in which the relationship is preserved, or alternatively brought to an end efficiently, economically and without acrimony.

Whatever the area of dispute, if arbitration is the appropriate procedure to use, the flexibility which is such a distinctive feature of the process can be used creatively and efficiently, speeding up the process, reducing cost, providing users with a service which meets their commercial or other needs. For example:

31

- hearings can be held in unconventional places (aboard a ship, in a factory, or house) or at unconventional times (during a weekend or over a public holiday);
- neutral territory can be selected to obviate suspicion or reluctance of the parties, or to give them confidence in the process (for example, a dispute between two different African states might be resolved according to English law in Switzerland);
- time-saving devices/fast-track procedures (written submissions, a video-linked hearing between parties in different countries, 'paperless' IT devices*) can be utilised;
- lawyers can be dispensed with (for example, in technical disputes).

There are infinitely various ways of dealing with the resolution of disputes imaginatively. This will depend on the skill, expertise, robustness and creativity of the arbitrator, and it is for him to manage the arbitration effectively and efficiently from the outset.

Other advantages of arbitration apart from its versatility and flexibility mentioned above, are that it can be very efficient and cost-effective. The arbitrator is an expert and thus will be familiar with the area of dispute, with current practices, technical terms, customs of the trade, technology etc, which will speed up proceedings. He is not subject to the restrictions which limit judges. Another advantage is that arbitration can be initiated much more quickly than litigation, which can be subject to lengthy delays (for example, judicial review). An arbitrator can arrange a hearing more advantageously than lengthy court lists—and anyone who has been

---

* The first paperless civil trial occurred in 1995 in the case of *Eagle Star v Mowlem*. D J Freeman acted for the successful party, Eagle Star, and Clifford Chance represented Mowlem. The case provoked intense interest as having made the greatest use of technology in the history of British civil litigation, using a computerised litigation support/IT system (Archea) unrivalled except by the Maxwell prosecution. Over 800,000 documents were imaged for electronic retrieval, scanned onto a computer and code-indexed by date, author, recipient etc. The computer was then able to answer questions, list relevant documents, flash them up and, when required, print copies. Thousands of documents were able to be stored on a single disc, highly portable in a lap-top computer. All the time-consuming (and costly) trawling through thousands of documents, making expensive sets of copies, binding them up and carting them backwards and forwards between counsel, witnesses and the court, was avoided. The authors are indebted to D J Freeman, Solicitors, for this most interesting information.

kept waiting outside a court on the first day fixed for a hearing only to be told that the previous case has overrun and that he will have to wait six months for a new booking, will appreciate the advantage of having an arbitrator firmly committed to starting a hearing on a fixed day. If a particular arbitrator is unavailable another arbitrator can be appointed who can comply with the timetable. (The rules of the London Maritime Arbitration Association provide that a party can force an arbitrator to retire if it cannot provide a hearing within a reasonable time.) Thus it can be quicker than litigation. Indeed a partner in one of the top ten firms of solicitors told one of the authors that, even though there might be cases where the actual costs would be heavier than if the dispute were resolved by the courts, this was the principal reason why they used arbitration.

Courts are open to the public, including the press. Arbitrations, unless both parties decide otherwise, are held in private so that, for example, trade secrets can be preserved and private disputes can be kept hidden from the public and competitors. Having their dispute heard in private may also help to preserve future commercial relationships between the parties. There are few openly published reports, and those that are occasionally published with the consent of the parties are carefully formulated so as to conceal the identities of the parties. While two recent cases in Australia (*Esso/BHP v Plowman* [1995] 11 *Arbitration International* 234 and *Commonwealth of Australia v Cockatoo Dockyard Pty Ltd* (1995) 36 NSWLR 662, both referred to in the DAC Report (February 1996) at pp 9 and 10) have thrown some doubt on the confidentiality of arbitration proceedings there, it is thought unlikely that the decisions, which were on special facts, will be followed in the English courts.

Arbitrators are the servants of the parties. Thus they conduct their proceedings with the convenience of the parties in mind. For example, as stated *above*, they can assist the parties by providing that they need not take time off work by handling the dispute on documents alone, or holding a hearing on a weekend, at the place of the dispute, eg on a building site. Arbitrators may also appear less intimidating in comparison with judges. They are, by and large, commercial men dealing with their like, resolving commercial disputes, although there are also many arbitrations which are conducted by retired judges who have had enormous experience both as practitioners and on the bench. Arbitrators produce a legally enforceable award. Certainty is what is required in order that people can get on with their business. (It is for this reason that many international arbitration agreements, for example, exclude the right to appeal.)

Arbitration is frequently the preferred means of resolving disputes by foreign powers who, for reasons of political prestige, do not want to be seen to be submitting to the jurisdiction of a foreign court.

Distinction between arbitration and valuation/ expert determination

Valuation or expert determination is a means by which parties to a contract jointly instruct a third party to determine an issue. It applies to a wide range of commercial transactions from rent reviews to breach of warranty claims, and from construction disputes to pension scheme transfers. The procedure is usually simple and is based on the wording of the specific contract. The process is used for technical as well as valuation disputes. It is quick, cheap and private. The individual is usually referred to as an expert, a valuer or a certifier. Such a person is engaged to effect valuation/ make a decision or to give a certificate that certain works have been completed on the basis of his own expertise.

Valuation and expert determination differ from arbitration in that they are subject to little or no control by the courts. There is usually no appeal from decisions. Experts are not clothed with judicial immunity (cf arbitrators, below), and may be liable for negligence. The decisions which they make have a completely different status from those made by judges or arbitrators; in particular, they cannot be enforced without further action. Such means of dispute resolution is therefore inappropriate for situations where international enforcement is required. It is important when setting out terms to see that the relevant clause is properly drawn, for example, is the reference to 'arbitrator' or 'expert'? While the use of express words is not conclusive, it can be very persuasive. While an arbitrator must be a readily identifiable individual, a partnership or a company can be an 'expert'.

Another process related to arbitration and increasingly used in the construction industry is adjudication. As generally understood, adjudication is a process of quick and temporary dispute resolution where a dispute may be referred to a third party, often named in the contract, which will make a quick decision on minimal submissions and evidence which is binding on the parties until the contract works are completed when it may be referred to arbitration or litigation for a final decision. At the time of writing a Bill is before Parliament which will make adjudication compulsorily available to parties to construction contracts, either by specific terms in a contract or by way of a statutory scheme. Final details are not yet available and it remains to be seen whether the provisions of the Bill, if and when enacted, will have the intended effect.

Arbitrators and how they are appointed

In theory anyone can be an arbitrator, whatever his age, disabilities or incompetence. Even 'lunatics, outlaws, perjurers and infants' can be arbitrators! (However, in the 9th.edition of Encyclopedia Britannica [1865] it states, 'Idiots, lunatics, infants and married women, who are under a general rule of disqualification in law, may all be arbitrators, for it is said, the parties have selected their own judges and must abide by their choice, ' (and see the acknowledgement to Michael Needham, who in the quoted article himself acknowledges his indebtedness to Michael D.Joyce for this information, later). However, under s 33 of the Act arbitrators are now required to act in a manner which will exclude the incompetent or the dishonest. Section 24(1) makes it clear that the parties may require the arbitrator to have certain qualifications and that the court may, upon application from a party, remove an arbitrator who may not be impartial, does not have the required qualifications or is, or may be, physically or mentally incapable of conducting the proceedings. (It does not specifically deal with the question of married women, however, something for which one of the authors is grateful!)

Clearly a person who has experience and expertise in a particular field will enhance the chances of the arbitration being conducted efficiently. It will also give confidence to the parties in the authority of his award. It is the parties who usually appoint the arbitrator(s), providing they can agree. Often it will be the parties' advisors who will have had dealings with someone they have used in the past to provide expert evidence and who has built up a reputation as an expert witness. In the eventuality of the parties failing to agree, or not knowing of an appropriately qualified expert in whom they can feel confidence, it is customary to apply to an appointing body, such as the Royal Institute of British Architects or the Chartered Institute of Arbitrators. The courts are available to assist where there is failure to agree an arbitrator. An arbitrator who acts in a judicial manner is immune from liability in negligence (see s 29).

II

Commentary

Chapter 4

Part I—Arbitration Pursuant to an Arbitration Agreement

Introductory

Section 1: General principles

1.1

Section 1 states that the provisions of Part I of the Act are founded on three principles and should be construed accordingly. Section 1(*a*) provides that 'the object of arbitration is to obtain the fair resolution of disputes by an impartial tribunal without unnecessary delay or expense;' s 1(*b*) provides that 'the parties should be free to agree how their disputes are resolved, subject only to such safeguards as are necessary in the public interest', and s 1(*c*) provides that 'in matters governed by [Part I] the court should not intervene except as provided by this Part'.

1.2

Section 1 is completely new. It is important in that it sets out right at the start the general fundamental principles on which the Act is founded. It makes clear that it will be construed in accordance with those principles. It does not define, but sets out the object of, arbitration. Fairness and impartiality are essential prerequisites because without such qualities arbitration would be discredited. It is interesting that the words 'fair' and 'fairness' are used in the Act, and that the words 'natural justice' have disappeared. (Lord Justice Saville has said that he stopped using the phrase 'natural justice' after being unable to answer Lord Mustill when asked by him to define the difference between natural and unnatural justice.) The parties have chosen arbitration rather than any other means of dispute resolution for what they perceive to be its advantages. These might relate to the privacy and confidentiality of proceedings, or to the flexibility of a procedure especially tailored to the parties' particular requirements. Their dispute should be resolved quickly and economically and this is something which the tribunal should keep in mind. Expense can only be kept down by speeding up proceedings and giving more autonomy to the tribunal. This provision encourages it to be more forthright, to take the initiative, to manage the case more effectively and efficiently. It also implies a duty on it to avoid delay and to be more cost-conscious. The duties to act fairly and impartially, and to avoid delay and unnecessary expense are set out in more detail in s 33. There is also a later provision (s 40) which sets out a corresponding general duty of the parties, for example, that they must comply without delay with directions of the tribunal. The message is clear to all users and the whole Act must be read and understood in the light of the declared object of arbitration.

1.3

To achieve the end set out in s 1(a) the two intertwined golden threads which run throughout this Part of the Act are clearly spelled out. The first is that it is the parties' arbitration and the process is consensual. Their autonomy is emphasised throughout. It is a key principle. The parties want the maximum flexibility so that they can make whatever agreement they like as to how their dispute shall be resolved. They will be in control of the process. They will decide on the most appropriate procedure for their particular dispute, subject only to such safeguards as are necessary for the public interest. The parties can, for example, agree to dispense with the strict rules of evidence, or even have their dispute settled not on legal grounds but on equitable grounds. They can dispense with a hearing and have the matter dealt with on documents alone, or on documents with a site meeting. They can exclude the right of appeal. It is up to the parties to decide (and in this they will be advised by the tribunal which will be conscious of its duty to save time and money.

However, fast-track procedures cannot succeed unless the parties want them to). The parties do not have absolute freedom, however. On the grounds of public policy certain provisions cannot be overridden. Section 4 deals with mandatory and non-mandatory provisions.

1.4

The second golden thread throughout this Part of the Act, and which is set out as a general principle, is that the courts are there to support the arbitral process, not to interfere with it. This corresponds to Article 5 of the UNCITRAL Model Law which states, 'In matters governed by this Law, no court shall intervene except where so provided in this Law'. By confining the circumstances in which the courts can intervene and setting them out in the statute, parties can know precisely and with confidence the limits of their power. They will not have the insecurity of some potential unexpected intervention based on a common law principle. In short, if the parties have chosen arbitration, then their decision should be respected and the courts should not generally be able to intervene. Such interventions are limited to those occasions when it is obvious that either the arbitral process needs assistance or that there has been, or is likely to be, a clear denial of justice.

1.5

It was Lord Denning in 1980 (*Japan Line Ltd v Aggeliki* [1980] 1 Lloyd's Rep 288) who asserted that as well as its statutory powers the court also had an inherent jurisdiction to supervise the conduct of arbitrators and could do so and provide remedies wherever such intervention was in the interests of justice. Note that s 1(c) says that the court 'should' not intervene, not 'shall' not. This might suggest that some overriding jurisdiction remains but must be used sparingly and only in the most exceptional circumstances? Support, rather than intervention, is the theme. The idea that the courts have some *general* supervisory jurisdiction over arbitrations, however, has been abandoned (see also s 12).

1.6

Not all users support the principle of party autonomy, ie that the arbitrator must follow the wishes of the parties so far as procedure is concerned, and provided they agree. Some might say that parties are rarely able to express an informed view about procedural matters. Many users think that it should be for the arbitrator to decide on the most appropriate procedure, although of course he should be careful to lead rather than to impose or dictate terms. He would of course listen to what the parties have to say but would not be bound by them. He should have the power to control procedure and override the ·vishes of the parties (or, more usually, their lawyers) in the final analysis, even to the extent of deciding that the matter could be resolved without a hearing, thus denying the parties their 'day in court'. Strong views were expressed for both arguments during the various consultation stages of the Act. However, despite these views, the drafters of the Act clearly considered that party autonomy was paramount, that it was their inalienable right to determine their own procedure, and that the principle should be preserved and strengthened.

1.7

Agreement of those concerned, ie party autonomy or contractual arbitration, is the basis of the Model Law. The parties should be held to their agreement and they should be able to decide how the arbitration should be conducted. Various rules, for example those of the International Chamber of Commerce, the London Court of International Arbitration, the International Centre for the Settlement of Investment Disputes, all uphold the parties' agreement as paramount in the determination of the arbitral procedure. If parties agree to resolve their dispute through the 'private sector' (arbitration) rather than the 'public sector' (the courts) then the courts should play no part in the process, save only to enforce an award in the same way as they enforce other contractual rights and obligations when this is necessary. To do otherwise would be to interfere in the parties' rights to resolve their dispute in the manner which they have specifically chosen. In parts of Europe, for example, the courts will only intervene if there has been a failure of due process—in short, if the arbitrator has not treated the parties fairly. There are, of course, arguments against this thesis, for example, that since the courts are there to prevent or correct injustices, then they should be allowed—

indeed it should be their duty—to interfere, if 'interference' means putting matters right (and see below, ss 42–45, which deal with the powers of the court in relation to arbitral proceedings).

1.8

A tribunal should act robustly and manage the arbitration effectively and efficiently. It should not allow parties or their representative to delay the process (see s 33(1) and (2), on the general duty of the tribunal, and s 40 on the general duty of parties, below). However, it may not override the wishes of the parties. Indeed, if it does, the court's powers can be invoked, (and see ss 67 and 68 which deal with challenging the award). None the less, if arbitration has been chosen rather than any other method of dispute resolution, it is because it is the preferred option. Parties, as Michael Needham, a distinguished and experienced arbitrator specialising in building disputes, said:

> '... expect all the advantages that are inherent in the process (of arbitration), that is privacy, flexibility, economy and so forth. They expect more, however: that their differences will be placed before someone who is highly experienced in the subject matter of their dispute, that the tribunal will apply appropriate technical and commercial standards; that the tribunal will understand the circumstances which arise during the course of the design and construction of a building or engineering project; that common sense will prevail; above all that there will be a fair and reasonable outcome to their differences' ('The Road to Kilkenny', *Arbitration*, February 1996 Vol 62 No 1, at p25).

The provisions of s 1, together with the remainder of the Act, should ensure this.

Section 2: Scope of application of provisions

2.1

Section 2 is new. It is important in that it defines the scope of Part I in relation to the location of the seat of the arbitration as defined below in s 3.

2.2

Section 2(1) states that the provisions of Part I apply where the seat of the arbitration is in England and Wales or

Northern Ireland. Note that England and Wales, which operate under a single statutory jurisdiction, are 'bracketed' together (by the use of the word 'and') whereas Northern Ireland, which like Scotland has a separate statutory jurisdiction within the United Kingdom, is treated separately. Arbitration in Northern Ireland has hitherto been governed by the Arbitration Act (Northern Ireland) 1937. This Act now consolidates the arbitration law applicable in England and Wales *and* in Northern Ireland. However, because Scotland has a separate law of arbitration, as a consequence of having adopted the UNCITRAL Model Law, the Act does *not* apply to Scotland except where specifically stated, such as s 108(3).

2.3

Section 2(2) defines those sections in Part I which will apply even though the seat of the arbitration is not in England and Wales or in Northern Ireland, or where no seat has as yet been designated or determined. They are ss 9 to 11 which deal with the stay of legal proceedings in favour of arbitration. Also included is s 66 which deals with the enforcement of arbitration awards in the same manner as judgments of the court. All the provisions of those four sections will therefore apply in any arbitration governed by the law of England and Wales or Northern Ireland, wherever the seat of the arbitration may be.

2.4

Section 2(3) states that certain powers of the court are also applicable even though the seat of the arbitration is not England and Wales or Northern Ireland or where no seat has as yet been been designated or determined. They are the powers to secure the attendance of witnesses in arbitration proceedings under s 43, and the powers exercisable by the court in support of arbitral proceedings under s 44. However, there is a proviso that the court may:

'refuse to exercise any such power if, in the opinion of the court, the fact that the seat of the arbitration is outside England and Wales or Northern Ireland, or that when designated or determined the seat is likely to be outside England and Wales or Northern Ireland, makes it inappropriate to do so'.

There are a number of court powers, not least the power to secure the attendance of witnesses, but also, for example, powers to make orders relating to property, which a court may well consider should not be exercised where the seat of the arbitration is not, or probably will not be, within the jurisdiction of England and Wales or Northern Ireland.

2.5

Section 2(4) gives the court a general discretion to exercise any powers conferred upon it by Part I in relation to arbitral proceedings, other than those specifically referred to in s 2(2) or (3), where:

'(a) no seat of the arbitration has been designated or determined, *and*
(b) by reason of a connection with England and Wales or Northern Ireland the court is satisfied that it is appropriate to do so' (emphasis supplied).

Note that this general discretion does *not* apply where the seat of the arbitration has been determined and it is outside England and Wales or Northern Ireland.

2.6

Section 2(5) states that s 7, which sets out the rules on the separability of an arbitration agreement from the contract containing it, and s 8, which sets out the effect of the death of a party, will apply 'where the law applicable to the arbitration agreement is the law of England and Wales or Northern Ireland even if the seat of the arbitration is outside England and Wales or Northern Ireland or has not been designated or determined'.

2.7

The overall effect of this section is that the provisions of Part I apply in their totality in any arbitration where the seat as defined in s 3 is in England and Wales or Northern Ireland. In addition, the court *will* enforce arbitration agreements and enforce awards, subject to the relevant provisions of the Act, wherever the seat of the arbitration is or may be. It *will* exercise its powers in support of arbitral proceedings wherever the seat of the arbitration is or may be, but may refuse to do so if the fact that the seat is or is likely to be outside of England and Wales or Northern Ireland makes it inappropriate to do so. It *may* exercise any other power conferred on it by Part I where the seat has not been determined and where it is satisfied that any connection of the proceedings with England and Wales or Northern Ireland, makes it appropriate to do so. The provisions of Part I relating to the separability of an arbitration agreement from the contract surrounding it and the effect of the death of a party *will* apply provided that the law of England and Wales or Northern Ireland governs the arbitration agreement. It is therefore only in the last case that a party might have to satisfy an arbitrator or a court that the arbitration agreement is governed by the law of England and Wales or Northern Ireland in order to show that the provisions in question apply.

Section 3: The seat of the arbitration

3.1

Section 3 is new. It provides that 'the seat of the arbitration' means the juridical seat of the arbitration designated:

'(a) by the parties to the arbitration agreement, or
(b) by any arbitral or other institution or person vested by the parties with powers in that regard, or
(c) by the arbitral tribunal if so authorised by the parties.'

It is a new concept (although used in a number of English cases and a familiar concept in international arbitrations). It does not necessarily mean it is the geographical area where the hearing takes place, although it frequently will be. The seat will dictate which law governs the procedure. The definition is also part of the definition of 'domestic arbitration' which appears in s 85.

3.2

Although parts of the arbitration hearing may take place in several countries, there can only ever be one seat of the arbitration. By having only one such seat, say in England, problems which might otherwise arise where the hearing of the arbitration is, say, in Bangkok, and where their procedural arbitration law might otherwise be imported into the proceedings, will be avoided.

3.3

It is the parties to the arbitration agreement who will decide the seat of the arbitration. If they do not do so, it will be the institution or person given the power to decide, for example, the President of the Law Society. Many parties use the standard terms of reference of a recognised arbitral body, such as the International Chamber for the Settlement of Investment Disputes, the International Chamber of Commerce Court of Arbitration or the London Court of International Arbitration. It may even be the tribunal itself, provided the parties agree. In cases where the choice has not been made in one of the ways described above, the seat will be determined having regard to the parties' agreement and to all the relevant circumstances. These might include the nationality or residence of the parties, where a company is incorporated, where the contract was made, where the subject matter of the dispute is, any presumptions that the parties intended the contract to be governed by a particular system of law, etc. Where the seat of arbitration is other than in England, Wales or Northern Ireland the court's powers are not only limited by those principles set out in s 1, but further limited by s 2(4) which '... makes it inappropriate to exercise that power'.

3.4

As we shall see later, parties are free to agree on the form of an award. However, in the absence of such agreement, the form of the award is set down by s 52. This includes the provision that the award shall state the seat of the arbitration. By s 53, unless otherwise agreed by the parties, where the seat of the arbitration is England and Wales or Northern Ireland, any award made shall be treated as made there, regardless of where it was signed, despatched or delivered. (In cases where there are three arbitrators, for example, at least one might be a national of/resident in another country, say France, and may sign the award after his return to France. He may deliver the award in Germany. This is of no consequence in the light of the above.)

Section 4: Mandatory and non-mandatory provisions

4.1

Section 4(1) states that the mandatory provisions are set out in Sched 1. Such provisions are to have effect notwithstanding any agreement by the parties to the contrary. Section 4 is new. It applies to Part I of the Act. A mandatory provision is one which cannot be displaced by the parties. An example of a mandatory provision is that relating to the application of the Limitation Acts (s 13). Whatever the parties feel about displacing the Limitation Acts and making their own provisions as to when proceedings might be brought for example, they cannot exclude statutory time limits. Other examples of mandatory provisions are ss 29 and 74 which confer immunity from suit on arbitrators and arbitral institutions which appoint them. Obviously, if parties could exclude these provisions by agreement they probably would, and they are therefore made mandatory. It is important to note, however, that the mandatory provisions of Part I are only mandatory in so far as the provisions of Part I apply.

4.2

The mandatory provisions are conveniently set out in list form in Sched 1. There are some 24 in all. They deal with the following areas:

- stay of legal proceedings;
- power of court to extend agreed time limits;
- application of the Limitation Acts;
- power of the court to remove arbitrator;
- effect of death of arbitrator;
- liability of parties for fees and expenses of arbitrators;
- immunity of arbitrator;
- objection to substantive jurisdiction of tribunal;
- determination of preliminary point of jurisdiction;
- general duty of tribunal;
- items to be treated as expenses of arbitrators;
- general duty of parties;
- securing the attendance of witnesses;
- power to withhold award in case of non-payment;
- effectiveness of agreement for payment of costs in any event;
- enforcement of award;
- challenging the award—substantive jurisdiction and serious irregularity;
- saving for rights of person who takes no part in proceedings;
- loss of right to object;
- immunity of arbitral institutions; and
- charge to secure payment of solicitors' costs.

4.3

Section 4(2) provides that all the other provisions in Part I, known as non-mandatory provisions, allow the parties to make their own arrangements. Therefore, a non-mandatory provision is one which the parties can choose whether to apply or not, in other words they are free to agree whatever procedure they consider to be the most appropriate for their particular circumstances. An example might be that the parties agree that their dispute be resolved on documentary evidence alone, without a hearing, and that it will be settled on non-legal grounds.

4.4

Section 4(2) goes on to say that if the parties choose not to, or fail to, make such an agreement, rules are provided in Part I which set out various default procedures which the parties can choose to accept, reject or modify. They are 'fall-back' provisions. If the parties have failed to agree on procedural and evidential matters, the tribunal will decide, for example, where and when any part of the hearing will take place, or what language will be used and whether the documents are to be translated. This provides for gaps in arbitration agreements to be filled—all part of the philosophy of the Act which is to avoid delay (and cost) by providing that at this juncture the arbitrator can move in with his own decisions, and to get the arbitration on track and make it work.

4.5

Section 4(3) provides that the parties may make such arrangements by agreeing to the application of institutional rules, or providing any other means by which a matter may be decided. They are not expected necessarily to draw up their own rules, although they may well do so in a smaller arbitration. They can agree that particular rules, for example those of GAFTA or LCIA, will apply to their dispute. The words 'providing any other means by which a matter may be decided', give wide discretion to the parties as to procedure. However, 'any other means' means pertaining to arbitration. They would not extend to deciding the dispute itself by other means such as mediation, as this would take the whole matter outside the scope of the Act.

4.6

Section 4(4) makes it clear that it is immaterial whether or not the law applicable to the parties' agreements under s 4(2) and (3) is that of England and Wales or Northern Ireland. In other words, even if the parties' agreement is governed, say, by French law, this will still have the same effect. If the parties have chosen a particular law to govern their agreement, or if such particular law is objectively determined in the absence of choice (express or implied) such law will be treated as having been chosen by the parties. In the example the parties, while having the hearing in England, have chosen French law to govern their rights and obligations under the contract in relation to the dispute. This will be taken to mean that the parties have agreed to the dispute being resolved according to French law. In other words, their choice of foreign law amounts to an agreement and this must be respected.

4.7

Section 4(5) makes it expressly clear that the choice of a foreign system of law as the law governing the subject matter of a non-mandatory provision is the same as having made an agreement providing for that matter.

Section 5: Agreements to be in writing

5.1

Section 5(1) sets out the requirement that in order to come within Part I of the Act an arbitration agreement, and any other agreement between the parties, must be in writing. It states that the words 'agreement', 'agree' and 'agreed' are to be construed accordingly. The words 'any other agreement' have been included to cover, for example, variations to the agreement.

5.2

The law in this respect is essentially unchanged. An arbitration agreement was (and is) required to be in writing in order to attract the statutory provisions. Section 32 of the 1950 Act, which has been followed, provided that '... the expression "arbitration agreement" means a written agreement to submit present or future differences to arbitration, whether an arbitrator is named therein or not'. The Act also follows Article 7(2) of the Model Law (but not the precise wording). Section 7 of the 1975 Act also required an arbitration agreement to be in writing. 'Writing' was not defined in either of the previous statutes but is now defined widely and in considerable detail in this section.

5.3

Considerable discussion took place as to whether Part I should be restricted to agreements in writing or whether to abandon the requirement. The DAC felt that since an arbitration agreement has the effect of depriving the parties of their basic right to seek redress through the courts (as they have chosen to arbitrate rather than to litigate), such an important matter should be recorded. Further, potential disputes as to whether or not the parties had in fact made an agreement, and what were its precise terms, would be avoided, or at least diminished, if the agreement was in writing. In *Zambia Steel v James Clark* [1986] 2 Lloyd's Rep 225, an oral agreement was made on the terms of a quotation sent by sellers to buyers which contained an arbitration clause. The Court of Appeal held that by their conduct the buyers had agreed to the quotation terms, which included the arbitration clause, and thus the agreement was 'in writing' as required.

5.4

Section 5(2) provides a widely drawn definition of 'writing'. It is wider than that found in the Model Law. There is an agreement in writing:

'(a) if the agreement is made in writing (whether or not it is signed by the parties),
(b) if the agreement is made by exchange of communications in writing, or
(c) if the agreement is evidenced in writing.'

It may be 'in writing', for example, if made by an exchange of letters, telex, faxes, or memos.

5.5

Section 5(3) states that where parties agree otherwise than in writing by reference to terms which are in writing, they make an agreement in writing. The agreement will be 'in writing' if it includes an oral agreement, say a telephone conversation between two merchants, which refers to written terms, such as the GAFTA Arbitration Rules. Another common example, helpfully provided in the DTI's Notes on Clauses, is an oral salvage agreement made by the master of a ship in distress incorporating Lloyd's Salvage Rules which contain an arbitration clause. This corresponds to the Model Law which provides that agreements which incorporate by reference the terms of a written form of agreement constitute valid arbitration agreements (and such contracts are separable from the main contract), and it codifies the existing common law rule. The use of the words 'otherwise than in writing by reference to terms which are in writing' cover an agreement by conduct. For example if, as is common in the building industry, a contractor sends a form of order to a subcontractor which contains reference to subcontract conditions embodying an arbitration clause, and the subcontractor fails to acknowledge the order but nevertheless goes on to carry out the work, the subcontract will have been confirmed by conduct and the arbitration clause will be a valid arbitration agreement (see also s 6(2)).

5.6

Section 5(4) states that an agreement is evidenced in writing if an agreement made otherwise than in writing is recorded by one of the parties, or by a third party, with the authority of the parties, for example by an arbitrator in procedural directions. This provision indicates no time constraints: it allows for the recording of an oral agreement, say incorporating changes to the agreed procedure by the parties after the hearing has begun, at any stage.

5.7

Section 5(5) follows (but not entirely) Article 7(2) of the Model Law. Where written submissions have been exchanged between parties in arbitral or legal proceedings in which one of the parties alleges that there is an arbitration agreement, and where that allegation is not denied by the other in his responses, then this will constitute an agreement in writing. The words 'written submissions' have been carefully selected rather than the much wider expression 'documents'.

5.8

Section 5(6) is again widely drawn. It states that reference to something being in writing 'include its being recorded by any means'. This means not only that courier services, e-mail, voice mail, fax, video-recordings, and any other electronic means by which information is recorded is within the provision, but also that any which might be developed in the future will be covered. In the light of the extraordinary and exciting experiments with all-electronic non-document litigation which is currently taking off in the City of London, demonstrating the astonishingly swift growth of technological development (see *above*), it is sensible to anticipate the future, particularly as we enter the third millenium.

5.9

If an arbitration is not in writing it is not completely ineffective, however. The common law recognises such agreements, but any such agreement would not be governed by the Act. An award would be enforceable, for example, only by way of an action for enforcement of the oral contract and not under s 66 of the Act. (See s 81(2) which provides that certain matters shall continue to be governed by the common law and *not* by Part I.)

5.10

Note s 23(4) which does not require writing for an agreement to terminate an arbitration. (Section 23 deals with revocation of the arbitrator's authority.)

The arbitration agreement

Section 6: Definition of arbitration agreement

6.1

Section 6 corresponds to Article 7 of the Model Law. Section 6(1) defines an arbitration agreement as 'an agreement to submit to arbitration present or future disputes (whether they are contractual or not)'.

6.2

This is in essentially the same terms as, although more informative than, s 32 of the 1950 Act, which defined an arbitration agreement as 'a written agreement to submit present or future differences to arbitration whether an arbitrator is named therein or not'. Section 7(1) of the Arbitration Act 1975 defined an arbitration agreement as 'an agreement in writing (including an agreement contained in any exchange of letters or telegrams) to submit to arbitration present or future differences capable of settlement by arbitration'.

6.3

It will be noted that the term 'disputes' replaces 'differences'. It is arguable that a 'difference' is wider than a 'dispute' and judicial *dicta* including *Sykes (F & G) Wessex Ltd v Fine Fare Ltd* [1967] 1 Lloyd's Rep 53 suggested that they were not the same. In any event the DAC considered that no change to the law was intended, but that the changed definition would be 'more informative'. Accordingly s 82, which contains minor definitions, makes it clear that 'dispute' includes any difference.

6.4

The definition also makes it clear that the dispute does not necessarily have to be one based on contract, and thus any kind of dispute, for example such as arising from allegations of negligence against a building contrator in tort and not in contract, or a dispute between neighbours about the location of a boundary fence, can be the subject of an arbitration agreement.

6.5

Section 6(2), which reflects Article 7(2) of the Model Law, provides that the reference in an agreement to a written form of arbitration clause or to a document containing an arbitration clause constitutes an arbitration agreement if the reference is such as to make that clause part of the agreement; in a nutshell, incorporation by reference. Section 5(3) deals with cases where parties make an oral agreement but one which incorporates by reference the terms of a written agreement. As discussed above, this constitutes 'an agreement in writing' even though it was in fact an oral agreement. Does it constitute an arbitration agreement? Section 6(2) says that it may be such an agreement as long as the reference 'is such as to make [the arbitration] clause part of the agreement'.This will be a question of fact, since there are any number of reasons why documents might refer to each other without necessarily becoming part of an agreement. Merely to refer to another document does not necessarily mean that its terms have been incorporated.

6.6

Section 6(2) corrects an unfortunate situation which had arisen fairly recently, particularly in building cases and notably in *Ben Barrett & Son (Brickwork) Ltd v Henry Boot Management Ltd* (1995) CILL 1026 where it was held (following *dicta* of Sir John Megaw in *Aughton Ltd v M F Kent Services Ltd* (1991) 57 BLR 1), that a reference to a standard form of subcontract in documents constituting a subcontract was not sufficient to incorporate into the subcontract so formed the arbitration agreement in the standard form. The argument was that, as an arbitration agreement is to be regarded as a 'self-contained contract collateral or ancillary to' the contract containing it, there had to be a specific reference to the arbitration clause itself in the documentation forming the subcontract in order for it to be incorporated. This decision understandably has caused considerable alarm and despondency among those concerned with construction disputes. Section 6(2) now makes it clear that this will no longer be arguable (if, indeed, it ever properly was, which is an open question). However, in *Aughton Ltd v Kent Services* which related to an agreement between a subcontractor and a sub-subcontractor, the reference in the documentation forming the sub-subcontract was to a form of subcontract which contained a clause providing for arbitration between the subcontractor and the main contractor. It was held there that, since the arbitration clause would require amendment in order for it to be appropriate to arbitration between the subcontractor and the sub-subcontractor, *that* did not constitute a valid arbitration agreement between those parties. That position remains unchanged.

Section 7: Separability of arbitration agreement

7.1

Section 7 states that unless otherwise agreed by the parties:

'an arbitration agreement which forms or was intended to form part of another agreement *(whether or not in writing) shall not be regarded as invalid, non-existent or ineffective because that other agreement is invalid, or did not come into existence or has become ineffective,* and it shall for that purpose be treated as a distinct agreement' (emphasis supplied).

In short, a contract and the agreement to arbitrate which it contains can be treated as separate and distinct if for some reason the main contract no longer exists, and, in this situation it is capable of surviving as an independent entity. The words emphasised above, '... whether or not ...' were added as otherwise it might be said that the section was only effective in relation to such other agreements which were in writing, and this was not the intention of the drafters.

7.2

The principle of separability is already part of English law (*Harbour Assurance Co (UK) v Kansa* [1993] 3 All ER 897). Section 7 corresponds to Article 16(1) of the Model Law. This recognises the independence of the arbitration clause from the substantive contract of which it is part. The consequence of this recognition is that if for some reason the substantive contract is rendered void, or contains some serious defect, this does not of itself make an otherwise valid arbitration agreement invalid. In this way the Model Law recognises 'separability' or 'severability' or 'autonomy' of the arbitration clause. Section 7 codifies the law on the separability of the arbitration clause from the main contract. It is not a mandatory provision which means that the parties can agree otherwise, ie they can exclude the provision.

7.3

Case law established that provided an arbitration agreement was validly made it would continue to exist even though the contract which contained it had ended in some way; for example, it could govern the rights of the parties even after the frustration of the contract *(Heyman v Darwins* [1942] AC 356). In *Harbour Assurance v Kansa* (above), it was held that the arbitrator could determine a dispute over the initial validity of the written contract provided the arbitration clause itself was not directly impeached. The question as to the initial illegality of the contract was also capable of being referred to arbitration provided that any initial illegality did not directly impeach the arbitration clause. 'In every case the logical question was not whether the issue of illegality went to the validity of the contract but whether it went to the validity of the arbitration clause' (*Harbour Assurance v Kansa*). The law is now codified.

7.4

By s 2(5), s 7 applies where the arbitration agreement is governed by, but the seat of the arbitration is *not in*, England and Wales or Northern Ireland.

7.5

The DAC considered that the doctrine of separability is quite distinct from the question of the degree to which the tribunal is entitled to rule on its own jurisdiction. The Model Law does not take this view. Section 30 deals with the competence of the tribunal to rule on its own jurisdiction.

Section 8: Whether agreement discharged by death of a party

8.1

Section 8(1) states that unless otherwise agreed by the parties, an arbitration agreement is not discharged by the death of a party and may be enforced by or against the personal representatives of that party. It reproduces the provisions of s 2(1) of the 1950 Act (but see below) but is not mandatory so that the parties can choose whether or not to adopt, adapt or dispense with it.

8.2

The common law rule is that an arbitration agreement is brought to an end by the death of one of the parties. Section 2(1) of the 1950 Act stated: 'An arbitration agreement shall not be discharged by the death of any party thereto, either as respects the deceased or any other party, but shall in such an event be enforceable by or against the personal representative of the deceased.' Section 2(3) of the 1950 Act stated: 'Nothing in this section shall be taken to affect the operation of any enactment or rule of law by virtue of which any right of action is extinguished by the death of a person.' The use of the word 'shall' indicated the mandatory nature of this provision. The technical term 'right of action' is not used in s 8. (It will be noted that the Act has tried to avoid all such 'legalese'.)

8.3

Apparently, the rather tortuous drafting of s 2(1) of the 1950 Act was to cover the case where there were two joint parties on one side and one party on the other, and where one of the joint parties died. The change made by s 8(1), reversing the common law rule, simplifies the earlier provision, referring to 'a party'. It also substitutes the word 'shall' (mandatory) for 'may' (discretionary).

8.4

Section 8(2) is based on s 2(3) of the 1950 Act. It has exactly the same effect, although expressed more felicitously. Where the obligation under the main contract is a personal one, and 'dies' with the person, the arbitration agreement still survives but does not affect the 'dead' obligation.

8.5

Section 8 deals only with the arbitration agreement. For the effect of death of a party on the appointment of an arbitrator see s 26(2).

8.6

By s 2(5), s 8 applies where the arbitration agreement is governed by, but the seat of arbitration is *not in*, England and Wales or Northern Ireland.

Stay of legal proceedings

Section 9: Stay of legal proceedings

9.1

Section 9 is in the schedule of mandatory provisions of Part I. It corresponds to Article 8 of the Model Law. It reproduces s 4(1) of the 1950 Act and s 1 of the 1975 Act with certain changes. It reflects United Kingdom Treaty obligations and other considerations. It deals with circumstances in which an application can be made to the court to stop legal proceedings being brought and to enforce the arbitration agreement.

9.2

Section 9(1) states that if a party to an arbitration agreement is being sued on a matter the parties agreed to resolve by arbitration, he may, providing notice is given to the other side, apply to the court to halt those proceedings. It also makes clear that the phrase 'against whom legal proceedings are brought' includes not only a claim but a counterclaim. 'Notice' is dealt with in s 80 (see below) and 'legal proceedings' are defined in s 82 as 'civil proceedings in the High Court or a county court'.

9.3

The drafting of s 9(1) is an improvement on s 4(1) of the 1950 Act which referred to 'any party to an arbitration agreement'. This meant that any party to the arbitration could apply for a stay whether or not it was being sued. The new provision makes it clear that only a party to an arbitration agreement against whom legal proceedings are brought may apply for a stay. It also makes it clear (see above) that legal proceedings may be brought by way of counterclaim as well, something which was not covered in the previous legislation.

9.4

The previous law on stay of legal proceedings was covered by s 4(1) of the 1950 Act and s 1 of the 1975 Act. The relevant words in s 4(1) of the 1950 Act read:

> '... any party to those legal proceedings may at any time after appearance and before delivering any pleadings or taking any other steps in the proceedings, apply to the court to stay the proceedings, and that court or judge thereof, if satisfied that there is no sufficient reason, why the matter should not be referred in accordance with the agreement, and that the applicant was, at the time when the proceedings were commenced, and still remains, ready and willing to do all things necessary to the proper conduct of the arbitration, may make an order staying the proceedings.'

'A step in the proceedings' might include appearing before a master asking for leave to defend a summons for judgment under Ord 14, or applying for security for costs.

9.5

Section 1 of the 1975 Act was basically the same but with significant differences in wording:

> '... any party to the proceedings may at any time after appearance, and before delivering any pleadings or taking any other steps in the proceedings, apply to the court to stay the proceedings; and the court, unless satisfied that the arbitration agreement is null and void, inoperative or incapable of being performed or that there is not in fact any dispute between the parties with regard to the matter agreed to be referred, shall make an order staying the proceedings.'

The 1950 Act was of general application, the court's powers were discretionary and the court had to be positively satisfied that there was no good reason why the matter should not be referred to the court, and that the applicant was and remained ready and willing to carry out the arbitration. The 1975 Act, on the other hand, had no application to domestic arbitration agreements, the court's powers were mandatory and the stay was to be granted unless the court was satisfied as to different matters than those set out in the 1950 Act.

9.6

Section 9(2) states that an application to stay can be made even though the matter will go to arbitration only after some other dispute resolution procedure has first been used. This would cover the case where the agreement provides for conciliation as a prerequisite to arbitration (as some consumer scheme arbitrations do). The conciliation (or other) procedure must first be exhausted, but the application to stay can be made notwithstanding (see *Channel Tunnel v Balfour Beatty* [1993] AC 334, in particular the *dicta* of Lord Mustill). In that case it was held that the court had an inherent power to stay proceedings brought before it in breach of an agreement to decide disputes by an alternative method and that accordingly, whether or not the procedure for resolving disputes agreed between the parties amounted to an arbitration agreement falling within s 1 of the 1975 Act, the court had jurisdiction which ought, in the circumstances, to be exercised to stay the action. The relevant clause in their particular contract provided for the initial reference of disputes or differences, including disputes as to the valuation of variations, to a panel of experts, and provided for final settlement by arbitration in Brussels. It said:

> '... such dispute or difference shall at the instance of either the employer or contractor in the first place be referred in writing to and be settled by a panel of three persons (acting

as independent experts but not as arbitrators) who shall, unless otherwise agreed by both the employer and the contractor within a period of 90 days after being requested in writing by either party to do so, and after such investigation as the panel think fit, state their decision in writing ...'

9.7

Section 9(3) provides for the timing of an application. It states that no application can be made by a person before taking an appropriate legal step to acknowledge the legal proceedings against him but also that no such application can be made *after* the applicant has taken any step in the legal proceedings to answer the claim. In other words, an application to stay legal proceedings can only be made after the applicant has acknowledged the legal proceedings (ie acknowledged the writ), but *before* he has entered a defence. Section 4(1) of the 1950 Act (see below) used the word 'appearance'. This word is no longer appropriate. Thus the word does not feature in s 9(3). No change in the law is made but the reference clarifies the pre-conditions by referring simply to 'the appropriate procedural step (if any) to acknowledge the legal proceedings'.

9.8

Section 9(4) provides that there is a mandatory duty on the court to grant a stay *unless* satisfied that the arbitration agreement is null and void, inoperative or incapable of being performed. This provision does not apply to a domestic arbitration agreement, in which case the court has an element of discretion (see s 86 and *caveat below*).

9.9

Section 9(4) effects two changes. The words in s 1 of the 1975 Act referred to above, '... there is not in fact any dispute between the parties with regard to the matter agreed to be referred ...', have gone. They are not required by the New York Convention on the Recognition and Enforcement of Foreign Arbitral Awards and were thought to be unnecessary and confusing, so are omitted from the Act. The second change is one relating to the burden of proof. Under s 4(1) of the 1950 Act (see above), the defendant to the court proceedings brought in breach of the arbitration agreement had to satisfy the court that arbitration was more appropriate than litigation. The new law turns the burden round. It is for the *plaintiff* to persuade the court that litigation is more appropriate. In other words, provided that the arbitration agreement is valid, it should be enforced unless there is a good reason not to.

9.10

Section 9(5) states that if the application to stay is refused by the court, any provision in the agreement that an award is a condition precedent to litigation in respect of any matter is of no effect.

9.11

If parties wish to make it certain that any dispute which arises in their contract will be settled by arbitration rather than by any other means, in particular litigation, they may insert a clause to that effect. A *Scott v Avery* ([1856] HL Cas 811) clause, as it is called, is a device used to ensure that disputes arising from the arbitration agreement are settled by arbitration. A typical example of such a clause might be: 'The making of an arbitration award shall be a condition precedent to the commencement of any action at law'. Section 24(3) of the 1950 Act recognised the validity of such a clause, giving the court power to strike it out only if it ordered that the arbitration agreement was to cease to have effect because the arbitrator was not impartial or the dispute involved a question of fraud. The provisions of s 9(5) give the court power to disapply such a clause when it refuses a stay on any grounds under this section or s 86.

9.12

By s 2(2), s 9 applies wherever the seat of the arbitration is.

Section 10: Reference of interpleader issue to arbitration

10.1

Section 10 is in the schedule of mandatory provisions. It reproduces s 5 of the 1950 Act, and complies with the New York Convention on the Recognition and Enforcement of Foreign Arbitral Awards. It deals with the concept of 'interpleader'. An example of interpleader arises, for example, where X has money, not his own, but deposited in his name in a bank. Y and Z each claim the relevant sum of money. X does not know to which of them he should account. He may 'interplead' and bring Y and Z to court. Thus interpleader arises where a person is obliged to one of two other persons but does not know to which one he is obliged, and the other two are in contention. 'Interpleader' is not defined in the Act. The use of the word is a departure from the Act's general avoidance of legal jargon, presumably because the drafters could find no satisfactory alternative expression.

10.2

Section 10(1) provides that where in legal proceedings relief by way of interpleader is granted and any issue between the claimants is one in respect of which there is an arbitration agreement between them, the court granting the relief must direct that the issue is determined in accordance with the arbitration agreement unless the circumstances are such that proceedings brought by a claimant in respect of any matter would not be stayed.

10.3

Section 10(1) is mandatory, and this differs from the 1950 provisions. The court must direct that the issue is determined in accordance with the agreement unless the position is that, under the circumstances, proceedings brought by a claimant would not be stayed. The court has no discretion to refuse the direction. This gives effect to the requirement of the New York Convention. It had not been included in the 1975 Act. It should have been. Note that by s 86(2) (below) the court has a wider discretion. In relation to domestic arbitration agreements the court can refuse the direction where a stay would be refused.

10.4

Section 10(2) deals with the situation where a *Scott v Avery* clause is included in the contract containing the arbitration clause. It states that where the above provisions apply but the court does not direct that the issues are determined in accordance with the arbitration agreement, any provision that an award is a condition precedent to the bringing of legal proceedings in respect of any matter shall not affect the determination of that issue by the court. In other words, it makes the same provision in relation to interpleader as s 9(5) makes in relation to stay.

10.5

Section 5 of the 1950 Act stated:

> 'Where relief by way of interpleader is granted and it appears to the High Court that the claims in question are matters to which an arbitration agreement, to which the claimants are parties, applies, the High Court may direct the issue between the claimants to be determined in accordance with the agreement.'

In other words, the court had a discretion to refuse the direction.

Section 11: Retention of security where Admiralty proceedings stayed

11.1

Section 11 is in the schedule of mandatory provisions. It reproduces the relevant parts (ie as relate to arbitration) of s 26 of the Civil Jurisdiction and Judgments Act 1982. It is concerned with situations where the court stays Admiralty proceedings in order to enforce an arbitration agreement and where property has been arrested or bailed or other security has been given to prevent or obtain release from arrest. It enables the court in England and Wales, or in Northern Ireland, to retain an arrested ship (or any bail or security given instead) as security for the satisfaction of a judgment of a foreign court which is enforceable in England where the ship was arrested in proceedings begun in England and subsequently stayed or dismissed on jurisdictional grounds. The arrest of a ship always recalls to one of the authors that dreadful howler of a law student who described such a process as being effected by 'nailing the writ to the master'.

11.2

By s 11(1) the court can order that the property arrested be retained as security for the satisfaction of any award given in the arbitration in respect of that dispute. Alternatively, the court can order the stay of those proceedings to be conditional on the provision of equivalent security for the satisfaction of any award.

11.3

By s 11(2) the same law and practice shall apply in relation to property held in pursuance of an order as would apply if it were held for the purposes of proceedings in the court making the order. This, however, is subject to any provision made by rules of court and to any necessary modification.

11.4

By s 2(2), s 11 applies wherever the seat of the arbitration is.

Commencement of arbitral proceedings

Section 12: Power of court to extend time for beginning arbitral proceedings, &c

12.1

Section 12 is one of the mandatory provisions in Sched 1. It reproduces s 27 of the 1950 Act with amendments, and sets out the powers of the High Court in certain circumstances to extend a time limit imposed by the arbitration agreement for the commencement of the arbitration. There are a number of changes in the law, the major one concerning the test that the court must apply before extending the time.

12.2

Section 12(1) states that where the agreement provides that the claim shall be barred, or the claimant's right extinguished, unless the claimant takes some step within a specified period to begin the arbitration proceedings or other dispute resolution procedures which must first be used before the arbitration can begin, the court may order the time for taking that step to be extended. In commodity trade arbitration agreements, for example, it is common to impose sharp time limits within which a claim to arbitration must be brought. The justification for doing this at a much earlier stage than ordinary limitation periods allow is that in certain commercial concerns it is considered necessary and important that each party knows quickly whether a claim is going to be brought against it. After all, arbitration was originally designed to allow commercial men to deal swiftly with disputes so that they could then return to business.

12.3

'Other dispute resolution procedures' in s 12(1)(*b*) is the same new phrase used in s 9 (stay of legal proceedings). The reference is to some initial step, such as conciliation, as prerequisite to arbitration. This is an increasingly common practice and the inclusion of this provision represents a small but logical extension to the previous law. However, only the two steps are covered by the section (beginning the proceedings or beginning, say, conciliation). If the step is something otherwise, then the section will not operate. The words 'barred, or the claimant's right extinguished' extend the provision in s 27 of the 1950 Act (see below), which simply provided that claims shall be 'barred'.

12.4

Section 12(2) provides that any party to the arbitration agreement may apply for such an order, provided notice is given to the other parties, but that it can only do this *after* a claim has arisen and *after* first exhausting any available arbitral process for obtaining an extension of time. The provision relating to 'other dispute resolution procedures' is also referred to in s 9(2) and reflects the increasingly common situation where arbitration may only be resorted to after other methods, such as conciliation, have been tried and failed. It is important that the applicant for the order is ready and willing to participate in the initial conciliation procedure. (A mediation clause is standard in all Hong Kong construction contracts of a certain kind, for example.) 'Notice' is dealt with in s 80. The words 'any available arbitral process' refer to situations where institutional rules apply and where they provide some process whereby an extension of time can be granted. In this case the applicant must first exhaust the procedure provided by those rules. Only if he is unsuccessful in obtaining the extension that he wants under those rules can he then approach the court. This is another example of the philosophy behind the Act, which is to support the arbitration process and to limit such applications as are made to the court to those that are really necessary.

12.5

Section 12(3) provides that the order will only be made if the court is satisfied that the circumstances are such that they were outside the reasonable contemplation of the parties when they agreed to the particular provision, *and* that it would be just to extend the time. Alternatively, the order will only be made if the court is satisfied that the conduct of one party makes it unjust to hold the other party to the strict terms of the relevant provision. The first two cases where the power would be justified have developed from the courts' interpretation of s 27 of the 1950 Act, while the third might be called 'consumer protection' and Part I of the Act is not concerned with this. The criteria will need to be interpreted in the light of the philosophy of the Act, and in particular that great care must be taken before interfering with the bargain which the parties have made.

12.6

Section 12(4) provides that the court may extend the time for such period and on such terms as it thinks fit. It may do so whether or not the time previously fixed (by the agreement or by a previous order) has expired.

12.7

Section 12(5) provides that an order under this section does not affect the operation of the Limitation Acts (which are dealt with in s 13).

12.8

Section 12(6) provides that the leave of the court is required for any appeal from a decision of the court under this section.

12.9

A *Scott v Avery* clause (see para 9.11) could be strengthened by introducing a time limit. For example, a clause in the agreement might read: 'Any claim hereunder must be in writing and the claimant's arbitrator appointed within three months of final discharge of the ship, failing which such claim will be deemed waived.' (See *Atlantic Shipping and Trading Co v Louis Dreyfus & Co* [1922] 2 AC 250.)

12.10

Section 27 of the 1950 Act (previously s 16(6) of the Arbitration Act 1934) gave the court the power to extend the time limit in certain cases, to mitigate the harshness of the contractual term and in particular where to enforce the agreement would cause hardship. (It could not, however, override normal limitation periods.) It stated:

> 'Where the terms of an agreement to refer future disputes to arbitration provide that any claims to which the agreement applies shall be barred unless notice to appoint an arbitrator is given or an arbitrator is appointed or some other step to commence arbitration proceedings is taken within a time fixed by the agreement, and a dispute arises to which the agreement applies, the High Court, if it is of opinion that in the circumstances of the case undue hardship would otherwise be caused, and notwithstanding that the time so fixed has expired, may, on such terms, if any, as the justice of the case may require, but without prejudice to the provisions of any enactment limiting the time for the commencement of arbitration proceedings, extend the time for such period as it thinks proper.'

12.11

The test in the 1950 Act, whether 'undue hardship' would otherwise be caused, was open to a wide range of interpretation. Changes have occurred over the years. Hardship was 'undue' if, for example, it was out of proportion to any fault of the claimant. In *Liberian Shipping Corporation v King & Son Ltd* [1967] 1 Lloyd's Rep 302, Lord Denning said, ' "Undue" simply means excessive. That is greater hardship than the circumstances of the case warrant. Even though a claimant has been at fault himself, it is an undue hardship on him if the consequences are out of proportion to his fault.' Criteria were laid down in 1981 and affirmed in 1985 (*Graham H Davies (UK) Ltd v Marc Rich & Co Ltd* [1985] 2 Lloyd's Rep 423) and these were to be used when a court decided whether or not to extend the time. They were:

- the length of the delay;
- the amount at stake;
- whether the delay was the applicant's fault;
- the degree of fault where the delay was caused by the applicant;
- whether the applicant was misled by the respondents;
- whether the delay has caused prejudice to the respondents.

There was dissatisfaction with the way in which the courts, in interpreting s 27 of the 1950 Act, were interfering with the bargain which the parties had made. Lord Denning, it will be recalled, had suggested (see comments in s 1) that the courts had some general power of supervisory jurisdiction over arbitrations (although see *Bremer Vulcan Schiffbau v South India Shipping Corporation* [1981] AC 909 and Lord Diplock's comments at p 983—at common law there is no general power to supervise arbitral proceedings). The position would now seem to be that the idea that the courts have some general supervisory jurisdiction over arbitrations has been abandoned.

12.12

Section 12 makes changes. The major change is that the previous test disappears. Instead, the court must now be satisfied before granting an extension of a time limit that circumstances have arisen which were outside the reasonable contemplation of the parties when they agreed the time limit and that it would be just to extend the time or that the conduct of one party makes it unjust to hold the other to the strict terms of their bargain. This is yet another example of the underlying philosophy of the Act which is that the parties have chosen to arbitrate, rather than litigate. They have made an agreement to that effect. It is their bargain. Party autonomy fits in with the general international understanding of arbitration. The courts should not interfere but should support the arbitration process. The parties should only be allowed to escape their contractual obligations if events arise which can clearly be said to fall outside that bargain. In other words, the courts will not override the parties' agreement unless such interference is fully justified.

12.13

The JCT Standard Forms of Building Contract contain a provision that, unless arbitration is commenced within a stated period after the issue of the Final Certificate, the certificate is 'conclusive evidence' as to certain important matters so that, while a party would not be barred from commencing arbitration, it would be unable to call any evidence to contravene the effect of the Final Certificate in respect of those matters. In *Crown Estate Commissioners v John Mowlem & Co Ltd* (1994) 70 BLR 1, the Court of Appeal (overruling *McLaughlin & Harvey plc v P & O Developments Ltd* (1992) 55 BLR 101) held that s 27 of the 1950 Act did not allow a court to extend that time limit. That position remains unchanged.

Section 13: Application of Limitation Acts

13.1

Section 13 is one of the mandatory provisions in Sched 1. It re-enacts ss 34(1), (2), (5) and (7)(*b*) of the Limitation Act 1980. There are small modifications which do not change the law, but merely restate it.

13.2

Section 13(1) states that the Limitation Acts apply to arbitral proceedings.

13.3

Section 13(2) provides that the court, where it has set aside an award or part of an award or declared it to be of no effect, may also order that in computing the time prescribed by the Limitation Acts for the purposes of determining whether legal proceedings in relation to the claim in question may be brought, the period between the commencement of the arbitration and the date of that order may be excluded.

13.4

Section 13(3) relates to a *Scott v Avery* clause (discussed above). Such a clause might be inserted into an agreement. The effect of this would be to allow a claim to be referred to arbitration and, if successful, enforced in court proceedings at any time, however late. The provisions of s 13(3)—that an award is a condition precedent to the bringing of legal proceedings in respect of a matter to which an arbitration agreement applies, shall be disregarded—changes this.

13.5

Section 13(4) defines the Limitation Acts to which this provision applies. It includes the Foreign Limitation Periods Act 1984. This avoids the imposition of an English limitation period where an applicable foreign law imposes a different period.

Section 14: Commencement of arbitral proceedings

14.1

Section 14 reflects to a degree Article 21 of the Model Law.

14.2

Section 14(1) and (2) states that the parties are free to agree when the arbitral proceedings are to be regarded as begun for the purposes of Part I and for the purposes of the Limitation Acts. If there is no agreement, default procedures are set out.

14.3

Section 14(3) states that where the arbitrator is named or designated in the agreement, the proceedings are begun when one party serves on the other party a notice in writing requiring him or them to submit that matter to the identified arbitrator. Service of notices is dealt with in s 76, and in particular s 76(6) says that 'a notice or other document' includes any form of communication in writing. The word 'matter' (ie 'in respect of a matter') is used rather than the word 'dispute'. This reflects the fact that a dispute is not the same as a claim (and see *Mustill & Boyd*, p 29). 'Matter' is a neutral word and will cover both. An arbitration clause which refers to 'claims' and one which refers to 'disputes' will therefore both be covered.

14.4

Section 14(4) states that where the arbitrator is to be appointed by the parties, the arbitral proceedings are commenced when one party serves on the other notice in writing requiring that other party to appoint an arbitrator or to agree to the appointment of an arbitrator. Again s 76 is relevant to the matter of service (but note that s 76 does *not* apply to the service of documents for the purposes of *legal* proceedings, because of course provision is made for this by rules of court; see the commentary on s 76 below).

14.5

Where an arbitration agreement provides that the parties are to agree an arbitrator but, where agreement is not reached within a certain time an application may be made to a third party to make the appointment, s14(4) will apply.

14.6

Section 14(5) states that where the arbitrator is to be appointed by a third party, the proceedings are begun when one of the parties gives notice in writing to that person (for example, the President or Vice President of the Chartered Institute of Arbitrators), requesting him to make the appointment.

14.7

Section 34(3) of the Limitation Act 1980 provided that an arbitration began when one party served on the other a notice requiring it to appoint an arbitrator or concur in the appointment of an arbitrator, or, where the arbitrator was identified in the arbitration agreement, when one party called on the other to submit the dispute to it. Section 10(2) of the 1950 Act, in part substituted by s 101 of the Courts and Legal Services Act 1990, also dealt with the power of the court in certain cases to appoint an arbitrator or umpire.

The arbitral tribunal

Section 15: The arbitral tribunal

15.1

Section 15 corresponds to Article 10 of the Model Law. This provides for the composition of the tribunal and lays down default procedures in the event that the parties fail to agree their own arrangements.

15.2

Section 15(1) states that the parties are free to agree on the number of arbitrators to form the tribunal and whether there is to be an umpire or a chairman. The distinction between a chairman and an umpire is set out in ss 20 and 21.

15.3

Section 15(2) states that, save where otherwise agreed by the parties, an agreement that the number of arbitrators shall be two or any other even number, shall be understood as requiring the appointment of an additional arbitrator as chairman. This is a sensible provision designed to avoid problems which might otherwise arise where the parties have expressly agreed even numbers of arbitrators. How a tribunal consisting of two arbitrators and a chairman is to arrive at its decision is set out in s 20. If the parties specifically wish the tribunal to consist of two arbitrators and an umpire s 21 applies.

15.4

Section 15(3) states that in the absence of any agreement as to the number of arbitrators, the tribunal shall consist of a sole arbitrator.

15.5

Article 10(1) of the Model Law provides that the parties are free to determine the number of arbitrators. The Act mirrors that provision. Article 10(2) of the Model Law provides that failing such determination, the tribunal shall consist of three arbitrators. In this respect s 15(3) parts company with the Model Law. The existing English rule provides that in the absence of agreement the default number shall be one. While parties should be free to choose three arbitrators if this is their wish, yet it was felt that this burden should not be imposed on them by default. Self-evidently the fees of three arbitrators will be three times as much as one!

15.6

Section 6 of the 1950 Act stated: 'Unless a contrary intention is expressed therein, every arbitration agreement shall, if no other mode of reference is provided, be deemed to include a provision that the reference shall be to a single arbitrator.' Section 8(1) of the 1950 Act stated: 'Unless a contrary intention is expressed therein, every arbitration agreement shall, where the reference is to two arbitrators, be deemed to include provision that the two arbitrators may appoint an umpire at any time after they are themselves appointed, and shall do so forthwith if they cannot agree.' Section 9 of the 1950 Act stated: 'Unless the contrary intention is expressed in the arbitration agreement, in any case where there is a reference to three arbitrators, the award of any two of the arbitrators shall be binding.' This last provision is substituted by s 6(2) of the 1979 Act. This was a patchy and incomplete system. Section 15, together with

ss 16 to 27 which deal with the procedure for the appointment of arbitrators, sweeps it all away and replaces it with a
new and comprehensive arrangement. The new provisions
fill certain gaps in the 1950 Act.

15.7

In domestic arbitrations the general practice is to appoint
one arbitrator, eg in building disputes. In maritime arbitrations sometimes two arbitrators are appointed: each party
appointing its 'own' arbitrator with an umpire to be
appointed by those arbitrators if they later fail to agree the
decision (*Laertis Shipping Corp v Exportadora* [1982] 1 Lloyd's
Rep 613). More commonly three arbitrators are appointed.
This is the international norm. One is appointed by each
party and one by the two party-appointed arbitrators. It is
often felt by foreign users that a three-person tribunal is an
insurance against a wholly unreasonable decision. In short,
to rely entirely on the decision of one person is too much of
a gamble and unwise. Furthermore, in disputes involving
foreign nationals they will sometimes feel more comfortable
with a 'mixed nationality' tribunal. Another advantage of
having a tribunal of three is where it may consist, say, of
two experts, each complementing the other in expertise where
the dispute involves highly technical matters, eg a dispute
relating to polluted land. The third arbitrator in such a
dispute might be a lawyer, particularly if he has specialised
in disputes of this kind.

15.8

The advantage of having three arbitrators, with each party
appointing one arbitrator and the two so appointed choos-
ing a third, is that time is not wasted while the parties try to
agree on a single arbitrator. However, the additional cost
and the difficulties of making arrangements for hearings etc
convenient to all three arbitrators as well as the parties, in
most cases greatly outweigh the advantages.

Section 16: Procedure for appointment of arbitrators

16.1

Section 16 expands upon Article 11(2),(3) (there is no equivalent to Article 11(1)) of the Model Law. Sections 16 to 18
provide default arrangements in the absence of agreement

between the parties, for appointing the tribunal and the procedure to be followed in the event of failure to appoint.

16.2

Section 16(1) states that the parties are free to agree on the procedure for appointing the arbitrator/s, including the procedure for appointing any chairman or umpire. Thus the section starts by setting out the basic philosophy of the freedom of the parties to choose their own procedure. Often institutional rules, for example the International Bar Association Rules, will be chosen by the parties to apply. The procedure will be set out and will become part of the arbitration agreement. Section 16(2) prescribes the fall-back procedures to apply in the absence of such agreement.

16.3

Section 16(3)–(7) sets out the default procedure if the parties have not agreed their own. Section 16(3) states that if the tribunal is to consist of a sole arbitrator, the parties shall jointly appoint him not later than 28 days after service of a request in writing by either party. The Model Law uses periods of 30 days, but the Act, anticipating the possibility of deadlines happening at weekends, introduces periods of 28 days. This is yet another example of the painstaking and immaculate attention to detail which is such a feature of this legislation, in this case anticipating difficulties which can be overcome by simple adjustments like numbers of days. See also s 78 for detailed instructions on reckoning periods of time stated in days.

16.4

Maritime arbitration users during the consultation process considered that 28 days was too long a period and that such a period might encourage abuse by the unscrupulous to delay matters. Parties tended to rely on statutory time limits and were not unhappy with the short period of seven days provided under the 1950 Act. It was felt, however, that arbitral institutions will in any event make their own provisions. The time limits set down in the Act are considered to be fair and reasonable for general purposes (for example, 28 days is probably the right period for the construction industry). Although ordinarily the court would not allow a departure from these time limits, there is a later provision, s 79, which provides for such time limits to be extended in certain circumstances.

16.5

Section 16(4) states that if the tribunal is to consist of two arbitrators, each party shall appoint one arbitrator not later than 14 days after service of a request in writing by either party to do so.

16.6

Section 16(5) provides that if the tribunal consists of three arbitrators, each party shall appoint one arbitrator not later than 14 days after service of a request in writing by either party to do so, and the two so appointed shall forthwith appoint a third arbitrator as the chairman of the tribunal, *not* as an umpire (see ss 20 and 21 for the distinction between the two).

16.7

Section 16(6) states:

> 'If the tribunal is to consist of two arbitrators and an umpire—
> (a) each party shall appoint one arbitrator not later than 14 days after service of a request in writing by either party to do so, and
> (b) the two so appointed may appoint an umpire at any time after they themselves are appointed and shall do so before any substantive hearing or forthwith if they cannot agree on a matter relating to the arbitration.'

Note the use of the mandatory 'shall' throughout until the provision relating to the appointment of an umpire, where the discretionary 'may' is introduced in relation to the timing of the appointment, with the important reinstatement of 'shall' compelling an appointment before a substantive hearing or following disagreement. See s 21(5) for the reason for this.

16.8

One of the perceived advantages of arbitration is that parties, anxious not to leave an important decision to a single 'judge' prefer to have their dispute resolved by a tribunal of three (see above). Thus the parties are free to select the number set down in the agreement or by any rules which they have agreed will govern the arbitration. It is not uncommon for each of the parties to appoint one arbitrator, leaving it to these two to appoint either a third arbitrator or an umpire. The distinction between an umpire and a third arbitrator is important, and the agreement should state clearly what is intended. An umpire, if the two appointed arbitrators fail to agree, replaces those arbitrators, ie the reference is to two arbitrators or one umpire and never involves a tribunal consisting of three members. An agreement for a reference to three arbitrators, on the other hand, takes effect in accordance with its terms, and under the previous and present law a majority decision is binding.

16.9

Section 16(7) states that in any other case, particularly if there are more than two parties, s 18 applies as in the case of a failure of the agreed appointment procedure. This is necessary in order to provide for multi-party situations where the arbitration agreements between pairs of parties only cover the case where there are two parties.

16.10

The 1950 Act made provisions about the appointment of arbitrators, failure to appoint arbitrators, and filling vacancies. It did not clearly distinguish between the different concepts. Section 16 is about appointing arbitrators and not muddled with other concepts. Its provisions simplify and clarify the previous law.

16.11

In s 74 (immunity of arbitral institutions) reference is made to bodies who appoint or nominate arbitrators. It might be appropriate here to examine the distinction between 'appointment' and 'nomination'. An appointment is where the arbitration agreement provides that the institution or person, say, the Chartered Institute of Arbitrators, is to appoint an arbitrator, often where the parties have failed to agree on an arbitrator themselves within a fixed time limit. Such an appointment by the institution is final and the parties have no right of subsequent objection. They have effectively agreed to relinquish their own ability to appoint an arbitrator to the

Chartered Institute of Arbitrators and must put up with whoever is so appointed by them. It is arguable—although there is no case law or other authority on the point which the authors can find—that a nomination is different. Here, the Chartered Institute of Arbitrators, for example, simply tells the parties whom they must appoint. The appointment is by the parties themselves, although they are bound by the nomination. There is probably little difference in practice, although some arbitrators who are appointed by an institution convey their acceptance of the appointment to the appointing authority and simply tell the parties that they have been appointed, stating their terms of acting. If they are nominated, however, they convey their acceptance to the parties themselves. In either case, unless the arbitration agreement specifically provides for it (such as the arbitration provisions in most current JCT contracts for building works), the authority, once having made an appointment or nomination, has no power to make another appointment or nomination if the first one fails, unless the parties make a fresh agreement that it should do so.

16.12

It appears to be an increasingly common practice for parties (or more particularly, their legal representatives) to 'interview' arbitrators before appointing them. The practice seems to be that two or three arbitrators are invited to submit their CVs, which are closely and carefully scrutinised, often, but not necessarily, by both parties. One, or possibly more, is then invited for interview. This gives the opportunity to evaluate the individual, to be reassured about his reliable availability etc. The authors know of some experienced arbitrators who will refuse to attend such an interview unless both sides are present, ie to avoid the possibility that any such appointment by one might be negatived by the other. They also know of instances where firm X has carried out this careful investigation of certain arbitrators, as has firm Y with other arbitrators (X and Y representing two parties), but where Y has been so confident in the evaluation process generally that he has in fact gone along with X's recommendation to appoint a certain arbitrator. Such co-operation is constructive and in the spirit of the Act.

17 Power in case of default to appoint sole arbitrator

17.1

This section deals with the power in case of default by each party to appoint an arbitrator. It deals with the case where two parties are each to appoint an arbitrator and one party refuses to do so. It replaces s 7(*b*) of the 1950 Act and simplifies and clarifies the previous law.

17.2

Section 17(1) states that where each of two parties to an arbitration agreement is to appoint an arbitrator and one refuses to do so, or fails to do so within the specified time, the other party, having appointed its arbitrator, may give notice in writing to the party in default that it proposes to appoint its own arbitrator to act as sole arbitrator. The section is prefaced by the usual words, 'unless the parties otherwise agree'. The word 'refuses' is used deliberately. If a party refuses, as opposed to fails to appoint, an arbitrator, then the non-defaulting party would not need to wait for the expiration of the relevant period within which the defaulting party may make such an appointment. It could apply under the provisions of s 17 forthwith.

17.3

Section 17(2) states that if, within seven clear days of issue of that notice, the party in default fails to make the appointment and notify the other party that it has done so, the other party may appoint its arbitrator as sole arbitrator. Note these two points: both to appoint *and* notify. Even if a party appoints, if it fails to notify the other party, that party can appoint its own arbitrator as sole arbitrator. That sole arbitrator's award shall be binding on both parties as if he had been appointed as sole arbitrator by the agreement.

17.4

Section 17(3) gives the right to the defaulting party to apply to the court which may set aside the appointment. It must give notice of its intention to apply to the court. Note that on such setting aside the arbitrator in question remains an arbitrator. What is set aside is his appointment as sole arbitrator.

17.5

Section 17(4) states that the leave of the court is required for any appeal from a decision of the court under this provision.

17.6

Section 7 of the 1950 Act said:

> 'Where an arbitration agreement provides that the reference shall be to two arbitrators, one to be appointed by each party, then, unless a contrary intention is expressed therein—
>
> (a) if either of the appointed arbitrators refuses to act, or is incapable of acting, or dies, the party who appointed him may appoint a new arbitrator in his place;
>
> (b) if, on such a reference, one party fails to appoint an arbitrator, either originally or by way of substitution as aforesaid, for seven clear days after the other party, having appointed his arbitrator, has served the party making default with notice to make the appointment, the party who has appointed an arbitrator may appoint that arbitrator to act as sole arbitrator in the reference and his award shall be binding on both parties as if he had been appointed by consent.'

Note that the defaulting party was under no obligation to say that it had made an appointment. The present position, set out above, is a significant improvement on the previous law.

Section 18: Failure of appointment procedure

18.1

Section 18 deals with failure of appointment procedure. It corresponds to Article 11(4) of the Model Law. It supersedes the relevant parts of ss 7 and 10 of the 1950 Act.

18.2

Section 18(1) sets out slightly more fully than previously the general principle that the parties are free to agree their own procedure. In particular this subsection deals with what is to happen in the event of a failure of the appointment procedure. It states that there is no failure if an appointment is duly made under s 17 (power in case of default to appoint a sole arbitrator) unless that appointment has been set aside under s 17(3).

18.3

Section 18(2) states that if the parties have been unable or unwilling to agree a procedure to cover the position as to what will happen if there is failure by one of them to appoint, then either/any of the parties may apply to the court. Again this reflects the philosophy of the Act: the parties can agree, and if they are unable or unwilling to, then the court is there to assist, to make the arbitration agreement work.

18.4

Section 18(3) sets out the powers which the court can exercise. The court can give directions as to the making of any necessary appointments. It can direct that the tribunal shall be constituted by such appointments (or any one of them) as have been made. It can revoke any appointments already made. The court can make any necessary appointments itself. These are very wide-ranging and give the court great flexibility to deal with particular situations. For example, such powers, and the use of the plural in the drafting ('appointments') could cover the case where there are more than two parties to the reference and where some, but not all, have appointed their own arbitrators. As to the power to revoke any appointments already made, this provision ensures that the parties will be treated fairly and equally. For example, if one party had its own arbitrator but the other had had its arbitrator imposed on it by the court, in circumstances which were no fault of its own, it might well feel aggrieved. By giving the court power to revoke any appointments already made, no such suggestions of unfairness could be made.

18.5

Section 18(4) states that an appointment made by the court under this provision has the same effect and status as if it had been made with the agreement of the parties. Section 18(5) again implies a limit to court intervention by stating that the leave of the court is required for any appeal from a decision of the court under this provision. The Model Law states that there should be no appeal from a decision of the court. The Act, however, permits such an appeal as it is felt that there may well be questions of important general principles which would benefit from authoritative appellate guidance.

18.6

The new provisions supersede the relevant parts of s 7 of the 1950 Act (referred to above) and s 10 of the 1950 Act which also dealt with the power of the court in certain cases to appoint an arbitrator or umpire. Parts of s 10 were substituted by s 101 of the Courts and Legal Services Act 1990.

Section 19: Court to have regard to agreed qualifications

19.1

Section 19 states that in deciding whether to exercise, and in considering how to exercise, any of its powers under s 16 (procedure for appointment) or s 18 (failure of appointment procedure), the court shall have due regard to any agreement of the parties as to the qualifications required of an arbitrator. It derives from Article 11(5) of the Model Law.

19.2

If the parties have made any such agreement it is obviously fair and proper for the court not only to take account of this, but also to preserve it as much as possible. It is most advantageous to the parties to be able to choose their own tribunal. Some firms of solicitors, for example, repose such confidence in certain experts whose integrity and reputation are beyond reproach and whom they have used over the years as experts or arbitrators (regardless of whether they have 'won' or 'lost') that they will continue to use them. The court can take account of various determining factors, such as professional qualifications and experience, availability, etc. They can also specify certain qualities or state that certain individuals are ineligible. In *Rahcassi Shipping Co SA v The Blue Star Line* [1969] 1 QB 173, the agreement stated, '... arbitrators and umpires shall be commercial men and not lawyers ...' Such agreement might relate to the arbitrator being on the panel of qualified members of the Chartered Institute of Arbitrators, or to being a practising lawyer, or a 'commercial man' (as opposed to a professional person who might lack a 'feel' for trade). In *Pando Compania Naviera SA v Filmo SAS* [1975] 1 QB 742 it was held that a full-time maritime arbitrator who had retired years ago as a practising solicitor, was a 'commercial man' under a charterparty arbitration clause. Maritime arbitrators will nearly always be members of the LMAA. The Centrocon arbitration clause, for example, states, 'All the disputes from time to time arising out of this contract shall, unless the parties agree forthwith on a single arbitrator, be referred to the final arbitrament of two arbitrators carrying on business in London who shall be Members of the Baltic and engaged in the shipping and/or Grain Trades, one to be appointed by each of the parties, with power to such Arbitrators to appoint an Umpire ...' In some trades, for example Federation of Oils, Seeds & Fats Association Ltd (FOSFA), arbitrators can only be appointed if they are on a panel. In others, for example Grain & Feed Trade Association (GAFTA), arbitrators merely have to be a member/employee of a member, and to be engaged/formerly engaged in the trade concerned. These are the sort of matters to which the court would have regard.

Section 20: Chairman

20.1

Section 20 is new. The previous Arbitration Acts did not provide for the office of chairman.

20.2

Section 20(1) deals with the concept of the office of chairman and provides that where the parties have agreed that there will be a chairman they are free to agree his functions in relation to the making of the decisions, orders and awards. Again the Act places reliance on the agreement of the parties. Section 20(2) states that in the absence of such agreement default provisions apply.

20.3

The default provisions are set out in Section 20(3) and (4). Decisions, orders and awards shall be made by all or by a majority of the arbitrators, including the chairman. The view of the chairman alone shall prevail in relation to a decision, order or award in respect of which there is neither unanimity nor a majority.

20.4

Under the 1950 Act the only provision relating to a disagreement amongst arbitrators where there was no umpire was s 9, amended by s 6(2) of the 1979 Act. This stated 'Unless the contrary intention is expressed in the arbitration agreement, in any case where there is a reference to three arbitrators, the award of any two of the arbitrators shall be binding.'

20.5

Under the previous law there could be either a chairman or umpire (although as stated above the previous legislation did not provide for the office of a chairman). This caused considerable confusion abroad, particularly in the USA, where the terms were used differently. Sections 20 and 21 set out the differences between the two.

Section 21: Umpire

21.1

By s 21(1) where the parties have agreed that there is to be an umpire they can agree what his functions are to be and in particular whether or not he is to attend the proceedings and when he is to replace the other arbitrators as the tribunal, with the power to make decisions, orders and awards.

21.2

Section 21(2) provides that if the parties have been unable or unwilling to reach such an agreement, then prescribed rules are laid down in the following subsections.

21.3

Section 21(3) states that the umpire shall attend the proceedings and be supplied with the same documents and other materials as are supplied to the other arbitrators (by s 82(1) 'arbitrator' includes an umpire). The word 'attend' the proceedings is used, rather than 'take part' or 'participate'. The saving of time and costs by this provision is discussed below.

21.4

Section 21(4) makes it clear that decisions, orders and awards shall be made by the other arbitrators. In other words, their authority continues. However, it only continues until they cannot agree a matter relating to the arbitration. Upon such disagreement, they must forthwith give notice in writing, both to the parties and to the umpire, stating that they are unable to agree. At that point the umpire steps in and the other arbitrators withdraw. The umpire thereafter acts as sole arbitrator (as he did under the previous law). Note that this provision is written in the mandatory mode, ie 'shall'. Note also that the moment any disagreement arises between the arbitrators, even on a minor procedural/interlocutory matter such as a period of time to be allowed, the umpire will take over and conduct the proceedings from then on as sole arbitrator. This puts a healthy pressure on the arbitrators not to fall out over minor matters but to make every effort to reach sensible agreements. In arbitrations with an umpire, therefore, if the parties do not agree to exclude or change this provision, then there will be strong pressure on the arbitrators to agree on everything except matters fundamental to the dispute, since as soon as they disagree they must retire from the case and the umpire will step in and take over.

21.5

Section 21(5) deals with the situation where the arbitrators cannot agree but fail to give notice of this fact, or one of them fails to join in the giving of notice which is required by s 21(4). In this case any party to the proceedings may apply to the court (the usual rules relating to notice being given to the parties and to the tribunal apply), which may make an order that the umpire shall replace the other arbitrators as the tribunal, with the power to make decisions, orders and awards as if he were the sole arbitrator. Note that this provision is framed in the discretionary mode, ie 'may'. Note also that it is narrower than s 8(3) of the 1950 Act which is set out below.

21.6

Section 21(6) adds the usual requirement that the leave of the court is required for any appeal from a court under this provision.

21.7

It was mentioned above that the distinction between an umpire and a third arbitrator is important, and that the agreement should clearly state what is intended. An umpire, if the two appointed arbitrators disagree, replaces those arbitrators. In other words, as we have seen, the reference is to two arbitrators or to one umpire/arbitrator and not to three. Section 8(1) of the 1950 Act stated, 'Unless a contrary intention is expressed therein, every arbitration agreement shall, where the reference is to two arbitrators, be deemed to include provision that the two arbitrators may appoint an umpire at any time after they are themselves appointed and shall do so forthwith if they cannot agree.' A term was also implied by s 8(2) of the 1950 Act, which was that if there were two arbitrators and they notified any party or the umpire, in writing, that they disagreed, the umpire might enter on the reference forthwith in place of the arbitrators. Section 8(3) of the 1950 Act stated, 'At any time after the appointment of an umpire, however appointed, the High Court may, on the application of any party to the reference and notwithstanding anything to the contrary in the arbitration agreement, order that the umpire shall enter upon the reference in lieu of the arbitrators and as if he were a sole arbitrator'.

21.8

The role of the umpire, then, is to make a decision in the eventuality of the arbitrators failing to reach agreement. He may be appointed at the time of the disagreement, whereupon he will have to listen to all the evidence again with the consequent waste of time and costs. On the other hand, if he is appointed at the beginning of the reference and sits in throughout the hearing, costs are similarly thrown away if no disagreement occurs. (In this situation, although he sits with the arbitrators and has the right to ask for clarification of the evidence, he takes no part in the deliberations until they have told him/the parties in writing that they are in disagreement.) The new provision requires that he attend and be supplied with all the materials which the arbitrators have before them. In the eventuality of a disagreement, he will at least have heard and read all the evidence by the time the disagreement arises so that the expenses which would otherwise have been incurred if he had to 'start wholly from the beginning' are thereby mitigated, if not avoided.

Section 22: Decision-making where no chairman or umpire

22.1

Section 22 is a short section which deals with decision-making where there are two or more arbitrators but no chairman or umpire. Section 22(1) states that where the parties agree that there shall be two or more arbitrators with no chairman or umpire, they are free to agree how the tribunal is to make decisions, orders and awards. In other words, express freedom is given to the parties to decide how the tribunal shall reach any decisions.

22.2

Section 22(2) provides that in the absence of any agreement, decisions, orders and awards shall be made by all, ie unanimously, or by a majority of the arbitrators. Clearly in each case, particularly where there is an even number of arbitrators, it is vital that the parties specify what is to happen if there is no majority in favour of any decision. Even where there is an odd number of arbitrators, in complex cases such as construction disputes there can often be a situation when all the arbitrators hold different opinions on individual issues.

Section 23: Revocation of arbitrator's authority

23.1

Section 23 deals with the circumstances in which the authority of an arbitrator may be revoked. It supersedes s 1 of the 1950 Act.

23.2

Section 23(1) states that the parties are free to agree in what circumstances the authority of an arbitrator may be revoked, and s 23(2) is constructed in the usual way by saying that where there is no agreement, default procedures (set down in the following subsections) apply, which rules will govern the revocation of his authority. For example, one party alone may revoke the appointment if the parties have agreed between themselves that that party has this power.

23.3

Section 23(3) sets out the only way such revocation can be effected. It states that the authority of an arbitrator may not be revoked except by the parties acting jointly, or by an arbitral or other institution or person vested by the parties with powers in that regard. Note here that, absent agreement to the contrary (see above), only the parties 'acting jointly' may revoke. 'An arbitral or other institution' would include, for example, the International Chamber of Commerce (ICC), the London Court of International Arbitration (LCIA), the American Arbitration Association (AAA), etc. The parties would have agreed, expressly or by implication, that the institution would deal with this matter by having referred in their agreement to being bound by such rules.

23.4

Section 23(4) states that revocation by the parties acting jointly must be agreed in writing *unless* the parties also agree (and this need not be in writing as the Act says 'whether or not in writing') to terminate the arbitration agreement. An agreement to end the arbitration agreement does not need to be in writing. The parties may simply mutually abandon it, and this might be inferred from their conduct. (The position where a claimant has shown inordinate and inexcusable delay in pursuing his claim is dealt with in s 41(3).)

23.5

Section 23(5) states that none of the above affects the powers of the court to revoke an appointment under s 18 (powers exercisable in case of failure to appoint) or to remove an arbitrator on the grounds set out in s 24 (see below). In other words, the powers of the court remain unaffected by this section.

23.6

Section 1 of the 1950 Act provided: 'The authority of an arbitrator or umpire appointed by or by virtue of an arbitration agreement shall, unless a contrary intention is expressed in the agreement, be irrevocable except by leave of the High Court or a judge thereof'. The arbitrator was given no power to resign nor had the parties any power to remove him, even by mutual agreement, without leave of the court. The rationale presumably was that, by accepting the appointment, the arbitrator had entered into a contract with the parties to carry out and complete the arbitration, (see *K/S Norjarl A/S v Hyundai Heavy Industries Co Ltd* [1991] 3 All ER 211). Such a contract would not be revocable unless all parties to it, including the arbitrator, agreed. If the arbitrator wished to resign he could not do so unless all parties to the arbitration agreed. If the parties wished to remove him they could not do so unless he agreed or unless they applied to the court to revoke his authority under s 1 of the 1950 Act. One solution which one of the authors has been known to be used effectively (although not against him as an arbitrator!) was for the parties to bring the arbitration to an end and start it again before a new arbitrator. However, such makeshifts were unsatisfactory and the new provisions will remove the need for them in the future.

Section 24: Power of court to remove arbitrator

24.1

Section 24 is one of the mandatory provisions in Sched 1. It corresponds to Articles 12–15 of the Model Law. The provision for the removal of an arbitrator, either by the parties acting together or by an arbitral institution such as the Chartered Institute of Arbitrators or, as a last resort, by the court, is new. The term 'misconduct' disappears although there is no change in the law.

24.2

Section 24(1) states that an application to the court by a party to the arbitral proceedings to remove an arbitrator, can be on one or more of the following grounds:

'(a) that circumstances exist that give rise to justifiable doubts as to his impartiality;
(b) that he does not possess the qualifications required by the arbitration agreement;
(c) that he is physically or mentally incapable of conducting the proceedings or there are justifiable doubts as to his capacity to do so;
(d) that he has refused or failed—
　　(i) properly to conduct the proceedings; or
　　　　(ii) use all reasonable despatch in conducting the proceedings or making an award.'

In addition to these grounds, the requirement is that substantial injustice has been or will be caused to the applicant. Notice must be given to the other parties, to the arbitrator concerned and to any other arbitrator. In this connection note s 73, which sets out circumstances in which parties forfeit their right to object to any irregularity regarding the tribunal or the proceedings—effectively it requires a person to 'put up or shut up' if a challenge is to be made.

24.3

The DAC Report (February 1996) made it abundantly clear that the ground set out in s 24(1)(*d*) '... only exists to cover what we hope will be the very rare case when an arbitrator so conducts the proceedings that it can fairly be said that instead of carrying through the object of arbitration as stated in the Act, he is in effect frustrating that object'.

24.4

Section 24(2) deals with the situation where an arbitral or other institution or person has been given the power to remove an arbitrator. It states that the court shall not exercise its power of removal unless satisfied that the applicant has first exhausted any available recourse to that institution or person. In other words, if the rules provide a mechanism for removal, they must first be used. Under LMAA Terms (1977), for example, a party can force a sole arbitrator to retire if he cannot offer a date for the hearing within a 'reasonable time', and if the parties cannot agree on a substitute the president will appoint one.

24.5

Section 24(3) states that the tribunal may continue the proceedings and make an award while such an application is pending. This is a practical provision designed to prevent a party deliberately trying to delay proceedings by making a groundless application to the court.

24.6

Section 24(4) states that where the court removes an arbitrator it may make such order as it thinks fit with respect to his fees or expenses, or the repayment of any fees or expenses already paid. This power would only be exercisable where the behaviour of the arbitrator is inexcusable and that this should result in him being deprived of all or some of his fees. This replaces s 13(3) of the 1950 Act which stated, 'The High Court may, on the application of any party to a reference, remove an arbitrator or umpire who fails to use all reasonable despatch in entering on and proceeding with the reference and making an award, and an arbitrator or umpire who is removed by the High Court under this subsection shall not be entitled to receive any remuneration in respect of his services'. Section 24(4) is much better drafted than s 13(3) of the 1950 Act and it gives the court a more flexible power. Note, however, that while an arbitrator may be deprived of his fees in whole or in part under this section, he cannot be sued for damages unless he has acted 'in bad faith' (and please see s 29—immunity of arbitrator).

24.7

Section 24(5) states that the arbitrator is entitled to appear and be heard by the court before it makes any order under this section. This is self-evidently fair. Statutory recognition has been given to what is in any event a current practice.

24.8

Section 24(6) states that leave of the court is required for any appeal from a decision of the court under this section.

24.9

Under the 1950 Act there were two alternative grounds on which an arbitrator might be removed by the court: delay and misconduct. Section 13(3) of the 1950 Act conferred power on the courts to remove an arbitrator. This stated:

> 'The High Court may, on the application of any party to a refer-ence, remove an arbitrator or umpire who fails to use all rea-sonable despatch in entering on or proceeding with the refer-ence and making an award, and an arbitrator or umpire who is removed by the High Court under this subsection shall not be entitled to receive any remuneration in respect of his services.'

In short, the removal could be on the grounds of delay. The power was discretionary. What was 'reasonable depatch' depended on all the circumstances, but the circumstances should relate to the parties and not to the arbitrator. Section 23(1) of the 1950 Act provided, 'Where an arbitrator or umpire has misconducted himself or the proceedings, the

High Court may remove him.' The word 'misconduct' caused some misunderstanding, implying as it does, a degree of moral turpitude. The words now used 'that he has refused or failed properly to conduct the proceedings' mean the same as 'misconduct' in the context of arbitration, but are much clearer and avoid the unfortunate implication.

24.10

Article 12 of the Model Law specifies justifiable doubts as to the 'independence' (as well as impartiality) of an arbitrator as a ground for revoking his authority. This is not specified as a ground in s 24. It might, of course, give rise to justifiable doubts as to the impartiality of the arbitrator. It was felt by the drafters of the Act that the inclusion of independence would give rise to endless arguments, as it apparently has in Sweden and USA. There were many reasons for its non-inclusion, for example, that there may be situations in which the parties wish their arbitrators to have familiarity with a specific field, rather than being independent.

Section 25: Resignation of arbitrator

25.1

Section 25(1) states that the parties are free to agree with an arbitrator as to the consequences of his resignation as regards his entitlement to fees or expenses, and to any liability for breach of contract incurred by him. The way in which this provision is drafted means that the agreement referred to is confined to an agreement as to the consequences of resignation. Suppose an arbitrator agreed not to resign, or only to resign in certain specified circumstances, with no further details as to what would happen if the promise was broken. This would not be within the subsection.

25.2

Section 25(2) makes the usual provision that if there is no agreement by the parties on this matter then default provisions apply which are set out below.

25.3

Section 25(3) states that provided he gives notice to the parties, an arbitrator who resigns his appointment may apply to the court to grant him relief from any contractual liability he has incurred, and to make such order as it thinks fit with respect to his fees or expenses. Note s 64 which deals with recoverable fees and expenses of arbitrators.

25.4

Section 25(4) states that if the court is satisfied in all the circumstances that it was reasonable for the arbitrator to resign, it may grant relief on such terms as it thinks fit. This is an important provision and is recognition of the fact that there may be circumstances when it is perfectly proper for the arbitrator to be allowed to resign. In particular, this might be the case in the light of s 34, which gives the parties freedom to agree any procedure they wish. Suppose they agree a wholly unworkable timetable about which the arbitrator had not been warned, which he thinks would be impossible to meet and which he considers would be in breach of his duty under s 33, he should be allowed to resign from his obligations. The court is given a discretion to grant relief as it thinks fit.

25.5

Section 25(5) requires that the leave of the court is necessary for any appeal from a decision of the court under these provisions.

25.6

Previously an arbitrator had no authority to retire unless he was entitled to do so under the arbitration agreement. His appointment was irrevocable. If he resigned he might be in breach of contract with the parties or with the person or institution who appointed him. He could not withdraw from his obligations merely because they had become onerous or inconvenient. It would be unlikely that the agreement would provide for his resignation, having accepted the appointment. However, he might retire if one of the parties asked him to. For example, it might be that 'without prejudice' material had been disclosed to him. It might be where circumstances had changed since his acceptance of the appointment, due possibly to a take-over, and where he might now have a financial interest in the outcome of the arbitration. Certain rules permit resignation of an arbitrator. For example, according to the Rules of the London Bar Arbitration Scheme an arbitrator must resign (unless the parties ask him to remain) if he is unable to offer a hearing date within a reasonable time. The previous Acts, while they conferred powers on the court to remove an arbitrator, provided no power for an arbitrator to retire, once he had accepted the appointment. (See also the discussion in para 23.6 above).

Section 26: Death of arbitrator or person appointing him

26.1

Section 26(1) is one of the mandatory provisions in Sched 1. It provides that the authority of an arbitrator is personal and ceases on his death.

26.2

Section 26(2) re-enacts s 2(2) of the 1950 Act. It states that unless otherwise agreed by the parties, the death of a person by whom an arbitrator was appointed does not revoke the arbitrator's authority. Section 2(1) of the 1950 Act permitted the arbitration agreement to be enforced by or against the personal representative of the deceased party. Section 2(2) of the 1950 Act stated, 'The authority of an arbitrator shall not be revoked by the death of any party by whom he was appointed'. Section 2(3) of the 1950 Act stated, 'Nothing in this section shall be taken to effect the operation of any enactment or rule of law by virtue of which any right of action is extinguished by the death of a person'. In other words, an arbitration agreement remained binding even though a party died, although in certain cases it might be that the death extinguished the right of action itself. Clearly the death of a party could have a significant effect on the conduct of the reference; for example, until a personal representative was appointed, who could enforce the award if this were necessary?

26.3

Section 26 complements s 8 (which deals with whether an arbitration agreement is discharged by the death of a party).

26.4

It is common for parties in long arbitrations to insure against the arbitrator's death. The financial consequences of such a death, possibly just as he was about to publish his award, can be very severe financially with the necessity to start the proceedings again from scratch before another arbitrator.

Section 27: Filling of vacancy, &c

27.1

Section 27 corresponds to Article 15 of the Model Law but also deals with other ancillary matters.

27.2

Section 27(1) states that where an arbitrator ceases to hold office, the parties are free to agree:

'(a) whether and if so how the vacancy is to be filled,
(b) whether and if so to what extent the previous proceedings should stand, and
(c) what effect (if any) his ceasing to hold office has on any appointment made by him (alone or jointly).'

27.3

Section 27(2) makes the usual provision that, in the absence of agreement between the parties, the subsections that follow will apply.

27.4

Section 27(3) states that the provisions of s 16 (procedure for appointment of arbitrators) and s18 (failure of appointment procedure) apply in relation to the filling of a vacancy in the same way as in an original appointment. For example, in the absence of any specific agreement to the contrary, if it is a sole arbitrator the parties must agree on a replacement within 28 days (s 16(3) which deals with procedure for the appointment of arbitrators) and if they fail to do so either party may apply to the court for an appointment under s 18(2) (failure of appointment procedure).

27.5

Section 27(4) states that the reconstituted tribunal shall determine whether and if so to what extent the previous proceedings should stand; for instance it may be necessary for the timing of any hearing fixed by the previous arbitrator to be changed. However, this does not affect any right of a party to challenge those proceedings on any ground which had arisen before the arbitrator ceased to hold office.

27.6

Section 27(5) states that his ceasing to hold office does not affect any appointment by him, alone or jointly, of another arbitrator, in particular any appointment of a chairman or umpire. The new arbitrator therefore cannot change such appointment already made.

27.7

The court's powers to fill a vacancy created by its removal of an arbitrator, contained in s 25 of the 1950 Act, are not reproduced. The original procedures for appointing an arbitrator are governed by ss 16 and 18, and the filling of vacancies must be effected by the same machinery. Section 25(1) of the 1950 Act applied where the court created the vacancy by removing one or more members of the tribunal. Provided that at least one arbitrator remained, or on the removal of an umpire who had not entered on the reference, the court could replace him on a party's application. The new law provides simpler and more clearly expressed rules about filling vacancies.

Section 28: Joint and several liability of parties to arbitrators for fees and expenses

28.1

Section 28 is one of the mandatory provisions in Sched 1.

28.2

Section 28(1) states that the parties are jointly and severally liable to pay the arbitrators such reasonable fees and expenses, if any, as are appropriate in the circumstances.

28.3

'Reasonable' and 'appropriate' suggest that one party could not therefore be responsible for unreasonably heavy fees which have been agreed to by the other party. 'Fees' would include the hourly or daily fee which has been agreed, including cancellation fees, and fees for travelling time, if this is on a different scale. Expenses would include travelling expenses, the cost of any legal or expert advice the arbitrator might have taken (and in particular note s 37(2) which concerns experts, legal advisors or assessers appointed by the tribunal), the cost of room hire if the arbitrator has agreed to arrange this, and the cost of any particular technical aid, eg electronic recording. (In respect of these last matters, arbitrators would be wise to leave this sort of arrangement to the parties.)

28.4

Section 28(2) states that provided notice is given to the other parties and to the arbitrators, any party may apply to the court which may order that the amount of the fees and expenses shall be considered and adjusted by such means and upon such terms as it may direct. Notice is covered by s 80.

28.5

Section 28(3) states that if the application is made after the amount has already been paid, the court may order the repayment of any amount as is shown to be excessive. However, it shall not do so unless it is shown that it is reasonable in the circumstances to order repayment. Note that this power gives the court power to adjust fees and expenses even *after* they have been paid. It would not be 'reasonable' to order repayment, for example, where an applicant delayed in making an application. See also s 56 (power to withhold award in case of non-payment) for the position where the arbitrator has refused to deliver an award until his fees are paid and the right of the parties to challenge the amount demanded at that stage.

28.6

Section 28(5) makes it clear that nothing in this section relating to the liability of parties to the arbitrator for his fees affects their liability to each other in respect of payment of the costs of the arbitration generally, including the arbitrator's fees and expenses (see ss 59 to 65 which deal with the costs of the arbitration and how they are ultimately to be allocated between the parties). It also makes it clear that nothing in the section 'affects ... any contractual right of an arbitrator to payment of his fees and expenses'. An arbitrator has a contract with the parties, and irrespective of this section he could sue the parties for payment of his fees and expenses as a matter of contract.

28.7

What this section does is to make it clear that *all* parties are jointly and severally liable to *all* the arbitrators for payment of their fees and expenses, but only to the extent that the fees and expenses are reasonable. Say, in a case where each of two parties has appointed an arbitrator, one of the parties has agreed with the arbitrator it has appointed a scale of fees which might objectively be thought excessive. The arbitrator concerned could pursue the party appointing him for fees on that scale as a matter of *contract*. However, if he could not obtain payment from that party, say because of insolvency, he could pursue the other party for payment of fees and expenses under the provision for 'joint and several liability' in this section. In that case he could only recover *reasonable* fees and expenses, not necessarily fees on the scale he had agreed with the party appointing him.

28.8

Section 28(5) also emphasises that the joint and several liability of the parties is owed to the arbitrator by the parties collectively. In other words, the relationship is between the arbitrator on the one hand and the parties on the other. How the parties share out those fees, and in what proportion, is a separate matter. If one of the parties agreed a very high fee with the arbitrator, notwithstanding the provision in s 28(1) which relates to 'reasonable fees', the arbitrator could still sue that party under general contract law.

28.9

Section 28(6) makes clear that reference to arbitrators includes an arbitrator who has ceased to act and an umpire who has not replaced the other arbitrators.

Section 29: Immunity of arbitrator
29.1

Section 29 is one of the mandatory provisions in Sched 1.

29.2

Section 29(1) states that an arbitrator is not liable for anything done or omitted in the discharge or purported discharge of his functions as arbitrator unless the act or omission is shown to have been in bad faith. The concept of bad faith was clarified in *Melton Medes Ltd v Securities and Investments Board* [1995] 3 All ER 880. It covered malice in the sense of personal spite or desire to injure for improper reasons, or knowledge of the absence of power to make the decision in question. The burden of establishing bad faith lies on the complainant.

29.3

This provision is completely new. It applies notwithstanding agreement by the parties to the contrary. For many years there has been a traditional view that an arbitrator should be treated like a judge, and be immune from liability for negligence or lack of ability in the discharge of his functions (see *below*) but the new provision makes his status clear.

29.4

Judges acting in their judicial capacity are immune not only from liability in negligence but even where they have acted maliciously or corruptly. The Act makes it clear, however, that immunity from suit is only available to an arbitrator to the extent that he has acted in good faith. If the act or omission for which he claims immunity can be shown by the party alleging it to have been in bad faith, such immunity will be lost. The burden will be on the party alleging; it will not be for the arbitrator to prove that he acted in good faith.

29.5

Difficulties have arisen in the past concerning claims for immunity, and in particular differentiating between persons acting as arbitrators and persons acting in other capacities, for example, valuers. An expert may be liable in negligence. However, in the case of arbitrators, the probability was that because of the judicial nature of their functions, they would not be liable for negligence. Problems arose when it was not entirely clear whether a person was acting in one capacity or another, for example, as a 'quasi-arbitrator'.

29.6

Doubts as to the immunity of arbitrators arose in two House of Lords decisions although in neither case was the person concerned an arbitrator. In *Sutcliffe v Thackrah* [1974] AC 727, a case which involved an architect acting as a valuer, the parties had agreed that certificates of the building owner's architect certifying that the work was done to the required standard, and that certain amounts were thus due, should be conclusive. The builder's work was defective; the builder went into liquidation. The house owner sued the architect for negligence. The architect had a duty to act fairly between the parties. However, he made his own investigations to determine whether or not the work had been properly done and what money was due. There was nothing judicial about his decision concerning whether the work was defective, there was no dispute, he was not jointly engaged by the parties, and they did not submit evidence to him. He was held not to be an arbitrator. Thus he was liable for negligently issuing interim certificates. In *Arenson v Arenson* [1977] AC 405, a case involving an auditor acting as a valuer, auditors had been expressly instructed to value shares as experts not arbitrators. In this case the court again considered the issue of immunity and set out various elements which might establish immunity from suit, for example, that there was a sufficient judicial element which would be established if the person were jointly engaged by the parties, that a dispute was submitted to him, that he did not merely investigate but examined and considered evidence, etc. The title 'arbitrator', however, is not conclusive as to the precise function concerned.

29.7

The uncertainty continued after the above cases. (See the full and interesting debate on the question in *Mustill & Boyd*, pp 224–231 which leaves the question very much open. Also see the most interesting analysis by Dr Julian Lew in his book, *The Immunity of Arbitrators* at p 21 onwards.) Various arbitration institutions advised their members to take out insurance cover in this respect. The Supply of Services (Exclusion of Implied Terms) Order 1985 (SI No 1) expressly stated that s 13 of the Supply of Goods and Services Act 1982 (implied undertakings to carry out any particular service for another with reasonable care and skill) did *not* apply to arbitrators. However, it still left open the question of liability at common law.

29.8

Granting immunity to arbitrators has not only made the law certain, it has underpinned the finality of the arbitral process. It was always open to a disappointed party to challenge the award by the backdoor method of suing an arbitrator in negligence. Now that door is closed.

29.9

Section 29(2) says that the above applies also to an employee or agent of an arbitrator as it applies to himself.

29.10

Section 29(3) states that nothing in this section affects any liability incurred by an arbitrator by reason of his resigning. The consequences of resignation are dealt with in s 25. Parties may agree with the arbitrator what the consequences of his resignation may be as regards 'any liability thereby incurred by him', and his immunity under s 29 will not protect him should that agreement contain provision for the parties to recover damages if he resigns. However, s 25(3) does enable him to apply to the court for 'relief from any liability thereby incurred by him' and this may provide some protection if the court, under s 25(4), considers that his resignation was reasonable in all the circumstances.

29.11

Section 29 should be read in the light of s 74 (immunity of arbitral institutions, &c) and also s 33 which sets out the general duty of the tribunal and provides checks and balances on the powers of an arbitrator.

Jurisdiction of the arbitral tribunal

Section 30: Competence of tribunal to rule on its own jurisdiction

30.1

Section 30 is based on Article 16 of the Model Law. It is entirely new.

30.2

Section 30(1) states that:

> 'unless otherwise agreed by the parties, the arbitral tribunal may rule on its own substantive jurisdiction as to:
> (a) whether there is a valid arbitration agreement,
> (b) whether the tribunal is properly constituted, and
> (c) what matters have been submitted to arbitration in accordance with the arbitration agreement.'

The first two examples go to the root of the tribunal's jurisdiction, ie whether there is a valid reference to arbitration at all on the basis of an arbitration agreement, and whether the tribunal itself has been properly appointed under that agreement. A decision in the negative on either of those points will bring the whole arbitration to an end. The third example is not so fundamental. A ruling that certain matters have not properly been referred to arbitration will mean that those matters cannot be considered, but the arbitration will continue on those matters which have been validly referred.

30.3

Section 30(2) states that any such ruling may be challenged by any available arbitral process of appeal or review or in accordance with the provisions of Part I. In other words, any ruling which might be made is not absolute. It may be challenged under any process of appeal or review available, ie under institutional rules (for example through the appeal procedure under the GAFTA Rules), or in the court under ss 32 (determination of preliminary point of jurisdiction) or 67 (challenging the award: substantive jurisdiction).

30.4

Article 16(1) of the Model Law states, 'The Arbitral tribunal may rule on its own jurisdiction, including any objections with respect to the existence or validity of the arbitration agreement. For that purpose, an arbitration clause which forms part of a contract shall be treated as an agreement independent of the other terms of the contract ...' Section 30 flows from, and is within the spirit of, Article 16 of the Model Law. In particular, it corresponds to Article 16(1) save that the concept of separability of the arbitration clause is not included as this is covered in s 7.

30.5

The section restates the existing law that an arbitral tribunal may rule on matters concerning its own jurisdiction, although the final decision rests with the court. 'The true principle is that the arbitrator may be empowered to determine questions of his own jurisdiction but that his ruling will, if challenged, be reopened by the English courts' (per Robert Merkin at para 7.2 in *Arbitration Law*, citing *Christopher Brown Ltd v Genossenschaft Oesterreichischer Waldbesitzer Holzwirtschaftsbetriebe Registrierte Genossenschaft mit Beschrankter Haftung* [1954] 1 QB 8). This is the doctrine of 'Kompetenz Kompetenz', the great advantage of which is that it avoids delays and difficulties when such a question is raised. Article 16(1) of the Model Law recognises this German doctrine. It permits the tribunal to rule on its own jurisdiction whenever the validity or existence of the main arbitration agreement is challenged. The arbitration can continue, and the state court cannot intervene, until the award is made. Article 16 is designed to cover jurisdictional attacks on a tribunal, for example, that the arbitrators are not 'commercial men' as the contract required. The rationale of the doctrine is that in circumstances where the arbitration agreement is invalid, arbitrators without such a suitable doctrine would be unable to rule on their own jurisdiction. In England, the comparable doctrine is merely to 'stay' proceedings, as an arbitration agreement can never oust the jurisdiction of the court. English law has not needed such a doctrine, achieving the same effect by different means.

30.6

In contrast to the Model Law the power of arbitrators to decide upon their own jurisdiction is made subject to contrary agreement by the parties. The parties may therefore by agreement *exclude* any right of the tribunal to rule on its own jurisdiction or on any one or more of the three aspects of jurisdiction listed in s 30(1).

Section 31: Objection to substantive jurisdiction of tribunal

31.1

This is a mandatory provision. It corresponds to Article 16(2) and to the first sentence of Article 16(3) of the Model Law.

31.2

Section 31(1) states that an objection that the tribunal lacks substantive jurisdiction at the outset of the proceedings must be raised by a party not later than the time it takes the first step in the proceedings to contest the merits of the matter to which the question of jurisdiction relates. The second paragraph in s 31(1) makes it clear that appointing or participating in the appointment of an arbitrator will not be considered to be such a step. If it were, it would in many cases frustrate the purpose of conferring authority on the tribunal to rule on its own jurisdiction in s 30. (For what is meant by 'substantive jurisdiction', see s 30(1).) The provision is limited to challenges to jurisdiction raised 'at the outset of the proceedings', ie, challenges brought at the very start when the arbitrator is being, or has been, appointed. Subsequent challenges are dealt with in s 31(2). A 'first step in the proceedings to contest the merits of [a] matter' would, for example, be the submission of a defence to a claim, when the challenge may be to the validity of the proceedings as a whole; in other words, a challenge to the validity of the arbitration agreement or to the constitution of the tribunal, or to an element of the claim. In short, the tribunal does not have jurisdiction in respect of *one* element of the claim although its jurisdiction is not challenged in respect of other elements.

31.3

Section 31 reflects in a different form Article 16(2) of the Model Law which states 'a plea that the arbitral tribunal does not have jurisdiction shall be raised not later than the submission of the statement of defence', and that 'a plea that the arbitral tribunal is exceeding the scope of its authority [ie that it is purporting to deal with matters outside its jurisdiction] shall be raised as soon as the matter alleged to be beyond the scope of its authority is raised during the arbitral proceedings'. The meaning is the same, but the provision in the Act appears better and more flexibly worded.

31.4

Section 31(2) states that if the arbitration proceedings have begun and there is an objection that the tribunal is exceeding its substantive jurisdiction, this must be made as soon as possible after the matter alleged is raised. Note that this is an objection that the tribunal is exceeding its jurisdiction, ie, an objection of the kind that the tribunal is given authority to rule on under s 30(1)(c). It is *not* an objection that the tribunal does not have jurisdiction *at all*. Any such latter objection must be raised at the outset under s 31(1), subject to the right of the tribunal to admit later objections under s 31(3).

31.5

The provisions of s 31(1) and (2) are sensible. If objections to jurisdiction are not raised as soon as possible there will be delay and increased cost. Taken together with s 73 (loss of right to object), they ensure that objections to jurisdiction are raised at the earliest stage possible. If the party having reason to object does not do so at the earliest opportunity, it will lose its right to raise the objection later, which in the past has frequently been done for tactical reasons (see the commentary on s 73).

31.6

Section 31(3) gives the tribunal the discretion to admit an objection later than the time specified above if it considers the delay justified. While the intention is to avoid delay and extra costs by having objections to jurisdiction raised at the earliest possible time, there must always be occasions where, for perfectly good reasons, this has not been possible. An example of this might be where the cause for challenge genuinely did not become apparent to the party seeking to make it when it theoretically should have done—perhaps because it has only now taken legal advice. It is obviously desirable to give the tribunal the power to entertain and deal with such late challenges where there is a good reason for doing so. However, the arbitrator must be careful to ensure that no unfairness to the other party will result from the admission of the later challenge.

31.7

Section 31(4) states that where an objection is taken to the tribunal's substantive jurisdiction and the tribunal has power to rule on its own jurisdiction it may (*a*) rule on the matter in an award as to jurisdiction or (*b*) deal with the objection in its award on the merits. However, if the parties have agreed which of these courses the tribunal should take, then the tribunal shall comply. Two methods have been provided as one might be more appropriate than another, and s 33 places a duty on the tribunal to adopt procedures suitable to the circumstances of the particular case, avoiding unnecessary delay or expense. Such rulings on jurisdiction can be challenged under s 67.

31.8

Article 16(3) of the Model Law provides that the tribunal may rule on a plea as to jurisdiction either as a preliminary question or in an award on the merits. The drafters of the Act were of the view that it was unnecessary to introduce a new concept of a 'preliminary ruling', and therefore s 31(4) only refers to awards. The effect, however, is substantially the same.

31.9

Section 31(5) states that the tribunal may in any case, and shall if the parties agree, stay proceedings, ie, put the arbitration 'on hold', while an application is made to the court under s 32. The stay becomes mandatory if the parties agree.

Section 32: Determination of preliminary point of jurisdiction

32.1

Section 32 is new. It is a mandatory provision.

32.2

Section 32(1) states that the court may, on the application of a party to arbitral proceedings determine any question as to the substantive jurisdiction of the tribunal. Notice must be given to the other parties. A party may lose the right to object (see s 73).

32.3

The tribunal is given power by s 30 to determine its own substantive jurisdiction. However, there may be circumstances when a party would be justified in making a direct approach to the court. This provision, then, without in any way detracting from the competence of the tribunal to deal with the matter, allows a party in certain limited circumstances to do this. The usual step would be for a party to approach the tribunal under s 31 and ask for an award on the matter. This would be given, and if it were then necessary, a challenge made through the court under s 67. Section 32 short-circuits the usual procedure and it sets out the third of the possible ways of dealing with a challenge to the jurisdiction. (The other two ways are set out in s 31.) It provides for exceptional cases only, as is shown in s 32(2).

32.4

Section 32(2) restricts the right to apply to the court in two ways. The application shall not be considered unless:

'(a) it is made with the agreement in writing of *all* the other parties to the proceedings, or
(b) it is made with the permission of the tribunal and the court is satisfied—
  (i) that the determination of the question is likely to produce substantial savings in costs,
  (ii) that the application was made without delay, and
  (iii) that [in addition] there is good reason why the matter should be decided by the court.'

What are 'substantial savings' will be a matter of fact dependent on all the relevant circumstances. These provisions allow parties who have genuine reasons to avail themselves of this more direct route. A 'good reason' might be where a non-participating party is clearly determined to challenge the jurisdiction subsequently. The other party could go straight to the court and have the question of jurisdiction determined there and then so that the arbitration could proceed with confidence. Note that *either* the agreement of the parties is required *or* that the court will need to be satisfied etc.

32.5

Section 32(3) says that unless the application is made with the agreement of all the other parties, ie, if it is made only with the permission of the tribunal, it shall state why it should be decided by the court. This is a sensible provision designed to assist the court to form a view as to the matters set out in s 32(2)(b).

32.6

Section 32(4) states that unless the parties agree otherwise, the proceedings may continue and the tribunal may make its award while an application to the court is pending. Where there is a power to choose, ie if the parties do not agree, the tribunal will be very mindful of its duty under s 33. The continuation of the proceedings will avoid delay (and expense) and these are important factors to bear in mind. Of course, the parties can agree that alternatively the proceedings can be put 'on hold' until the decision has been made, in which case the tribunal must comply.

32.7

Section 32(5) states that no appeal lies from a decision of the court as to whether the conditions set out in s 32(2) are met, unless the court gives leave.

32.8

Section 32(6) states that the decision of the court on the question of jurisdiction shall be treated as a judgment of the court for the purposes of appeal. However, such an appeal is restricted by the further provision that no appeal lies without the leave of the court which shall not be given unless the court considers that the question involves a point of law which is one of general importance or one which for some other special reason should be considered by the Court of Appeal. In short, appeals which are made to waste time (delay the day of reckoning?) are deterred.

The arbitral proceedings

Section 33: General duty of the tribunal

33.1

This section is completely new. It is one of the mandatory provisions. It corresponds in part to Article 18 of the Model Law.

33.2

Section 33(1) states that:

'The tribunal shall—
(a) act fairly and impartially as between the parties, giving each party a reasonable opportunity of putting his case and dealing with that of his opponent, and

(*b*) adopt procedures suitable to the circumstances of the particular case, avoiding unnecessary delay or expense, so as to provide a fair means for the resolution of the matters falling to be determined.'

33.3

Section 33(2) states that the tribunal shall comply with this general duty in conducting the arbitral proceedings, in its decisions on matters of procedure and evidence and in the exercise of all other powers conferred on it.

33.4

The Act uses the words '... giving each party a reasonable opportunity ...' whereas the Model Law refers to '... full opportunity ...' It was considered by the drafters that the word 'full' might give a party an opportunity to delay matters. The word 'reasonable' on the other hand gives the tribunal the opportunity to decide whether or not the time a party is asking for to take some step in the arbitration is unreasonably long and would be detrimental to the s 1(*a*) requirement that the arbitration should proceed 'without unnecessary delay or expense'. Article 18 of the Model Law states, 'The parties shall be treated with equality and each party shall be given a full opportunity of presenting his case'.

33.5

Section 33 corresponds to the general principles set out in s 1. It is the pivotal centre of the Act. The intention is to allow the tribunal the widest possible discretion in its conduct of the arbitration, subject to compliance with the basic principles of justice—ie, fairness, impartiality, and the avoidance of unnecessary delay (since justice delayed is justice denied, as is also justice obtained at great and unnecessary cost). The great advantage of arbitration is its flexibility, enabling it to be structured in the most appropriate way to resolve the particular dispute. This provision encourages tribunals to use this flexibility, and not slavishly to follow more rigid procedures, such as exist in litigation.

33.6

The provision is mandatory since it would clearly be against the principles set out in s 1 for parties to be able to agree that the tribunal should not act in the manner stated.

33.7

It will be noted that there is no requirement that the tribunal be 'independent' of the parties (see Article 9 of the Model Law). This is considered by the authors to be a wise omission since 'independence' is a concept easy to recognise but impossible to define or limit. For instance, can a party-appointed arbitrator be considered to be 'independent' if he is dependent upon the party for the appointment? He may well look to that party for further appointments in the future. The arbitrator must nevertheless be both 'fair' and 'impartial', which is to say he must not allow his dependence on one of the parties for his appointment, or his hopes for the future, to influence his decisions. He must put them out of his mind and reach all decisions which he is required to reach on the basis of strict fairness and impartiality. It would be better for an arbitrator not to receive future appointments from a party that is prepared to penalise him for acting fairly and impartially (or worse, to threaten him with such penalties if he does not lean in the party's favour).

33.8

The relationship between ss 1(*b*) (party autonomy), 33 and 34(1) (the tribunal decides procedural and evidential matters subject to the agreement of the parties), should be most carefully studied. Indeed s 33, being central to the Act in setting out the duties and obligations of the tribunal should constantly be referred back to when considering other provisions. (It must be remembered, however, that it only applies to Part I of the Act, having no relevance to the other Parts.)

33.9

The DAC's comment on this provision in its Report is worth repeating:

> 'It has been further suggested that this part of the Bill will cause the demise of the amateur arbitrator. If by this is meant the demise of people who purport to act as arbitrators but who are either unable or unwilling (or both) to conduct the proceedings in accordance with what most would regard as self-evident rules of justice, then we indeed hope that this will be one of the results. But since these rules of justice are generally accepted in our democratic society, and are not merely theoretical considerations that concern lawyers alone,

we can see no reason why the Bill should discourage anyone who is ready, willing and able to apply them. Indeed we consider that the Bill will encourage and support all such people.'

33.10

Failure by the tribunal to comply with s 33 may constitute serious irregularity on which the award can be challenged by a party (see s 68).

Section 34: Procedural and evidential matters

34.1

Section 34 corresponds to Articles 19, 20, 22 to 24 and 26 of the Model Law but goes into far greater detail in specifying the powers of the tribunal in default of agreement of the parties as to procedure. It is one of the key provisions of the Act.

34.2

Section 34(1) states that it is for the tribunal to decide all procedural and evidential matters, subject to the right of the parties to agree any matter.

34.3

The only references to the procedural powers of the tribunal in the previous law were contained in s 12(1)–(3) of the 1950 Act. The language of s 12(1) was drafted in wide terms. It provided, inter alia, that:

> 'the parties ... shall, subject to any legal objection, submit to be examined by the arbitrator ... on oath or affirmation, in relation to the matters in dispute, and shall ... produce before the arbitrator or umpire all documents within their possession or power respectively which may be required or called for, and do all other things which during the proceedings on the reference the arbitrator or umpire may require.'

(Note that it was the parties who were required to be examined; what about their witnesses? What about examination by someone other than the arbitrator, such as the other party?) The contrast with the new provisions could not be more marked. The previous provisions posed more questions about an arbitrator's powers than they answered. For example, 'witnesses may be examined on oath'—but were they able to be examined in the first place? Were parties obliged to obey *anything* the arbitrator might require, or only those things which might be considered reasonable?

34.4

Note the wording of s 34(1). The usual opening words, 'Unless otherwise agreed by the parties' are *avoided* in favour of the words used which would appear to suggest that it is ultimately for the tribunal to decide on procedural and evidential matters, possibly against the wishes of the parties. However, this would be contrary to the general principle of party autonomy as stated in s 1(*b*). The intention is clearly that the tribunal should take the initiative in procedural and evidential matters—and all arbitrations must be carried out as expeditiously, efficiently and inexpensively as possible—but that ultimately the tribunal's decisions must be subject to the overriding right of the parties to agree how their arbitrations should be conducted. The parties may agree at any time but, by s 5(1), for any such agreement to be effective it must be in writing as defined in that section. The section also acknowledges by implication that arbitration is an entirely different process from litigation and that it can, and should, take many forms, from 'look-sniff' commodity arbitrations, to maritime or consumer disputes resolved entirely on the documents with no hearing. Arbitrations do not have to be conducted like court hearings, and indeed many of them are very different.

34.5

In the consultation which took place before the Act was published as a Bill there was pressure from some quarters to give the tribunal the ultimate power to decide on procedural and evidential matters, even against the wishes of both parties. However, not only would that be contrary to the principle of party autonomy but it would also be impractical. How could the tribunal enforce its wishes against the combined wishes of the parties? Ultimately, if an arbitrator considers that he cannot, in all conscience, and perhaps in accordance with what he sees as his duty under s 33, conduct the arbitration in the manner the parties wish him to, his only proper course is to resign. If what the parties propose is so outrageous, they will have difficulty in finding another arbitrator of suitable ability, experience and standing to do what they wish, and they might well have to return to their original arbitrator and admit that he was right.

34.6

Section 34(2) states that procedural and evidential matters include:

'(a) when and where any part of the proceedings is to be held;
(b) the language or languages to be used in the proceedings and whether translations of any relevant documents are to be supplied;
(c) whether any and if so what form of written statements of claim and defence are to be used, when these should be supplied and the extent to which such statements can be later amended;
(d) whether any and if so which documents or classes of documents should be disclosed between and produced by the parties, and at what stage;
(e) whether any and if so what questions should be put to and answered by the respective parties and when and in what form this should be done;
(f) whether to apply strict rules of evidence (or any other rules) as to the admissibility, relevance or weight of any material (oral, written or other) sought to be tendered on any matters of fact or opinion, and the time, manner and form in which such material should be exchanged and presented;
(g) whether and to what extent the tribunal should itself take the initiative in ascertaining the facts and the law; and
(h) whether and to what extent there should be oral or written evidence or submissions.'

34.7

The list in s 34(2) is illustrative, and not exhaustive, as the word 'includes' indicates. The parties know that if they do not exclude in writing any particular power set out in sub-paragraphs (a)–(h), then the tribunal will have that power. This list gives arbitrators as much power as possible, with a corresponding reduction in the powers of the court compared to those in the 1950 Act. However, a power must always be balanced against a corresponding duty, and readers should remind themselves of those duties and obligations under s 33. The following are examples which might be included but all are subject to the parties' contrary intentions.

34.8

Section 34(2)(*a*) gives the tribunal power to set the hearing date; to decide, for example, not to sit every Friday; to have the hearing on board ship (something Cedric Barclay, the well-known and much admired maritime arbitrator did frequently), or in a particular country, or in several countries simultaneously by means of video-linking. Article 20(1) of the Model Law states that, in the absence of agreement between the parties, 'the place of arbitration shall be determined by the arbitral tribunal having regard to the circumstances of the case, including the convenience of the parties'. The reference to 'convenience' is not repeated in s 34(2)(*a*) since consideration of the convenience of the parties is already implicit in the provisions of s 33. The DAC in its Report also points out that the convenience of the parties must be a consideration in other matters listed in s 34(2) such as s 34(2)(*b*). Unlike the Model Law (which only refers to where the place of the arbitration is), this provision refers to '*when* and where'. An arbitration need not be held at the 'seat' of the arbitration. The 'seat' only defines the law which is to apply to the arbitration and govern its proceedings. The actual hearing or meetings and hearings on interlocutory matters may be held at some quite different location.

34.9

Section 34(2)(*b*) allows the tribunal to decide the language to be used. In deciding which documents, if any, need to be translated, the arbitrator will be mindful of the possibility of this lengthening the hearing, delaying the outcome and of the cost to the parties. He will also be mindful of their convenience, and how such a decision might affect 'a fair means' of resolving the dispute. In short, he will constantly be conscious of his duties and obligations under s 33.

34.10

Section 34(2)(*c*) gives the arbitrator power, for example, to order that the 'pleadings' be in the form of a Scott or 'Official Referee's' Schedule. In cases where the dispute concerns the pricing of individual items or where many individual items are in issue, it is sometimes convenient for the claimant to set them down separately in a list, and for the respondent to indicate against every item the extent to which he agrees or disagrees with the claim, with his comments.

34.11

In any dispute resolution process the first step after appointment of the tribunal will be for each party to set out its case. This subsection only refers to 'statements of claim and defence' and this accords with Article 23(1) of the Model Law. In English arbitrations, as in litigation, there is a tradition of allowing the claimant to serve a statement of reply to the defence enabling him to have 'the last word' in the written statements, as he will do at the hearing (if there is one). Whether this tradition is to be continued, or whether there is really any need for it to continue, will no doubt be a matter for debate. In the authors' view it is a tradition which deserves at least to be questioned and claimants should be persuaded to set out the whole of their case in a single document. A properly prepared statement of claim should lead to there being no need for a reply to the defence to it; it should already have anticipated and covered everything which is likely to be raised in the defence. (Of course for 'statements of claim and defence' read also 'statements of counterclaim and defence'.)

34.12

Before the recent moves towards reform, statements in larger arbitration proceedings tended to take the form of pleadings in litigation, ie formal documents which 'should contain only assertions of fact (at any rate in theory), and shall not comprise arguments, evidence or propositions of law' (*Mustill & Boyd*, p 318). Recently, however, statements in arbitrations have tended to take the form of full written statements of each party's case, setting out not only the bare facts relied upon but also the full history of the matter, brief reference to the evidence which will be put forward to support the facts, and propositions of law which will be relied upon with references to authorities. These statements also tend to be accompanied by lists of the documents which will be relied upon with copies of the principal documents attached to the statements and cross-referenced to them (cf 23(1) of the Model Law). Properly prepared statements of this kind, which are now required by many institutional rules (see, for instance, the LCIA Rules, Article 6), take longer to prepare than formal pleadings and require more care. However, they have the benefit of enabling each party fully to understand the other party's case from the outset. They will enable the tribunal to have a far better knowledge of the real nature of the dispute, to know which matters are likely to be hotly contested and those matters upon which some agreement between the parties is already apparent and which may well fall away as the arbitration progresses.

34.13

In smaller cases full statements of case may not be necessary and less formal means may be used for each party to convey the essence of its case to the other party and to the tribunal. A simple exchange of letters may be all that is necessary, or even a meeting between the parties and the arbitrator at which the parties can explain their respective cases orally to the arbitrator who will then set them out himself in a document which both parties can agree as representing the essence of the dispute between them.

34.14

As stated below in considering s 34(2)(*h*), some smaller cases may most speedily and economically be dealt with by way of written submissions and documentary evidence only, without a hearing. Clearly, in 'documents only' cases the written statements of each party must set out the whole of its case with great care since the arbitrator will be deciding the matter on the basis of those statements alone without the opportunity for either party to expand upon them or explain them at a hearing. As a result, paradoxically, the statements of case in a 'documents only' arbitration may take longer and be more expensive to prepare than they would be in a much larger arbitration with a hearing. However, the extra expense in preparing the statements will be far outweighed by the saving resulting from not having a hearing. In such cases the claimant should normally be permitted to serve a statement of reply to the defence so as to preserve 'the right to the last word'.

34.15

Hitherto it has been common in arbitrations, as in litigation, for parties to serve upon each other 'Requests for Further and Better Particulars' on the grounds that the other party's case has not been stated 'with sufficient particularity' to enable the responding party to know fully the case it has to answer. If there was resistance to such a request the arbitrator might be asked to order that the party respond to the request perhaps within a specified time limit. This could often raise difficult questions for the arbitrator who might be called upon to decide whether or not a particular request was justified or should be resisted on the grounds that the case was already sufficiently pleaded and the request was only a 'fishing expedition' to try to get evidence in advance.

34.16

There has been an increasing trend towards the view that there is no proper place in arbitration for such requests, and that they should in any case be unnecessary if proper statements of case are prepared by each party. It is notable that the Model Law does not give the tribunal power to order a party to amend or supplement a claim or defence, although Article 23(2) allows parties to do so of their own volition (and also gives the tribunal power to prohibit such amendment 'having regard to the delay in making it'). This is now reflected in the words, 'and the extent to which such statements can be later amended'. (The Model Rules, on the other hand, do give the tribunal power 'to decide which further written statements, in addition to the statement of claim and the statement of defence, shall be required from the parties or may be presented by them ...'.) This could be read as giving the tribunal power to order parties to provide further or supplementary statements which might be in the form of further and better particulars, but the preferred view is that it simply gives the tribunal power to order, for instance, that the claimant may serve a reply to the defence. It should be noted, in any case, that the Model Rules substantially pre-date the Model Law, and the law may therefore be taken to represent more recent thinking on what the powers of the tribunal should be in relation to the control of statements of case.

34.17

The philosophy of the Model Law, now reflected in the Act, would seem to be that it is for each party to decide how it should present its case without interference from the tribunal and then to prove it at hearing or otherwise. If a party has not presented its case with sufficient clarity it will find it difficult to prove when it comes to hearing. If the respondent finds it difficult to understand the case he has to answer he must say so in his defence. There will then be a choice. The claimant will have to decide whether to clarify his case by amendment or to take the risk of carrying on and losing his case precisely because it has not been properly set out and cannot therefore be properly proved. Alternatively, he will have to pay the costs of the inevitable delays when the respondent justifies his complaint at a later stage in the proceedings and the claim then has to be amended in any case—provided that the tribunal does not then prohibit the amendment on the grounds that it is too late and that it would result in injustice to the respondent if the amendment were allowed.

34.18

Section 34(2)(*d*) is important. This gives the arbitrator wide powers with regard to what is generally known as 'discovery', ie, the disclosure by each party to the other of documents relating to the matters at issue.

34.19

Until quite recently it was common for arbitrators as a matter of course to order 'general discovery', ie the production of all documents within the 'possession, custody or power' of each party having any bearing upon the issues in the arbitration. This power was conferred by s 12(1) of the 1950 Act, although *Mustill & Boyd*, p 323, footnote 6 points out that the word 'custody' which, in relation to High Court proceedings, appears in RSC Ord 24 r 1, did not appear in the 1950 Act. This may be because of doubts as to whether an arbitrator should have power to order production of documents belonging to third parties. This possible lacuna was originally filled by s 12(6)(*b*) which gave the High Court power to order 'discovery of documents' which could be discovery within the meaning of RSC Ord 24 r 1, ie the court would have the power at its discretion to order production of documents within a party's custody. However, this power was removed when the provision was abolished by the Courts and Legal Services Act 1990.

34.20

'General discovery' means that each party must disclose, usually by way of a detailed list, *all* documents within its possession, custody or power having any bearing on the issues, whether favourable or unfavourable to its case.

> 'Any document is disclosable which it is reasonable to suppose contains information which may enable a party either to advance his own case or to damage that of his adversary, or if it is a document which may fairly lead him to a train of enquiry which may have either of these two consequences (*Mustill & Boyd*, pp 323–4 quoting Esher MR in *Compagnie Financiere et Commerciale v Peruvian Guano Co* (1882) 11 QBD 55 at 62).'

This case has led to the test for discovery becoming known by the curious appellation of 'the *Peruvian Guano* test'—leading many to wonder what South American bird droppings have to do with English litigation.

34.21

The *Peruvian Guano* test has led increasingly to voluminous discovery in litigation and in arbitration, going far beyond what should strictly be necessary. While the test is only for the initial listing of documents for inspection by the other party, and it is not necessary for all documents listed to be produced at trial, it has become customary for all listed documents to be made available at the trial or hearing 'to be on the safe side'. This has been compounded by the development of fast and efficient copying machines which has led to its being easier and cheaper to copy all documents rather than to go through voluminous files and pick out those documents which are really relevant. It is common for less than 10 per cent of the documents produced on discovery and copied actually to be referred to at trial or hearing.

34.22

There has been an increasing tendency in recent years for arbitrators to be encouraged to limit discovery. Courts also are becoming disillusioned by the results of the application of the *Peruvian Guano* test and are increasingly limiting discovery strictly to relevant documents only. The LCIA Rules, for example, require the parties' statements of case to be 'accompanied by copies (or if they are especially voluminous, lists) of all essential documents on which the party concerned relies and which have not previously been submitted by any party' (art 6.6); and then give the tribunal power to 'order any party to produce to the tribunal, and to the other parties for inspection, and to supply copies of, any documents or classes of documents in their possession or power [not 'custody'] which the tribunal determines to be relevant', (art 13.1(i)). Thus the parties initially produce those documents which they each wish to produce to support their respective cases. The tribunal may subsequently determine what, if any, further documents should be produced either of its own volition or on the application of a party which may have reason to believe that documents exist in the possession and control of the other party that have not been produced and which may help its case.

34.23

It should be noted that neither the Model Law nor the Model Rules contains any provision whatever for the tribunal to order production of documents. Article 24.3 of the Model Rules has sometimes been read as giving such a power, but in fact it only gives power to the tribunal to specify the period of time within which 'documents, exhibits or other evidence' are to be produced. It does not empower the tribunal to order their production.

34.24

While, therefore, the Act does not go to the length of the Model Law in omitting any specific power conferred on the arbitrator to order production of documents, it is clearly intended that the power which it does confer should be used discretionally and judicially, and that it is not intended that blanket *Peruvian Guano* discovery should be ordered.

34.25

The normal process of discovery has been that each party produces a list of the documents which it is required to disclose by the arbitrator's order. The documents are then inspected by the other party which will request copies of those documents which it needs in order to prepare its own case, copying charges being paid by the party requesting them and then forming part of the costs of the arbitration.

The parties will then normally be directed to produce an 'agreed bundle' of the documents which will be produced as evidence at the hearing. The fact that the documents in the bundle are 'agreed' means that they do not have to be proved as documents, ie, the signatory of a letter will not have to be called to prove that he signed it. The fact that a document is included as 'agreed' does not mean that its contents are accepted as proving the truth of whatever it says. The value of the documents is evidential only, and the truth of any statements in the documents may still have to be proved by other evidence. This can cause problems when the hearing is *ex parte*, ie in the presence of one party only, when there will be no 'agreed bundle' and, strictly speaking, each document will have to be individually proved. However, the need for this has been called in question in the case of *Fairclough Building Ltd v Vale of Belvoir Superstore Ltd* 56 BLR 74, where it was held that an arbitrator ought to have accepted documents in an *ex parte* hearing as proved by the conduct of the signatories and others present and by their general acceptance in other evidence.

34.26

In future, if it becomes common practice for parties to produce copies of principal documents with their statements, the need for discovery will only relate to documents which a party has not produced voluntarily. For instance, in a construction dispute, the building owners may not have produced clerk of works' reports which clearly are known to exist and the contractors may ask for them to be produced. The arbitrator will then probably order that the reports be produced for inspection by the contractor who can then request the arbitrator to order that they be produced in evidence if they indeed prove favourable to his case.

34.27

Certain types of documents are currently protected by 'privilege', ie as a matter of public policy a party will not be required to disclose them to its opponent. This is largely confined to communications between a party and its legal advisors or between solicitors and counsel (see the commentary on s 36 relating to communications with non-legal advisers). Other types of communications between the parties themselves may not be produced to the arbitrator without the consent of the originating party, such as offers of settlement, such documents commonly being endorsed 'without prejudice'. However, the simple fact that a document is so endorsed does not necessarily mean that it may not be produced if it can be shown that it does not constitute a genuine offer of settlement or should not be protected for some other valid reason (see also the commentary following s 62, relating to documents endorsed 'without prejudice save as to costs').

34.28

Section 34(2)(*e*) empowers the arbitrator to order what are known as 'interrogatories'. The 1950 Act did not specifically empower arbitrators in this way except by the general power under s 12(1) but it did originally give the courts the power under s 12(6)(*b*) until that section was abolished by the Courts and Legal Services Act 1990. Interrogatories enable a party to ask its opponent specific questions in advance of the hearing, presumably on the ground that a truthful answer will so damage the opponent's case in whole or in part as to dispose of it completely or leave it requiring little time to dispose of at the hearing. In litigation they would be answered by affidavit.

34.29

Interrogatories are rare in litigation and not very common in arbitration either. However, they are sometimes used and can be useful in disposing of issues which really should never come to hearing. The authors respectfully agree with John Tackerberry QC that 'if the arbitrator considers that (most unusually) they [interrogatories] will truly assist in disposing of an issue fairly, expeditiously and cheaply, and are not being used merely for a fishing expedition or as a delaying or harassing tactic, or by way of anticipatory cross-examination, he should be prepared to allow them' (*Bernstein's Handbook*, p 228).

34.30

The new provision does not use the word 'interrogatories', presumably because it is one of the technical legal terms which the drafters have sought to avoid. It gives the arbitrator wide powers to decide how they should be administered and answered. The authors again agree with John Tackerberry (above) that 'so far as the formalities are concerned, in most cases the same object can be achieved if they are administered and answered by letter [ie rather than being answered by affidavit] provided that it is made clear to the party answering them that he will be bound by the answers'.

34.31

Section 34 (2)(*e*) is framed in such general terms—'whether any and if so what questions should be put to and answered by the ... parties and when and in what form this should be done'—that this goes far beyond the sort of questions discussed above. For example, in a technical dispute where the parties are not legally represented, an arbitrator might dispense with a preliminary hearing, gathering all the relevant information he requires at that stage by sending the parties a list of questions to which he requires answers. This power can also be useful if the arbitrator, in an attempt to clarify certain issues, puts written questions to the parties to which he requires specific answers. Once knowing the general area of dispute he might frame specific questions to the parties, the answers to which might narrow the issues, or assist the parties in their drafting of their statements of case and defence. In a simple consumer or other dispute, for example, where the claimant has failed to be sufficiently particular (and where as a consequence the respondent has not been able to answer the generality of the complaint), the arbitrator can set out a list of specific questions to which he requires specific answers rather than allowing the dispute to become bogged down with what might amount to a request for 'further and better particulars' from the respondent. The wide powers given to the arbitrator to decide all procedural and evidential matters (subject of course to the right of the parties to agree otherwise) are to enable him more effectively to comply with the mandatory duty imposed on him by s 33(1)(*b*) which is to avoid unnecessary delay and expense. To try to limit the issues in contention by seeking specific information from the parties in the way described above can be an efficient and effective way of managing the resolution of the dispute.

34.32

Section 34(2)(*f*) gives the arbitrator, unless the parties agree otherwise, wide powers to decide what evidence to admit and what weight should be attached to it. It also empowers him to give directions as to how such evidence should be presented.

34.33

With regard to admissibility of evidence, this will enable the arbitrator at his discretion to disregard the so-called 'hearsay rule' (see, for instance, *Pickwick Papers*: 'You must not tell us what the soldier or any other man, said, sir', interposed the judge; 'it's not evidence'). The rule was really designed for jury trials where a lay jury might be misled into accepting hearsay evidence as good evidence of the facts alleged in the statement, and was in any case widely misunderstood. 'What the soldier said' could be good evidence if the fact that he said something goes to support other evidence. It was only hearsay if it was adduced to prove the truth of what he actually said, not the fact that he said it. A competent arbitrator, in any case, will be perfectly well able to distinguish between direct and hearsay evidence and to attach correspondingly less weight (or possibly even none at all) to the latter than to the former.

34.34

This provision will also enable an arbitrator to admit other kinds of evidence which would arguably be inadmissible under strict rules. For example, to save time and costs he might admit statements from witnesses unable to attend the hearing without going through the procedures of the Civil Evidence Act 1968, provided, of course, that he ensures no unfairness results to the other party from the admission of such evidence. He would also have to attach appropriately less weight to such evidence than he would to evidence given in person at the hearing, having regard to the fact that no cross-examination to test it is possible and having given proper warning to the party putting it forward that he will do so.

34.35

The DAC in its Report (February 1996) also rightly points out that this provision will put an end to arguments that the question of whether there is material evidence to support a finding of fact is a matter of law and therefore appealable.

34.36

As to the 'time, manner and form' which evidence should take, this again gives the arbitrator wide powers to order exchange of witness statements both of fact and opinion in advance of hearing. As to evidence of witnesses of facts it has been the practice for some years now in the Commercial Court, as well as in arbitrations, for witness statements to be exchanged in advance, sometimes with a second exchange of statements of rebuttal. It is often the practice also for witness statements to be 'taken as read' so that there will be no evidence to be given in chief at the hearing, the witness being made available immediately for cross-examination on his statement. This practice can be unfairly detrimental, particularly where a witness is unaccustomed to giving evidence when a short examination-in-chief can enable him to settle down and get used to the atmosphere of the hearing so that he may do himself and his evidence more justice in cross-examination. It is suggested that the possibility for a short examination-in-chief, perhaps restricted to questions for clarification only or to ask the witness to update his statement, should be left open.

34.37

It has long been the practice for evidence of opinion in the form of expert reports to be exchanged in advance of hearing. The practice has also developed of ordering that experts of like discipline meet before the hearing to discuss their evidence and see whether and to what extent they can agree on their opinions. Such meetings are normally on a 'without prejudice' basis so that the experts can talk frankly to each other without the inhibition of knowing that what they say might be repeated at the hearing. Sometimes experts are required to exchange their reports initially in draft only and then to meet before producing final reports, or even to produce a single joint report after meeting, setting out matters on which they agree and matters on which they disagree, with reasons for the latter. All these may save a great deal of time at the hearing.

34.38

Section 34(2)(*g*) is an extremely important and significant new provision. It effectively entitles the arbitrator, subject to the agreement of the parties, to adopt an 'inquisitorial' as opposed to 'adversarial' form of procedure ie, to conduct an enquiry itself into the facts of the matter, taking a proactive role rather than adopting the traditional practice of the courts and arbitrators in England and Wales of allowing the parties to present their respective cases and deciding the issues solely on the evidence and submissions put forward by the parties.

34.39

It was felt by many that arbitrators already had the necessary powers in relation to the above. The traditional rule, however, was that arbitrators were bound to adopt an adversarial procedure unless there was an express or implied contrary agreement. In *Chilton v Saga Holidays plc* [1986] 1 All ER 841 it was held to be actual misconduct for an arbitrator, without the consent of both parties, to adopt an inquisitorial procedure. In this case a Registrar sitting as an arbitrator refused to allow a witness for an unrepresented party to be cross-examined directly by a solicitor for the other party, insisting that all questions should be put through him. He was held to have misconducted the proceedings. And in *Bremer Vulkan v South India Shipping* [1981] AC 909 it was held that in the absence of express or implied agreement to the contrary, an arbitral tribunal must adopt an adversarial as opposed to inquisitorial procedure. ICC Rules and LCIA Rules contain the necessary agreement to the contrary. However, there were potential, if not actual, problems with *ad hoc* London arbitration agreements with foreign arbitrators where there was no contrary agreement, or arbitrations under institutional rules where there was no contrary agreement expressed. Lord Steyn has said (1990 Bernstein Lecture), 'it is entirely contrary to the spirit of international commercial arbitration that the arbitrators should be bound by the local rules of evidence of the venue'. He also went on to say that '... there is widespread concern in the commercial community that the existing procedures are too time consuming and costly ...' and that 'arbitrators with inquisitorial powers are entitled to limit the discovery and evidence, and set time limits on the length of the hearing'. Lord Mustill has blamed the decline of arbitration on arbitrations being 'parodies of court proceedings'. Sir Francis McWilliams blamed the English adversarial system for making arbitration much more confrontational (see 'Flip Flop Costs—A Tonic to Revive Arbitration' by Richard Bloore, *Arbitration*, Vol 61, No 2, May 1995). Lord Steyn has said that the adoption of litigation-style procedures is the greatest cause of delay and cost in arbitration proceedings. 'Civil Justice on Trial—The Case for Change' (report by the joint working party of the Bar and Law Society, 1993) recommended that judges should adopt a more interventionist role in order to limit the issues, reduce delays and avoid court time being wasted.

34.40

Section 34(2)(*g*) provides a new power and makes it clear that arbitrators are allowed to act inquisitorially. However, it is certainly one to be exercised sparingly, in suitable cases and after very full discussion at least with the parties and their legal or other advisers. The authors consider there is no doubt that it will be a very useful power, particularly in smaller disputes where parties are not represented or in larger disputes where the issues are primarily technical rather than legal. In that case an arbitrator-expert in the subject matter can reach a proper judicial decision far more quickly by conducting an enquiry with experts of like discipline rather than a formal hearing with all evidence being presented through counsel. (This also has in the past been regarded as 'misconduct', see *Town & City Properties v Wiltshier* 44 BLR 109.)

34.41

Section 34(2)(*h*) contemplates that there may be occasions when oral evidence is unnecessary and where the dispute can be satisfactorily resolved on documents alone, or on documents with a site visit. One of the more important distinguishing features between arbitration and litigation is the provision for arbitrations to be conducted on documents alone, for example, by the exchange of files, or on bundles of documents produced by each party. Thousands of consumer arbitrations have been and are conducted in this way. Normally a 'documents only' procedure is not suitable where a party will need to produce evidence from witnesses of fact to support its case, since if fairness is to be done the other party should normally have an opportunity of testing that evidence at a hearing. However, even in such cases it may be possible to conduct the matter on 'documents only' with written statements of evidence if the parties are able to exchange statements in rebuttal of the evidence contained in the other's witness statements so that the arbitrator may read the original evidence and that in rebuttal, and form a view as to which he should accept.

34.42

In exercising all the vitally important powers now conferred upon him by this subsection, the arbitrator must always be guided by the overriding obligations imposed on him by s 33, 'to act fairly and impartially as between the parties, giving each party a reasonable opportunity of putting his case and dealing with that of his opponent', and to 'adopt procedures suitable to the circumstances of the particular case, avoiding unnecessary delay or expense, so as to provide a fair means for the resolution of the matters falling to be determined'. If he bears these principles firmly in mind and applies them in deciding on the exercise of the powers set out in this subsection, he will not go far wrong.

34.43

Section 34(3) states that the tribunal may fix the time within which any directions given by it are to be complied with and may, if it thinks fit, extend the time (whether or not it has expired). The arbitrator should clearly consult the parties in fixing those limits, but in default of any agreement he must fix them himself, having due regard to the practicalities, the convenience of the parties and the obligation to avoid 'unnecessary delay or expense'. Too short time limits may lead to wasted time later if they do not give the parties a proper and reasonable opportunity to prepare their case.

34.44

The power to extend time limits once fixed, which would normally be at the request of a party, should be used with discretion. However, it is generally preferable to allow a party further time if it requests it unless it is obviously a time-wasting ploy. Again the arbitrator must decide whether to refuse the request, as an extension of time may prevent a party from preparing its case properly and may lead to unfairness or to waste of time later. He should ask himself whether it is fair and right to refuse the application rather than to grant it.

34.45

Is there a potential for conflict between ss 34(1) and 40 (general duty of the parties)? In the authors' opinion the answer is, No. Any agreement made pursuant to s 34(1), consistent with s 33, will define the scope of s 40. The relevant words are 'to do all things necessary for the proper and expeditious conduct of the arbitral proceedings' (see s 40). If the tribunal exceeds its powers or fails to conduct proceedings in accordance with the procedure agreed by the parties, or fails to comply with the requirements as to the form of the award, it may be challenged on the ground of serious irregularity (see s 68).

34.46

This new clarity as to the tribunal's powers in the absence of the parties' agreement otherwise should do much to assist the efficient running of arbitrations by knowledgeable and experienced tribunals.

Section 35: Consolidation of proceedings and concurrent hearings

35.1

Section 35(1) provides that the parties may agree that the proceedings are consolidated with other arbitration proceedings or that concurrent hearings shall be held. However, s 35(2) states that unless they agree to give such power to the tribunal, it has no power to order either consolidation or concurrent hearings.

35.2

The problem of concurrent proceedings on one or more related disputes with common parties is often encountered in the construction and maritime areas. In construction disputes there are often similar issues between the main contractor and the building owner, and between a sub-contractor and the main contractor, involving much the same facts and with separate arbitration agreements. The same applies in maritime disputes between charterers and owners on the one hand and sub-charterers on the other. If the disputes are heard by separate tribunals there is the danger not only of conflicting decisions but also of thrown away costs. Attempts have been made to overcome this problem in legislation in other jurisdictions, eg The Netherlands, but without notable success. Certain sets of procedural rules contemplate a very limited form of consolidation, for example, those relating to multiparty disputes and the provisions of LMAA Terms (1987). However, disputes involving more than two parties frequently end up before the courts.

35.3

There was considerable pressure on the DAC to include provisions either enabling arbitrators to order consolidation of proceedings where they have been appointed in both disputes or, alternatively, to give the court power to order consolidation of separate but related arbitration proceedings at its discretion and on the application of one or more of the parties involved. The DAC concluded that it would be a negation of party autonomy to confer such powers on the court and that to endeavour to draft provisions conferring the power on arbitrators which would suit every eventuality was impracticable. This provision therefore allows the parties to make their own arrangements on consolidation and/or concurrent hearings in related disputes, which can be done *ad hoc* when the situation has arisen, or by careful drafting in related arbitration agreements in, say, standard form main and sub-contracts, or by way of rules. This would need most careful consideration since contracts which provide for joinder of other parties in certain circumstances could not be enforced against strangers—this is the doctrine of privity of contract—and the question of privacy might also arise. The key word above, however, is 'related'.

Section 36: Legal or other representation

36.1

This provision is new. It makes it clear that the parties are free to be represented in arbitration proceedings by *anyone* they choose, in contrast to litigation in the higher courts where parties may appear in person but must otherwise be represented by lawyers, usually counsel. In technical disputes not involving difficult issues of law it may be to a party's advantage to be represented by an expert in the subject matter of the dispute rather than by a lawyer, particularly where the arbitrator is also an expert in the particular field.

36.2

The section has been carefully worded to avoid the impression that a party may stubbornly insist on being represented by a particular person whose lack of availability may lead to unreasonable delay in the proceedings. In deciding who is to represent them, parties must have regard to the overriding requirement in s 1 that the object of arbitration is to obtain the fair resolution of disputes 'without unnecessary delay or expense', reflected also in the tribunal's obligations under s 33(1)(*b*) (adopt procedures suitable to the circumstances of the particular case) and the parties' own obligations under s 40 (the parties shall do all things necessary for the proper and expeditious conduct of the arbitral proceedings).

36.3

There is one possible difficulty in appointing non-lawyer representatives, and that is that communications with them may not be protected by the same degree of privilege as applies in communications with, and between, legal advisers. (The rule is that neither client nor solicitor can be compelled to produce documents or answer questions about communications which passed between them in their capacities as solicitor and client, regardless of the nature of the matter— assuming it was *bona fide* concerned with legal advice— whether contentious or non-contentious. The privilege attaches to the client and not to the solicitor, ie, only a client could waive such privilege.) The DAC considered that to try to provide for privilege to be extended in this way would raise difficult questions of general principle. It is to be hoped that arbitrators will use their power under s 34(2)(*d*) (whether documents should be disclosed between the parties), to limit disclosure of documents as between the parties so as to protect, as far as may be reasonable, the necessary degree of confidentiality as between parties and their immediate advisers and representatives.

Section 37: Power to appoint experts, legal advisers or assessors

37.1

Section 37 is new. Section 37(2) is one of the mandatory provisions of Sched 1. It reflects and expands the power under Article 26 of the Model Law for the tribunal to appoint experts 'to report to it on specific issues'.

37.2

Section 37(1) provides that unless the parties agree otherwise, the tribunal may appoint expert or legal advisers to report to it and to the parties, or appoint assessors to help it on technical matters. It may allow such expert, legal adviser or assessor to attend the proceedings and the parties shall be given a reasonable opportunity to comment on any information, opinion or advice offered by him/them.

37.3

In contrast to the Model Law there is no express power of the tribunal to 'require a party to give the expert any relevant information or to produce, or provide access to, any relevant documents, goods or other property for his inspection'. However, s 37 adds the very important provision lacking in the Model Law, that 'the parties shall be given a reasonable opportunity to comment on any information, opinion or advice offered by any such person'.

37.4

Section 37(2) states that the fees and expenses of such a person appointed by the tribunal are expenses of the arbitrators for the purposes of Part I.

37.5

The parties may by agreement remove the tribunal's rights and s 37(2) appears to oblige the parties to pay the fees as part of the tribunal's expenses payable under s 28 (joint and several liability of parties to arbitrators for fees and expenses). However, the protection afforded to the tribunal by the mandatory nature of s 37(2) is not quite as far-reaching as it appears, since the parties' obligation under s 28 is limited to 'such reasonable fees and expenses (if any) as are appropriate in the circumstances'. If, therefore, the tribunal's appointment of an expert or assessor is, objectively considered, unreasonable in the circumstances of the particular case the parties may be able to avoid the apparent obligation to pay his fees. Any arbitrator is therefore well advised to consult the parties and seek their agreement before taking the step of appointing an expert or assessor. Note in respect of s 37 that s 28 (joint and several liability of parties to arbitrators for fees and expenses) and s 56 (power of the tribunal to withold an award in case of non-payment of fees) apply.

37.6

It is interesting to note that the power to appoint assessors, ie people who will sit with the tribunal during the hearing and advise on particular issues during the preparation of the award, is limited to assistance in respect of *technical* and not legal matters. Legal advisers must report both to the tribunal and to the parties. It should also be noted that by s 37(1)(*b*) the parties are to be given 'a reasonable opportunity to comment on *any* information, opinion or advice offered by *any* such person' (emphasis added), ie by assessors as well as by advisers. It has often been the case in the past that an assessor, having sat in on the hearing, has given advice to the arbitrator 'behind the scenes' in private. This will no longer be possible and all advice given to the tribunal must be given openly so that the parties may comment on it. This is right and proper. The function of an assessor is to advise. The function of the arbitrator is to make a decision on the evidence before him. The parties must know the extent of all the evidence on which the arbitrator is relying, including the advice the assessor gives to the arbitrator, and having heard it, it is only fair that they should be given the opportunity to voice their disagreement, if any.

Section 38: General powers exercisable by the tribunal

38.1

Section 38, apart from s 38(5) is new. It confers upon the tribunal important powers which were formerly only exercisable by the court under s 12 of the 1950 Act. It reflects Article 17 of the Model Law. It reverses the House of

Lords decision in *SA Coppee Lavalin NV v Ken-Ren Chemicals and Fertilisers Ltd* [1994] 2 WLR 631.

38.2

Section 38(1) makes it clear that the parties may agree to confer any special powers upon the tribunal that they wish and s 38(2) makes the usual provision that, in the absence of agreement, the tribunal has powers which are set down in the following subsections. Since the parties can agree, modify or exclude any of the fall-back procedures, it is clear that they may by agreement exclude the powers otherwise conferred on the tribunal by s 38(3)–(6).

38.3

Section 38(3) gives the tribunal the power to order a claimant (which by s 82(1) includes a counterclaimant) to provide security for the costs of the arbitration, ie to provide security by way of a cash deposit, bank guarantee or other suitable instrument for the respondent's anticipated costs for which the claimant may become responsible if he loses the arbitration. While formerly parties could give arbitrators the power to order security (and many institutional rules and arbitration agreements in standard contracts did give arbitrators that power), in the absence of such agreement only the court could order a party to provide security for costs under s 12(6)(*a*) of the 1950 Act.

38.4

It is important to note that the costs for which security should be ordered are the respondent's costs of defending the claim and not his costs of pursuing any counterclaim. The same consideration applies as between counterclaimant and counter-respondent.

38.5

It is also important to note that the power is to order security for 'the costs of the arbitration', which, by s 59(1)(*a*), include the arbitrator's own fees and expenses. It appears therefore, that an arbitrator now has power under the Act to order a claimant or counterclaimant to provide security for his own fees and expenses. Previously, if an arbitrator wished to have a right to secure such security, he had to include it in his terms for agreement with the parties at the outset of the arbitration unless procedural rules gave him that power. The power now given is obviously one to be exercised with discretion. The authors suggest that he should still seek to establish with the parties, at the outset of the arbitration, the amount and type of security he will require and when it is to be lodged to avoid taking the parties by surprise later. At all costs an arbitrator should avoid giving an impression of greed and a concern to protect his own interests at the expense of the parties'.

38.6

The clause as originally included in the Bill when published in December 1995 restricted the power to ordering security only to where the court would have such power in litigation and provided that the tribunal should exercise the power on the same principles as would the court. However, this was felt to be too restrictive and far from 'user friendly', particularly for foreign parties since the circumstances in which the court will exercise the power are determined by substantial case law and extensive provision in the Rules of Supreme Court (the *White Book*).

38.7

As it now appears in the Act the provision is clearly intended to give arbitrators the widest possible discretion as to ordering security for costs. However, such discretion must be exercised judicially and must take into account the overriding requirements of ss 1 and 33, ie fairness, speed and economy. Improper use of the power may lead to an application for removal of the arbitrator under s 24(1)(a)—on the grounds that it gives rise to justifiable doubts as to his impartiality.

38.8

The power is a judicial power which may have serious results for the claimant or counterclaimant ordered to provide security. The arbitrator must, as in his consideration of the substantive issues in dispute, give each party 'a reasonable opportunity of putting his case and dealing with that of his opponent' (s 33(1)(a)).

38.9

In litigation an application for security for costs is seldom, if ever, heard by the judge who will actually try the case. This has traditionally been because, in giving reasons in support of his application, a defendant may wish to reveal matters which, if they became known to the trial judge, might prejudice his eventual decision on the substantive issues, for example, that a payment had been made into court by the defendant which might lead the judge to assume a lack of faith in his case. The applicant/defendant may also wish to persuade the judge hearing the application that the plaintiff has little chance of succeeding in the action, and the judge may therefore be asked to form a view on the merits which it would be improper to ask the trial judge to do before hearing evidence at the trial itself. However, these are only some of the considerations which the arbitrator may be asked to take into account, and those who drafted the Act clearly took the view that arbitrators may be trusted not to be influenced by such considerations as being made aware that an offer of settlement has been made. (This is an important point because the fact that the arbitrator has inadvertently become aware that an offer of settlement has been made has often been used by respondents, anxious to delay matters, to suggest that he has become irretrievably prejudiced by the knowledge and that he should withdraw or be removed. This should no longer occur. Offers of settlement are frequently made for purely commercial reasons to get rid of an inconvenient and expensive dispute without any admission or implication of acceptance of liability for the amount offered, or any amount. No arbitrator worth his salt will be influenced by the knowledge that an offer has been made).

38.10

The point about being asked to form a view of the merits of the parties' respective cases in advance of a proper hearing or consideration of the evidence is a more serious one. It is suggested that arbitrators should avoid at all costs being persuaded to form, or above all to express, a view on the merits which might justifiably then be used by the claimant as grounds for an application for his removal under s 24(1)(*a*) (justifiable doubts as to his impartiality).

38.11

The main factors which should be considered by an arbitrator when dealing with an application for security for costs in *favour* of granting the application are:

- if there is a real prospect that the claimant would be unable to pay the respondents' costs if called upon to do so by the eventual award;
- if an offer of settlement of an amount which could well exceed the amount eventually awarded in the claimant's favour has been made and rejected (although respondents will generally be wary of revealing the amount of an offer to the arbitrator so that this will not often be a consideration which the arbitrator will be aware of);
- if the claimant's main assets are lodged outside the jurisdiction of the English courts.

Note that the fact that the claimant is an individual normally resident abroad or a company having its central management and control abroad is expressly excluded from consideration. This is in order to comply with European Union regulations which forbid discrimination against foreign parties and also so as not to discourage foreign parties from conducting arbitrations in the United Kingdom under English law.

38.12

The main factors which should be considered by an arbitrator when dealing with an application for security for costs *against* the application are:

- whether there is a real prospect that the claimant will be unable to continue with the arbitration and therefore have to abandon his possibly justifiable claim if required to provide security (applications for security are frequently made with just this aim in mind—though not, of course, expressed);
- whether the claimant is an individual rather than a limited company (the courts will rarely order an individual to provide security for costs, particularly the costs of a limited company);
- whether the arbitration is to be conducted on written submissions and documents alone without a hearing ('an arbitration on documents will not normally attract an order for security unless the documents and contentions are unusually elaborate' (*Mustill & Boyd*, pp 336 and 337)).

38.13

However, the overriding factor is simply whether it is fair in all the circumstances to order the claimant to provide the security. The arbitrator who decides the matter by applying that principle alone will not go far wrong.

38.14

Section 38(4) provides that the tribunal may give directions in relation to any property which is the subject of the proceedings and which is owned by/in the possession of a party to the proceedings. The directions can be '(a) for the inspection, photographing, preservation, custody or detention of the property by the tribunal, an expert or a party,' or '(b) ordering that samples be taken from, or any observation be made of, or experiment conducted on, the property.'

38.15

This is a modification of powers which were reserved to the court under s 12(6)(g) of the 1950 Act. Note that the present power extends not only to property which is the subject matter of the proceedings but also to property 'as to which any question arises in the proceedings'. It must be property 'which is owned by or is in the possession of a party to the proceedings'. While in general, therefore, the power does not extend to property owned by or in the possession of third parties, property owned by third parties may be the subject of an order if it is in the possession of a party. Note also that a direction for inspection, photographing etc under s 38(4)(a) may order that it be done by the tribunal itself, an expert or a party.

38.16

Section 38(5) directs that a party or witness shall be examined on oath or affirmation. It repeats with modifications s 12(2) and (3) of the 1950 Act. It is usual in arbitrations of any substance for evidence to be taken on oath or affirmation although there is no known case of a prosecution for perjury arising from false evidence given in an arbitration. A court will sometimes enquire the reason for a witness preferring to affirm rather than take the oath, the traditional reason being lack of fixed religious belief. However, it is strongly suggested that is an inappropriate question for an arbitrator to ask. Unless there has been prior agreement that evidence will not be taken on oath or affirmation, an arbitrator should arm himself at the hearing with the necessary equipment for the taking of oaths, ie a New Testament Bible, a complete Bible and a copy of the Koran, and should have the text of the normal forms of oath and affirmation clearly written on cards for the witnesses to read. It is for the parties or their representatives to ensure that the wording of, and necessary equipment for, less usual forms of oath are provided if required.

38.17

Section 38(6) gives the arbitrator power to give directions for the preservation of any evidence in a party's custody or control for the purposes of the arbitration. This is an important power (not previously available to arbitrators, or expressly to the court) if there is any danger of evidence being destroyed. This might be for innocent reasons, for example, that its importance, while apparent to the party wishing it to be preserved, is not apparent to the party having its custody or control.

38.18

See s 44 and the commentary for court support in respect of some of these powers.

Section 39: Power to make provisional awards

39.1

Section 39 is a new provision. It confers a power on the arbitrator which he did not have previously under common law (see, for instance, the judgment of Goff J (as he then was) in *The Kostas Melas* [1981] 1 Lloyd's Rep 18 at 26). It is the power to make a provisional order for relief of a kind which he could grant in a final award, ie it must be a relief actually sought by one of the parties in the arbitration. The relief may be by way of an order for the payment of money by one party to the other, either by way of the costs of the arbitration or of money in dispute, or for the disposition of property between them, such as a division of assets in a partnership dispute. The order would not be an award and its effect can be corrected, changed or completely negated by any future interim or final award which, by s 39(3), must deal with the effect of the order, for example, direct that money directed to be paid under the order be repaid. (In the authors' view the words 'final award' in s 39(3) must also include a partial award under s 47 which would be final in respect of the matters with which it deals—see below.) The power only exists if the parties expressly agree that the arbitrator should have it, whether in the arbitration agreement or by subsequent agreement when the occasion arises. This is made clear by s 39(4) which expressly excludes the power unless the parties agree that the arbitrator should have it.

39.2

It is important to distinguish this from a partial award which the arbitrator may make under s 47 ('If the tribunal does so, [make more than one award] it shall specify in its award the issue, or the claim or part of a claim, which is the subject matter of the award'). It is a temporary or a provisional order, whereas any partial award dealing only with some of the issues in dispute will be final as regards the arbitrator's decision on those issues which it covers. It is intended to be used sparingly and probably following an application from the party seeking the order. It should be used only where the arbitrator forms a view that it would not be fair for a party to be kept out of money claimed, or should continue to bear its costs of the arbitration so far, until a final decision is made on the merits of the dispute. It might be exercised, for instance, in favour of an impecunious claimant where the other party is a major company and the claimant would have difficulty in pursuing the arbitration unless he was given relief of this kind—even though in the end he may lose and have to repay the money. The arbitrator must obviously be very careful to ensure that injustice is not done to the respondent by the granting of such relief.

Section 40: General duty of parties

40.1

Section 40 is new and mandatory. It has no parallel in the Model Law.

40.2

Section 40(1) states that the parties shall do all things necessary for the proper and expeditious conduct of the arbitral proceedings. It imposes on the parties the reciprocal obligations in regard to the conduct of the arbitration to those imposed on the arbitrator by s 33. It is mandatory because, as the DAC has pointed out in its Report, 'the ability to contract out of it would be a negation of the arbitral process'. It is therefore central to the purpose of the Act.

40.3

The duty is to 'do *all* things necessary', that is to say, to act in accordance with the principles laid down in s 1.

40.4

The matters set out in s 40(2) are only examples of what the parties should do, but they are important. Section 40(2)(*a*) imposes a duty of prompt compliance with decisions of the arbitrator on procedural and evidential matters and with his orders and directions generally. The sanctions for non-compliance with this provision are set out in s 41 (powers of tribunal in case of party's default) and s 73, by which a party may lose certain rights if it fails to act promptly.

40.5

Section 40(2)(*b*) imposes a duty to take promptly 'any necessary steps to obtain a decision of the court on a preliminary question of jurisdiction or law' under ss 32 and 45. No time limits are imposed in those sections for applications made under them, and this provision imposes the obligation to make such applications promptly so as not to impede the arbitration process. As will be noted later under the commentary on s 73 (loss of right to object), that section does impose an effective time limit on applications relating to the arbitrator's jurisdiction.

40.6

Taken together with s 1, setting out the general object of arbitration to 'obtain the fair resolution of disputes ... without unnecessary delay or expense', and s 33, relating to the basic duty of the tribunal to avoid unnecessary delay and expense, this section is central to the Act. By imposing an obligation on the parties themselves also to 'do all things necessary for the proper and expeditious conduct of the arbitral proceedings' it binds them also to the obligation not to impede their proper and expeditious conduct. In marked contrast to the position before the Act came into force, an arbitrator, faced with delaying tactics by a party, will now be able to point to the party's obligation under this section and use the powers now conferred upon him to make and enforce orders designed to secure the proper and expeditious conduct of the proceedings. He will be safe in the knowledge that, if the party concerned seeks to have him removed or otherwise to challenge his authority, he may cite this section in justification of his actions.

Section 41: Powers of tribunal in case of party's default

41.1

Section 41—apart from s 41(3) which reproduces in different form s 13A of the 1950 Act as inserted by s 102 of the Courts and Legal Services Act 1990—is new. It reflects Article 25 of the Model Law but goes considerably beyond it in important respects.

41.2

Section 41(1) provides that the parties are free to agree on the powers of the tribunal in case of a party's failure to do something necessary for the proper and expeditious conduct of the arbitration. Section 41(2) provides that in the absence of agreement, a default procedure (set down in s 41(3)) will apply.

41.3

Section 41(3) gives arbitrators the same power as was conferred on them by s 13A of the 1950 Act, which is the power to dismiss a claim 'for want of prosecution', ie for inordinate delay in pursuing it. Prior to the insertion of s 13A in the 1950 Act by the 1990 Act, arbitrators did not have this power (*Bremer Vulcan Schiffbau etc v South India Shipping Corporation* [1981] Lloyd's Rep 253). It was possible for the parties to confer the power on arbitrators by agreement, but this was seldom done even in institutional rules. (The JCT Arbitration Rules 1988 were a notable exception, not only giving the power to the arbitrator to make an award dismissing the claim if not delivered within a specified time limit, but also actually obliging him to do so and to make an order compelling the claimant to pay the arbitrator's fees and expenses and any other costs incurred by the respondent.)

41.4

Section 41(3) gives the arbitrator power to dismiss a claim if he is satisfied that there has been 'inordinate *and* inexcusable delay on the part of the claimant in pursuing his claim'. Both factors must be present if the power is to be exercised. It is not sufficient for the delay to be inordinate. It must *also* be inexcusable, ie there must be no reasonable cause for the delay. These are the primary factors. If they both exist the arbitrator must also take *one* of two other factors into account. The delay must either give rise, or be likely to give rise, to 'a substantial risk that it is not possible to have a fair resolution of the issues in that claim', or to have caused, or be likely to cause, 'serious prejudice to the respondent'. Effectively this means that the arbitrator must form the view that so much time has passed since the subject matter of the claim occurred that it will simply no longer be possible to have a fair trial of the issues because, for example, witnesses have died or forgotten all about the subject matter, and documents will have been lost or destroyed. Serious prejudice to the respondent may result if, for example, he had justifiably assumed that the claim had been dropped and had therefore no longer taken steps to preserve evidence which may have contravened the claim.

41.5

One other factor should be borne in mind in deciding whether to dismiss the claim under this provision, ie whether any statutory period of limitation has expired in relation to the dispute. If the period of limitation has not expired so that the claimant, if his claim were dismissed under this provision, could simply give a fresh notice of arbitration, it is suggested that an arbitrator should be reluctant to dismiss the claim. Any possible unfairness to the respondent would be mitigated by the fact that the respondent as a matter of common prudence should have preserved his records and kept in contact with possible witnesses and so forth while the other party's right to commence litigation or arbitration in respect of the contract remained.

41.6

Section 41(4) gives the arbitrator the power to proceed *ex parte*, ie in the absence of a party, if that party 'fails to attend or be represented at an oral hearing of which due notice was given' or 'where matters are to be dealt with in writing, fails after due notice to submit written evidence or make written submissions'. The power is to 'continue the proceedings in the absence of that party or, as the case may be, without any written evidence or submissions on his behalf, and may make an award on the basis of the evidence before it'.

41.7

Prior to the Act it had long been considered that arbitrators had the power to proceed *ex parte* in such circumstances. Few institutional rules therefore gave any express power to do so (again, with the notable exception of the JCT Arbitration Rules 1988, Rule 12.1.4 and also the ICE Arbitration Procedure 1983, Rule 11.4). However, some doubt was cast on this by s 5 of the 1979 Act which enabled arbitrators or parties to apply to the High Court for the arbitrator to be given power 'to continue with the reference in default of any appearance or of any other act by one of the parties in like manner as a judge of the High Court might continue with proceedings in that court where a party fails to comply with an order of that court or a requirement of rules of court'. Why, it was asked, give the right to apply to the High Court for an order conferring such power on an arbitrator if he already had it at common law? Fortunately the matter is now put beyond doubt by s 41 before too much harm has been done.

41.8

As with all such powers, an arbitrator will be well advised to take great care in exercising it and should only do so where justice to the non-defaulting party demands it. It should only be exercised after ample notice has been given to the defaulting party, preferably more than once, and the arbitrator has taken reasonable steps to assure himself that the notice has been received by the defaulting party, not only in compliance with the requirements for service of notices in s 76, but also by taking all other available steps such as delivery by Recorded Delivery Post with confirmation of receipt or by courier with signature on receipt, the courier being instructed to accept a signature only from the addressee and not from anyone else on his behalf.

41.9

In litigation, failure by a party to appear at trial will normally result in a judgment in favour of the other party. That is not necessarily the case in arbitration. The arbitrator still has a duty to consider the evidence before him and decide on the merits of the case as presented by the non-defaulting party. It is not unknown for a claim in *ex parte* proceedings to be dismissed or substantially reduced (see, for example, *Fox v PG Wellfair Ltd* [1981] 2 Lloyd's Rep 514— although the award in that case was set aside on other grounds).

41.10

Section 41(5) empowers an arbitrator to make a 'peremptory order' where a party has failed to comply with an order in ordinary form. The order should prescribe a time for compliance and failure to comply within that time limit will bring the provisions of s 41(6) and (7) into effect.

41.11

This regularises a form of order which has frequently been used by arbitrators in the past but with some doubt as to their powers in the event of non-compliance. Sometimes called an 'unless order', it is an order issued where there has been a failure to comply with a previous order, stating a time limit for compliance and stating the consequences of non-compliance. For example, where the order is for service of a defence, it may say that if the defence is not served within the specified time limit the arbitration will proceed without a defence and any defence served subsequently will be disregarded. The efficacy of such orders, and the question of whether an arbitrator really would have the power to disregard any defence subsequently served, have been questioned in the past. Section 5 of the 1979 Act helped to some extent and applications were made under it for orders giving arbitrators such power in particular cases. However, it was a clumsy and time-wasting system.

41.12

Section 41(6) provides that, if the peremptory order under s 41(5) is for security for costs, the arbitrator may make an award dismissing the claim. Where there has been a failure to comply with an order for security made by a court, the normal course was for the proceedings to be stayed. However, in the Commercial Court this has now been changed and the court will make an order dismissing the action. It is clearly considered unfair that an arbitration should continue in existence indefinitely and may be revived by the claimant at any time in the future on provision of the security ordered. In the interests of certainty and justice to the other party, where it has been considered that there are good grounds for ordering that security for costs be provided and it is not provided within a set time limit or a reasonable time, the arbitration should be brought to an end.

41.13

Section 41(7) defines the powers available to the arbitrator if a peremptory order is not obeyed. The courts' further powers of enforcement are defined in s 42 (below). There are four courses of action open to him.

41.14

He may 'direct that the party in default shall not be entitled to rely upon any allegation or material which was the subject matter of the order'. For example, if the order is for service of the defence and the respondent has not complied within the time limit but has submitted a defence much later, the arbitrator may direct that he will not be able to pursue that defence at the hearing or otherwise and will be debarred from producing any evidence in support of it. Alternatively, if the order is for witness statements to be exchanged and one party has not complied, the arbitrator may direct that that party will not be able to rely on the contents of any subsequent statements, or call the witnesses at the hearing.

41.15

The arbitrator may draw 'such adverse inferences from the act of non-compliance as the circumstances justify'. For example, if the order is for the production of a particular document and it is not produced, the arbitrator may assume that its contents were unfavourable to the defaulting party's case and base his award accordingly.

41.16

The arbitrator may 'proceed to an award on the basis of such materials as have been properly provided' to him. The operative word is 'properly', ie, provided in accordance with his order. Materials provided out of time may be disregarded by him in arriving at his award.

41.17

He may 'make such order as [he] thinks fit as to the payment of costs of the arbitration incurred in consequence of the non-compliance'. For example, if he considers that justice requires that he should not issue a direction that the party in default shall not be entitled to rely on, for instance, witness statements served late, but allows the evidence to be given, he may award that the other party's and his own costs of any resulting delay be paid by the defaulting party in any event.

41.18

All these powers are discretionary and must be exercised judicially. An arbitrator should not, for example, automatically exercise them in the event of any non-compliance, even with a peremptory order, without considering whether fairness might suggest leniency. The power to award costs under s 41(7)(*d*) is valuable in that regard as it may allow the arbitrator to be lenient to the defaulting party without substantial injustice being done to the other party which will be compensated in costs. In extreme cases costs in such a case may be awarded on the indemnity basis (see commentary to s 61 below).

Powers of court in relation to arbitral proceedings

Section 42: Enforcement of peremptory orders of tribunal

42.1

Section 42 is new. It has no parallel in the Model Law. Section 42(1) provides that unless the parties have agreed otherwise the arbitrator and the parties have the right to ask the court to enforce any peremptory order made under s 41. This would then have the force of an order of the court and the normal sanctions for contempt will be available should the order continue to be disobeyed.

42.2

By s 42(2) an order under this section may be applied for:

(a) by the arbitrator himself—but he must give notice to the parties before doing so;

(b) by the party seeking enforcement of the order—but only with the permission of the arbitrator, and having given notice to the defaulting party (and any other party);

(c) if the parties have expressly agreed in advance that the powers of the court shall be available.

This last provision means that, while the parties may agree that the court's powers under this section shall not be available to them, if they positively agree that they *shall* be available, either the arbitrator or the party seeking enforcement may apply without notice or permission.

42.3

Section 42(3) provides that no application shall be made to the court unless all possibilities of pursuing the matter through the medium of the arbitration have been exhausted. It is obviously undesirable for a party to be able to go to the court when remedies are available through the arbitral process, and those remedies have not been exhausted.

42.4

Section 42(4) contains the fairly obvious proviso that the court will make no order under this section unless it is satisfied that the peremptory order has not been obeyed. If there is no time limit for compliance stated in the order (which should be unusual), the court will determine whether a reasonable time has been allowed.

42.5

Section 42(5) provides that there can be no appeal from an order made by the court under this section without leave of the court. If the peremptory order has been properly considered and drawn up in the first place, and all conditions set out in the section have been met, there should be little scope for appeal in any case.

Section 43: Securing the attendance of witnesses

43.1

Section 43 is mandatory. It reflects Article 27 of the Model Law and s 12(4) and (5) of the 1950 Act.

43.2

Section 43(1) provides that parties to arbitral proceedings may use the same processes as are available to parties in litigation to compel the attendance of witnesses to give evidence.

43.3

The legal jargon of *subpoena ad testificandum, subpoena duces tecum* and, even worse, writ of *habeas corpus ad testificandum* have been left out of the Act for the greater understanding of laymen and foreign users. Apart from that, however, the effect is the same as the 1950 Act provisions, ie, the court would act in respect of normal witnesses required to give oral evidence or produce documents or other material evidence by way of *subpoena* and the power would include that of having a prisoner brought from prison to give evidence (an arbitrator, having no jurisdiction in criminal matters, would have no power to do this himself).

43.4

Section 43(2) is new and provides that a party may only apply to the court for the exercise of the powers under s 43(1) with the permission of the arbitrator or, alternatively, with the agreement of the other party or parties.

43.5

Section 43(3)(*a*) provides, as in the 1950 Act, that the court procedures in s 43(1) may only be used if the witness is in the United Kingdom, including Scotland. Section 43(3)(*b*) is new and provides that such procedures may only be used if the arbitral proceedings are being conducted in England and Wales or Northern Ireland. Note that if the seat of the arbitration under s 3 is in England, Wales or Northern Ireland but the proceedings are actually being conducted elsewhere, including Scotland, the powers cannot be invoked.

43.6

Section 43(4) repeats the provision in the 1950 Act that a person cannot be compelled under this section to produce documents or other materials which he could not be compelled to produce if the matter were in legal proceedings rather than arbitration. A person cannot therefore be compelled, for example, to produce material which, in legal proceedings, would be protected by legal privilege.

43.7

By s 2(3), the court may exercise these powers even if the seat of the arbitration is *not* in England and Wales or Northern Ireland, subject to the proviso set out in s 2(3) (see commentary on s 2).

Section 44: Court powers exercisable in support of arbitral proceedings

44.1

Section 44 reflects Article 9 of the Model Law and repeats in part s 12(6) of the 1950 Act.

44.2

Section 44(1) confers the same powers on the court in aid of an arbitration as it has for the purposes of court proceedings. With the exception of the sale of goods, the granting of interim injunctions or the appointment of a receiver, all the powers given to the court in this section may also be exercised by the arbitrator unless the parties agree otherwise under s 38. (For the arbitrator's power as to what amounts to injunctive relief generally, see para 48.6.) With the exceptions stated, the court's powers are therefore supplementary to the arbitrator's powers and the intention is that they should be exercised only where, for any reason, the arbitrator is unable to exercise them effectively. It may also be necessary for some of the powers to be exercised against a third party, such as the preservation of property and of evidence. This would not be within the powers of the arbitrator which are confined to 'property ... which is owned by or is in the possession of a party to the proceedings' (s 38(4)), and evidence 'in [a party's] custody or control' (s 38(6)).

44.3

The court's powers under the 1950 Act to order security for costs and for the amount in dispute have been omitted. The arbitrator now has power to order security for costs subject to the parties' agreement otherwise (see s 38(3)). However, it appears that there is now no power for either an arbitrator or the court to order security for the amount in dispute.

44.4

The powers exercisable by the court are as follows:

'(a) *The taking of evidence of witnesses.* The former power under s 12(6)(c) and (d) of the 1950 Act was 'the taking of evidence by affidavit' and 'the examination on oath before an officer of the High Court or any other person, and for the issue of a commission or request for the examination of a witness out of the jurisdiction'. The simple phrase now used would seem to cover both those former provisions. As to evidence by affidavit, 's 12(6)(c) seems to assume that evidence in arbitration cannot be given by affidavit, unless the arbitration agreement so provides' (*Mustill & Boyd* p 356, footnote 5), and, of course, unless the court orders it. The question of whether an arbitrator can order evidence by affidavit would appear still to be in doubt since his power under s 38(5) is to 'direct that a party or witness shall be examined on oath or affirmation'. Affidavit evidence is not obtained by examination. However, it is suggested that the power would still lie with the court under this section and the need would only arise where a witness for any reason cannot be called to give evidence in person or where the inconvenience or cost of his doing so would not be justified. Of course, evidence can always be taken by affidavit if both parties agree.

(b) *The preservation of the evidence.*

(c) *Making orders relating to property which is the subject of the proceedings in parallel with those the arbitrator may make under s 38(4) and (6).* As stated above, this would probably be done in relation to evidence and property in the possession or control of third parties. The

151

court would also be able to issue Mareva (an injunction to stop the dissipation of assets) or Anton Piller (a pre-trial discovery injunction) orders for protective measures to preserve assets or evidence.

(d) *The sale of any goods the subject of the proceedings.* This is not within the powers of an arbitrator.

(e) *The granting of an interim injunction or the appointment of a receiver.* A party may well wish the court to exercise these powers, which for obvious reasons only a court and not an arbitrator should be able to exercise, for its protection in the arbitration proceedings.

44.5

Section 44(3) gives the court power, in cases of urgency, to make orders for the preservation of evidence or assets (eg Anton Piller or Mareva orders) not only during the course of arbitration proceedings but also before they are commenced, provided of course that arbitration is in contemplation.

44.6

Section 44(4) makes it clear that, except in cases of urgency, the court shall act only on the application of a party while the arbitration proceedings are in progress and then only upon notice to the other party or parties and the arbitrator. The permission of the arbitrator is *also* required unless the other party or parties have agreed to the application being made.

44.7

Section 44(5) further makes it clear that the court shall only act if the arbitrator had no power to make an order of the kind sought or is unable to do so effectively. All these provisions are to ensure that the court does not officiously intervene in matters which should be within the arbitrator's province, in accordance with the principle as to court intervention set out in s 1(c).

44.8

Section 44(6) is a new and radical provision giving the arbitrator power to order that an order of court made under this section shall cease to have effect. Not only that, but the same power may be exercised by an institution or trade organisation if the rules under which the arbitration is being conducted empower it to act in relation to the subject matter of the order. That an arbitrator or organisation may terminate the effect of an order of court in this way is an entirely new concept and illustrates the radical nature of the thinking behind so much of this Act. The intention is that the court should have power to step in to assist the arbitrator where needed but should then, in appropriate cases, retire gracefully and leave it to the arbitrator or other authority with similar powers to decide when the effect of the order should be brought to an end.

44.9

Section 44(7) provides that there can be no appeal from an order made by the court under this section without leave of the court.

44.10

By s 2(3), the court may exercise these powers even if the seat of the arbitration is *not* in England and Wales or Northern Ireland, subject to the proviso in s 2(3) (see commentary on s 2(3)).

Section 45: Determination of preliminary point of law

45.1

Section 45 reproduces—but with important changes—s 2 of the 1979 Act which in turn replaced with changes the old 'consultative case' procedure under s 21(1)(a) of the 1950 Act. It has no parallel in the Model Law. Subject to stringent conditions, it enables a party to request the court to determine a question of law arising during the course of the arbitration proceedings.

45.2

Section 45(1) enables the parties to agree that the court should not have jurisdiction to determine a point of law under this provision. However, by s 87 (effectiveness of agreement to exclude court's jurisdiction), in a domestic arbitration as defined in s 85, such agreement may only be made *after* the arbitration has commenced as defined in s 14. It follows that in non-domestic arbitrations the agreement can be made *before* as well as after the commencement of the arbitration. See further the commentary on s 87 on this point; but see also the commentary to s 88 concerning possible repeal of that Part of the Act.

45.3

Section 45(1) also contains the important condition that the court must be satisfied that the question of law 'substantially affects the rights of one or more of the parties'. The court will not have the power to entertain any question of law which does not fulfil that condition.

45.4

Section 1(4) of the 1979 Act stated, in relation to appeals on questions of law arising from awards:

'The High Court shall not grant leave under subsection (3)(*b*) above unless it considers that, having regard to all the circumstances, the determination of the question of law concerned could substantially affect the rights of one or more of the parties to the arbitration agreement; and the court may make any leave which it gives conditional upon the applicant complying with such conditions as it considers appropriate.'

Section 2(1) of the 1979 Act stated:

'Subject to subsection (2) and s 3 below, on an application to the High Court made by any of the parties to a reference—

(*a*) with the consent of an arbitrator who has entered on the reference or, if an umpire has entered on the reference, with his consent, or

(*b*) with the consent of all the other parties, the High Court shall have jurisdiction to determine any question of law arising in the course of the reference.'

Section 2(2)(*b*) stated:

'The High Court shall not entertain an application under subsection (1)(*a*) above in respect to any question of law unless it is satisfied that ... (*b*) the question of law is one in respect of which leave to appeal would be likely to be given under s 1(3)(*b*) above.'

45.5

In the Report of the DAC, para 219, it stated, 'However, under s 45(1), unless the parties agree, the Court must now be satisfied that determination of the given question of law will substantially affect the rights of one or more of the parties'. It goes on, 'This last point is a departure from the 1979 Act, s 1 of which made this pre-condition in relation to an appeal in respect of questions of law arising out of the award, but s 2 of which did not impose it in relation to the determination of a preliminary point of law'. However, what about the convoluted route of a cross-reference in s 2(2)(*b*) of the 1979 Act ('... would be likely to be given under s 1(3)(*b*) ...') to the circumstances in which leave to appeal would be granted under s 1(4) ('... the determination of the question of law concerned could substantially affect the rights of one or more of the parties ...') in which leave would be granted under s 1(4) (but only if the application was not made with the consent of the other parties)? Professor Rhidian Thomas, in his masterly exposition on the Arbitration Act 1979 in *The Law and Practice Relating to Appeals from Arbitration Awards*, says (at p 387)

> 'There are, however, many difficulties associated with any attempt to bring s 1(2) appeals and s 2 applications within a policy framework. One sphere of the discretion under s 1(3)(*b*) emphasises that leave to appeal is more likely to be given where the question of law is of importance because of its general interest to the public at large or to a segment of the public. In contrast, the orthodox rationale of s 2 as a statutory measure assisting the efficiency of the arbitration process strongly suggests that the issue of importance of a question of law may on occasions be a more polarised concept and closely tied to the interests of the parties to a reference.'

Whether the limitation did or did not appear in the previous law, s 45(1) *now* makes it absolutely clear that, unless the parties agree, the court must be satisfied that determination of the given question of law will substantially affect the rights of one or more of the parties.

45.6

Section 45(1) goes on to provide that if the parties have agreed to dispense with reasons for the arbitrator's eventual award under s 52(4), this shall be considered to be an agreement to exclude the court's jurisdiction to determine questions of law under this section. An agreement to dispense with reasons must sensibly be taken effectively to be an agreement not to apply for determination of a question of law or to seek an appeal on a question of law arising from an award. By s 87 (effectiveness of agreement to exclude court's jurisdiction) such agreement will only have this effect in a domestic arbitration if it is reached *after* the arbitration has begun.

An agreement to dispense with reasons contained in the domestic arbitration agreement itself will therefore only have this effect if reaffirmed after the arbitration has begun. (Note that this is correct at the time of writing. However, the distinction may be removed by order made under the provisions of s 88 and may indeed have already been removed by the time the Act comes into force (see para 88.1).

45.7

Section 45(2) provides that the court may not consider an application under this section unless it is either made with the agreement of all parties or is made with the permission of the arbitrator. In the latter case (but not the former) the court must be satisfied '(i) that the determination of the question is likely to produce substantial savings in costs', *and* '(ii) that the application was made without delay.' This latter proviso (ii) did not appear in the 1979 Act.

45.8

Section 45(3) provides that, unless the application is made with the agreement of all parties, it must 'state the grounds upon which it is said that the question should be decided by the court'. This provision did not appear in the 1979 Act. The court, in considering the application, must obviously know why the party is making it, if it is made without the agreement of the other parties.

45.9

Section 45(4) empowers the arbitrator, unless otherwise agreed by all the parties, to continue with the arbitration while the application is pending—which will be of great value in avoiding delay. This provision did not appear in the 1979 Act.

45.10

Section 45(5) provides that there shall be no appeal from a decision of the court as to whether the conditions for allowing the application set out in s 45(2) are satisfied, except with the leave of the court. This repeats s 2(2A) of the 1979 Act which had been inserted by s 148 of the Supreme Court Act 1981.

45.11

Section 45(6) provides that a decision of the court on a question of law under this section is to be treated as a judgment of the court for the purposes of appeal against it. However, no such appeal will be allowed without leave of the court which shall not be given unless the court considers that the question of law is one of general importance or is one which 'for some other special reason should be considered by the Court of Appeal'. This would be if the question has a significance which goes beyond the circumstances of the particular arbitration and is one, the final determination of which on appeal, is in the general public interest and possibly will have an influence on many future arbitrations. The examples given by the DAC in its Report are questions which arose from the closure of the Suez Canal in 1956 and the United States embargo on the export of soya beans, both of which had important implications in a number of maritime and trade arbitrations at the time.

The award

Section 46: Rules applicable to substance of dispute

46.1

This is a new provision and it corresponds to Article 28(3) of the Model Law.

46.2

Section 46(1) provides that the tribunal shall decide the dispute (*a*) in accordance with the law chosen by the parties as the applicable law or (*b*) if the parties agree, in accordance with such other considerations as are agreed by them or determined by the tribunal.

46.3

Section 46(1)(*a*) gives the parties the right to choose the law which is applicable to the substance of the dispute. The 'applicable' law means the law which governs the substantive rights of the parties. They will normally choose this. However, sometimes the parties intention in the agreement is unclear. If it is unclear then it can be inferred that they chose the system of law most closely associated or connected with the particular transaction. Various matters, such as the place in which the subject matter of the contract currently lies, the place in which the contract is to be performed, the language which is used in the agreement, will be relevant. This matter could be clarified by the arbitrator who will try to ascertain the parties' choice.

46.4

Section 46(1)(*b*) says that, alternatively, if the parties agree, the dispute may be decided in accordance with 'other considerations' as are agreed by the parties or determined by the tribunal. This means that the parties might want their dispute decided not under a recognised system of law but under what are often referred to as 'equity clauses', which is not uncommon in international commercial contracts.

46.5

Article 28(3) of the Model Law (drafted more boldly than UNCITRAL Rules, Article 33(2)) states, 'The arbitral tribunal shall decide *ex aequo et bono* or as *amiable compositeur* only if the parties have expressly authorised it to do so'. The expressions do not derive from English law or arbitration practice and it was felt inappropriate to incorporate them into the Act, all the more so since Latin and French phrases have been studiously avoided in the Act in the interests of simplicity and understandability. (In Australia it was thought necessary to translate these phrases as 'considerations of general justice and fairness', s 22 of the Victorian Commercial Arbitration Act 1984.)

46.6

An example of such an 'equity clause' might be, 'The tribunal shall reach its decision by reference to the principles of equity and fair dealing', or 'the tribunal shall decide according to the customs and usages of the trade', in effect, deciding otherwise than in accordance with established and determinable principles of law.

46.7

In 1979 Lord Devlin called for the recognition of such clauses, (see *The Judge*, p 104). *Mustill & Boyd* (at pp 74–86) discuss such clauses, and Stewart Boyd QC, a member of the DAC, in the Bernstein Lecture in 1989, said:

'The fact is that arbitration, unlike the courts, depends for its vigour on market forces, and the market in which English arbitration operates is an international market where equity clauses are almost universally recognised. If London will not accommodate equity clauses (and I believe it can), Alsatia undoubtedly will.'

(He was referring to the case of *Czarnikow v Roth I Schmidt & Co* [1922] 2 KB 478 at p 488, where Lord Justice Scrutton said, 'There must be no Alsatia in England where the King's writ does not run'. The authors are indebted to Lord Steyn's reference to this in the Ronald Bernstein Lecture of 1990 on 'Arbitration Law Reform').

46.8

Awards based on equity clauses are enforced in our courts and there appeared no good reason to exclude such a provision from the Act. It has been suggested that there is a widespread desire in the commercial community for such a flexibility of approach, although there is little hard evidence (for example from the experience of ICC) to support this. However, it is interesting to note that the contract for the Channel Tunnel, one of the biggest civil engineering enterprises ever to be undertaken, contained such an equity clause (*Channel Tunnel v Balfour Beatty* [1993] AC 334). Note that the parties, by agreeing that their disputes are to be resolved in this way, have effectively excluded their right to appeal (since there will be no question of law against which they could appeal). However, since s 87 (effectiveness of agreement to exclude court's jurisdiction) does not specifically refer to this section, such an agreement may presumably be made before, as well as after, the arbitration proceedings have commenced, in domestic as well as international arbitrations.

46.9

Section 46(2) provides that the choice of laws of a country means its substantive laws and not its conflict of laws rules. This provision adopts the rules found in Article 28 of the Model Law.

46.10

Section 46(3) provides that if there is no choice or agreement then the tribunal must decide what conflict of laws rules apply. The tribunal must then use them in order to determine what is the applicable law. This again is the language of the Model Law. The DAC in its Report (February 1996) said, 'It has been suggested ... that more guidance be given as to the choice of a proper law, but it appears ... that flexibility is desirable, that it is not our remit to lay down principles in this highly complex area and that to do so would necessitate a departure from the Model Law wording'.

Section 47: Awards on different issues &c

47.1

This 'very important provision' (DAC Report, February 1996) resembles s 14 of the 1950 Act which gave arbitrators, unless the parties agreed otherwise, the power to make what were called 'interim awards'. It has no parallel in the Model Law, Article 31 of which appears to assume that there will be only one award. The Report (Febraury 1996) of the DAC said, 'we have been careful to avoid the use of the term "interim aw.ard" which has become a confusing term, and in its most common use, arguably a misnomer'. In what follows we shall use the term 'partial award' to describe the sort of award authorised by this section.

47.2

Section 47(1) states that, unless otherwise agreed by the parties, the arbitrator 'may make more than one award at different times on different aspects of the matters to be determined'. Where, as is common in major arbitrations, particularly in the construction field, the dispute involves a number of issues, this gives the arbitrator power, unless the parties agree otherwise, to deal with each issue or groups of issues in a series of awards before bringing the matter to a final conclusion in the final award.

47.3

Section 47(2) provides two examples of what a partial award might cover. Section 47(2)(*a*) may be an award relating to an issue affecting the whole claim. Often the whole, or the major part, of a party's case will depend upon a single proposition of fact or law. To dispose of that issue may well settle the whole matter, or it may enable the parties to reach a settlement of the dispute in the light of an award on that single issue. For example, in a building contract dispute the contractor may be claiming entitlement to additional payment in respect of a particular delaying event, the defence being that the event either did not delay the works or, if it did, that the contractor was not entitled to additional payment in respect of it. If the arbitrator makes a partial award upholding either of those defences, the contractor's claim will fail, and much time and expense will have been avoided in the arbitration by the fact that the quantum of the contractor's claim will not have had to be examined. If the partial award finds that the works were delayed by the event and that the contractor is entitled to additional payment, the parties may well be able to agree quantum for themselves in the light of the decision, without having to spend time and money fighting it in the arbitration.

47.4

Section 47(2)(*b*) relates to a part only of the claims or cross-claims submitted to the arbitrator for decision. It may be possible to divide up the dispute into discrete packages and to deal with each in turn or in groups in separate partial awards. However, caution must be exercised that in doing so the arbitrator does not award payment to one party of more than that party would receive when all claims and counterclaims are taken into consideration. In most circumstances it would be most unjust, for example, to direct in a partial award that a sum of money be paid by the respondent in respect of the claimant's claim when a counterclaim against the claimant remains to be determined. If this were the case, eventually a far lesser sum may become payable by the respondent, or even a sum become payable by the claimant where the final award on the counterclaim exceeds the award on the claim. On the other hand, it would be permissible, and in some circumstances could be useful to the parties and lead to a settlement of the whole dispute, for a partial award to state that a sum of money is found to be due on the claim with no direction for its actual payment. When in due course any sum is found to be due on the counterclaim, that sum could be offset against the amount found to be due on the claim and a final direction be given for payment of the balance by one party to the other.

47.5

It is important to distinguish between partial awards under this section and provisional orders under s 39 (power given by the parties to the tribunal to make provisional awards). An order under s 39 is not intended to be final as to any of the issues in the arbitration and its effect would be capable of being changed or even cancelled out by any eventual award, whether final or partial. By s 58 (effect of award), a partial award under this section will be final in respect of all issues which it covers and will not be capable of further review. It is for that reason that s 47(3) requires the arbitrator to specify in any partial award 'the issue, or the claim or part of the claim, which is the subject matter of the award', so that there should be absolute certainty as to what the partial award does and does not cover and in respect of what issues and claims it is intended as final.

Section 48: Remedies

48.1

This provision is largely new and has no parallel in the Model Law.

48.2

Section 48(1) provides that the parties have absolute freedom—'parties are free to agree'—to decide what remedies the arbitrator may direct in his award. This is an extremely important and far-reaching provision since it includes injunctive relief and even remedies which would not be available in court proceedings.

48.3

Section 48(2) states that unless otherwise agreed by the parties, the arbitrator will have the powers as to remedies set out in s 48(3), (4) and (5), ie the usual fall-back-provisions formula.

48.4

By s 48(3) the arbitrator has power to 'make a declaration as to any matter to be determined in the proceedings'. This gives him power, for example, to make declarations as to the meaning to be given to terms of a contract or as to ownership of property. Such declarations, unless they dispose of the whole subject matter of the dispute, will often be made by way of partial awards under s 47 (awards on different issues) and will often assist the parties to reach a settlement of the remainder of the dispute.

48.5

Section 48(4) gives the arbitrator power to 'order the payment of a sum of money, in any currency'.

48.6

Section 48(5) gives the arbitrator the same powers as the court to make three kinds of orders. By s 48(5)(*a*) he may 'order a party to do or refrain from doing anything'. For example, in a dispute between neighbours about the removal of a boundary fence the arbitrator may order it to be replaced. In a dispute over blockage of access he may order the removal of the obstruction. The power allows him to order what would amount to injunctive relief, for instance, by ordering a party not to trespass on another's land.

48.7

Section 48(5)(*b*) gives the arbitrator the power 'to order specific performance of a contract (other than a contract relating to land)'. This repeats s 15 of the 1950 Act and retains the prohibition as to contracts relating to land. The power to order specific performance is one to be used with caution. The arbitrator should be careful not to put himself in a position where he may effectively become a certifier as to satisfactory performance. For example, an arbitrator may award that certain work under a building contract is incomplete and should be completed by the builder; but then what is the building owner's remedy if the completion work is unsatisfactory? The arbitrator may consider that the answer is to make a partial award for specific performance of the completion work and to make a final award when it has been completed. However, if by doing so he gives himself the responsibility of deciding whether or not the completion work is satisfactory and in accordance with the contract, he may effectively be making himself an expert certifier and possibly no longer protected by the immunity conferred by s 29. A possible answer may be for the arbitrator to direct that the completion work be supervised or inspected by an independent surveyor or architect and to make a final award on the basis of the supervisor's certificate that the work is satisfactory.

Section 49: Interest

49.1

Section 49 amends ss 19A and 20 of the 1950 Act (the first of which was inserted by s 15 and Sched 1, Part IV of the Administration of Justice Act 1982) in important respects. It has no parallel in the Model Law.

49.2

Section 49 now gives arbitrators far wider powers in relation to the award of interest than the courts have at the time of writing (although the authors have little doubt that similar powers will soon be extended to the courts, particularly in respect of the award of compound, rather than simple, interest).

49.3

Section 49(1) gives the parties power to agree on the powers the arbitrator should have regarding the award of interest. They may decide for their own reasons, for example, that the arbitrator should not have power to award interest at all or should only do so at a certain fixed rate or should only award simple and not compound interest. In default of such agreement the arbitrator is to have the powers set out in s 49(3)–(5).

49.4

It is worth setting out a brief history of arbitrators' powers to award interest. Originally (for some reason except in cases within the jurisdiction of the Admiralty Division of the High Court), neither arbitrators nor the courts were empowered to award interest at all (*London Chatham & Dover Railway Co v South Eastern Railway Co* [1893] AC 429 HL). Power to award interest on sums directed to be paid in a judgment was given to the courts by the Law Reform (Miscellaneous Provisions) Act 1934. From then until the Administration of

Justice Act 1982 came into force on 1 April 1983, arbitrators were considered to have a common law power to award interest on principal sums awarded, by analogy with the power of the courts to do so under that Act (see *Chandris v Isbrandtsen-Moller Co Inc* [1951] 1 KB 240 (CA)). That power was confined to interest on principal sums awarded and did not extend to sums claimed but paid before the award. The position was regularised and extended to interest on sums claimed but paid before the award by the insertion of s 19A into the 1950 Act. However, in Northern Ireland the position remained the same until the coming into force of the present Act, as s 19A was not incorporated into the Arbitration Act (Northern Ireland) 1937. Interest was simple and not compound interest since the courts regarded the award of 'interest upon interest' to be abhorrent to English law.

49.5

Section 49(3) gives the arbitrator power to award compound or simple interest, in place of the former power under the 1950 Act which was to award simple interest only. The rate should be stated as should the 'rests', ie the intervals at which interest is to be compounded, eg quarterly.

49.6

In the case of interest on an amount ordered to be paid in an award, by s 49(3)(*a*) the terminal date for interest must be not later than the date of the award itself. Interest thereafter is dealt with in s 49(4). The starting date is to be determined by the arbitrator, but would normally be the date when, in the arbitrator's view, the money should have been paid. For example, in a building contract this would be the date payment would have become due under a payment certificate issued after the expenditure or loss was incurred or the work was carried out. The important words in this provision are, 'as it considers meets the justice of the case'.

49.7

By s 49(3)(*b*) in the case of interest on amounts claimed in the arbitration and outstanding at the start of the proceedings under s 14 (commencement of arbitral proceedings), and paid *before* the award was made, the starting date again will be when, in the arbitrator's view, the money should have been paid. The finishing date will be the actual date of payment.

49.8

In both cases the authors recommend that the arbitrator, unless there are special reasons against it, should calculate the interest and state it in his award so as to avoid later arguments between the parties as to the calculation. In fairness he should also state the rate, the starting and finishing dates and the rests. If the arbitrator gets the calculation wrong he can correct it under the 'slip rule' in s 57. (One of the reasons for an arbitrator not to calculate the amount may be that the parties have excluded his power to correct slips under s 57(1)).

49.9

It should be noted that an arbitrator does not have to award interest for a continuous period, for example from the date when the money should have been paid to the date of the award. If the arbitrator considers it just, periods may be excluded, perhaps because in the arbitrator's view there was an unreasonable delay by the claimant in pursuing the claim in the arbitration, and the respondent should not pay interest for that period (for a similar decision on slightly different grounds see *Rees & Kirby Ltd v Swansea City Council* 25 BLR 129 (QBD); 30 BLR 1 (CA)).

49.10

Section 49(4) gives the arbitrator power to award simple or compound interest, at whatever rates and at whatever rests he considers just, on the outstanding amount of any award until it is paid, the principal amount to include costs and interest included in the award. Section 20 of the 1950 Act only provided that 'a sum directed by an award to be paid shall, unless the award otherwise directs, carry interest as from the date of the award and at the same rate as a judgment debt'. It was held that the phrase, 'unless the award otherwise directs', only permitted an arbitrator to direct that the award should not carry interest and did not permit him to change the rate (*London & Overseas Freighters v Timber Shipping Co SA* [1971] 1 Lloyd's Rep 523). It should be noted, however, that interest will now only apply if the arbitrator so directs. It will not now apply automatically unless he directs otherwise.

49.11

By s 49(5) interest may be awarded to be paid on an amount not actually awarded but becoming payable from a declaratory award under s 48(3). An award may not actually direct the payment of a specific sum, but it may be the consequence of a declaration as to the rights of the parties that a sum of money becomes due from one party to another, for instance a declaration that a contract is not binding because of some defect and a reimbursement of money which a party had paid in advance for a service which he now does not receive. It is only fair that interest should be payable on that sum as it would be if the sum were actually directed to be paid.

49.12

Section 49(6) preserves the power to award interest other than under this section. For instance, the contract between the parties may actually provide that interest be paid on overdue monies (see for example, the ICE Conditions of Contract for Civil Engineering Works 6th Edition, cl 60(7)). Institutional rules, under which the arbitration is being conducted, may themselves give the arbitrator the power to award interest (see the current LCIA Rules, Article 16.5).

49.13

It is important to note that the powers under this section relate to the awarding of interest on any sum awarded in a partial or final award. It does not affect the power to include in any amount awarded interest claimed as special damages, such as interest on an overdraft incurred as a result of simple failure to make payment in accordance with the terms of the contract. This is subject to compliance with the rule in *Hadley v Baxendale* (1854) 9 Ex 341, ie that the loss was a direct result of the failure to pay and was in the reasonable contemplation of the parties, or would have been had they applied their minds to it, at the time the contract was entered into (see *Wadsworth v Lydall* [1981] 1 WLR 598 and *La Pintada* [1984] 2 Lloyd's Rep 9, and the commentary in *Mustill & Boyd* at p 393). For special consideration of this subject in building contracts see also *F G Minter Ltd v Welsh Health Technical Services Organization* 11 BLR 1 (QBD); 13 BLR 1 (CA), and *Rees & Kirby Ltd v Swansea City Council* 25 BLR 129 (QBD) and 30 BLR 1 (CA).

49.14

The power to award interest under this section must always be exercised judicially. The rates and rests should be based on normal commercial considerations and standards, such as those adopted by banks when lending money. Punitive rates or rests should not be awarded. The purpose should simply be to compensate the claimant for being kept out of his money. This is particularly the case now that compound interest can be awarded, which removes the former difficulty so usefully discussed in *Mustill & Boyd* at p 392.

49.15

On the other hand interest should always be awarded in appropriate cases whether specifically claimed or not (see *Tehno-Impex v Gebr van Weelde Scheepvaartkontor BV* [1981] 1 Lloyd's Rep 587 and *La Pintada* (above)). If interest is not awarded where, on ordinary reading of the award it would appear appropriate, clear reasons should be given for the omission.

Section 50: Extension of time for making award

50.1

Section 50 replaces and extends s 13 of the 1950 Act. It has no parallel in the Model Law.

50.2

Section 50(1) empowers the court, unless the parties agree otherwise, to extend any time limit for the making of an award which appears in the arbitration agreement or is subsequently fixed, subject to conditions.

50.3

Section 50(2) provides that an application for an order under this section may be made by the arbitrator upon notice to the parties, or by any party to the arbitration upon notice to the arbitrator and the other parties. An application can only be made if any process available under the arbitration for extending the time has been exhausted. Most institutional rules contain time limits for the making of an award and also contain provision for extension of those time limits. For example, under the ICC Rules of Arbitration, Article 18, the normal time limit of six months may be (and almost invariably is), extended by the ICC Court in Paris. Under the JCT Arbitration Rules 1988, Rule 6.9.1 provides that the time limit of 28 days may be extended by the arbitrator himself on notice to the parties before the original time limit has expired. All such machinery for extension of time must have been exhausted before the court will entertain an application under this section.

50.4

By s 50(3) the court may only make an order extending the time limit if 'a substantial injustice would otherwise be done'. It appears to the authors that, despite this condition, the courts will invariably grant at least some extension of time since it is almost axiomatic that injustice will be done to at least one of the parties if, by the expiry of a time limit, the arbitrator is prevented from making an award. However, there may be circumstances in which it would be unjust to one of the parties to extend the time limit, and it appears to us that the courts are likely in practice to have regard to that consideration rather than whether injustice would be done by not extending the time limit.

50.5

Section 50(4) empowers the court to specify the period of the extension granted and any conditions attached to the extension. They may extend the time, irrespective of whether the original, or any previously extended, time limit has expired. Parties may therefore apply for an extension even though the original time limit has not expired, or after it has already expired.

50.6

Section 50(5) provides that leave of the court is required for any appeal against a decision under this section.

50.7

See commentary on s 12 (power of the court to extend time

for beginning arbitral proceedings) and s 79 for extensions of time generally.

Section 51: Settlement

51.1

Section 51 is new. It reflects Article 30 of the Model Law.

51.2

Section 51(1) provides that the requirements of the section may be set aside by agreement between the parties. Such agreement can be reached at any time.

51.3

Section 51(2) provides that upon notification of the settlement the arbitrator is to terminate the proceedings and, if so requested by the parties, shall record the terms of the settlement in an agreed award (sometimes called a consent award). The provision that an agreed award will only be issued if the parties request it, is because if the parties trust each other to observe the terms of the settlement they may save costs by not having its terms recorded in an award. The value of embodying a settlement in the form of an award means that, should the agreement not be complied with, the award could be enforced in the usual way. Without such an award the parties would be forced back to their contractual rights.

51.4

The words, 'if ... not objected to by the tribunal' are important. They empower the arbitrator not to issue an agreed award if, in his view, it contains terms which are objectionable or illegal and he does not wish to be associated with it. However, if the parties still wish to go ahead with the settlement they can do so and simply dispense with the award.

51.5

Section 51(4) and (5) states that an agreed award under this section has the same status and effect as any other award on the merits and all other provisions in ss 52–58 apply. For example, it is final and binding under s 58 and can be enforced by one party against the other under s 66 (which empowers the court to enforce an award in the same manner as a judgment) if the terms of the settlement are not honoured. The award must have the same form as any other award (s 52), and the provisions regarding the place where the award was made (s 53), the date (s 54), notification (s 55), the power of the arbitrator to withhold it until payment of his fees (s 56), and correction or power to make additional awards (s 57), apply. Also, by s 51(5), all provisions relating to costs in ss 59–65 apply, so that the arbitrator will retain his powers in relation to costs as set out in those sections unless, of course (as will almost invariably be the case unless the parties are exceptionally foolish or they wish to leave costs to the arbitrator's discretion in the light of the terms of the settlement on the issues), the parties have agreed on distribution of responsibility for costs in the settlement.

Section 52: Form of award

52.1

Section 52 corresponds to Article 31 of the Model Law.

52.2

Section 52(1) states that the parties can agree the form of the award. Section 52(2) states that if they do not agree, the following provisions apply.

52.3

Section 52(3) states that the award shall be in writing and signed by all the arbitrators or all those assenting to the award, ie it allows arbitrators who dissent from the award to decline to sign it.

52.4

Section 52(4) says that the award shall contain the reasons for the award unless it is an agreed award or the parties have agreed to dispense with reasons.

52.5

Section 52(5) states that the award shall state the seat of the arbitration and the date when the award was made. (The seat of the arbitration is defined in s 3 and the word is used here in order to correspond with earlier provisions. Of course, the seat is only of importance in international arbitrations or where an award has to be enforced abroad.)

52.6

Excluding statutory arbitrations, for example those under the Agricultural Holdings Act 1986, English law imposed no legal requirements as to the form of a valid award. Parties could not compel an arbitrator to give reasons except through an application to the court under s 1(5) of the 1979 Act, where it applied. It is up to the parties to agree what they want incorporated in the award. To the extent that they do not agree then, as stated above, there are legal requirements which are now imposed, eg, that it should be in writing and signed etc.

52.7

There were and are—other than those set out above—no legal requirements as to the form of an award. It should, of course, be signed (s 52(3)) and, although not strictly necessary, many sole arbitrators also have their signatures witnessed. The witness need not actually be present when the award is signed but the arbitrator should confirm that it is his signature when asking the witness to sign it. It will need to set out the arbitration agreement, the date and the method of appointment of the arbitrator. The whole object of an award is to tell the parties what decision the arbitrator has reached, whether the claim has succeeded in entirety, whether the counterclaim has succeeded, and whether the amount claimed is recoverable in full. It will tell them how much is to be paid in compensation, whether specific performance is to be ordered, who will pay the arbitrator's costs, who will be responsible for the costs of the reference, whether interest will be paid on the sum, and if so how much and to cover what period, etc. It will then entitle the successful party, should the unsuccessful one refuse to comply with its terms, to enforce it through the courts. It is the culmination of the arbitrator's work and thereafter he will have no more authority. It is therefore essential that the award complies with all the terms of the agreement and that it is complete, certain, consistent, final and clear.

52.8

As to the requirement for reasons, it has long been felt that a basic rule of justice is that those who determine the rights and obligations of others should explain how they have reached their decisions. The policy of the 1979 Act was to encourage reasoned awards but an arbitrator was not obliged to give reasons even if asked to do so by the parties. Section 1(5) of the 1979 Act provided that on the application of a party, either with the consent of the other party or with leave of the court, an arbitrator might be required to give, or amplify, his reasons for an award. This was in order to determine whether any question of law arose from them.

52.9

Section 52(4) appears to suit most commercial interests—most cases of substance, and many consumer awards contain reasons—but rent review arbitrators have voiced doubts, saying that parties only want valuation. However, in this case they would simply agree to dispense with reasons if that was their wish. As to the form reasons might take, the arbitrator must state as simply as he can why he reached his conclusions. In *Bremer Handelsgesellschaft v Westzucker (No 2)* [1981] 2 Lloyd's Rep 130, Donaldson LJ (as he then was) said:

> '... the task is not a formidable one ... no particular form of award is required ... All that is necessary is that the arbitrators should set out what, on their view of the evidence, did or did not happen and should explain succinctly why, in the light of what happened, they have reached their decision and what that decision is.'

In *Antaios Compania Naviera SA v Salen Rederierna* [1985] AC 191, Lord Roskill commented, referring to some 96 pages of reasons, that businessmen were more interested in the decision than in the underlying philosophy. In *Hayn Roman & Co SA v Cominter (UK) Ltd (No 2)* [1982] 2 Lloyd's Rep 458 at p 464, Goff J (as he then was), said:

> '... it is incumbent upon arbitrators, in giving their reasons, to explain on what basis they have rejected contentions that have been advanced before them. They are not being asked to go into great detail, they are simply being asked to deal with submissions which have been advanced before them because this is just the kind of matter on which the parties, if their contentions are rejected, may wish to pursue an appeal.'

52.10

Will the requirement for reasons lead to a flood of applications for leave to appeal? This is not expected to be the case.

Both the philosophy of the Act and the added restrictions regarding access to the courts and, in particular, the abolition of the special categories, make this unlikely to happen. The parties, of course, are free expressly to exclude the right to appeal or to tell the arbitrator that they do not require a reasoned award. And, as seen in the commentary to s 46 (concerning rules applicable to the substance of the dispute), the parties, in agreeing to have their dispute decided under an 'equity clause', are in effect excluding their right to appeal, there being no 'question of law' for the court to decide.

Section 53: Place where award treated as made

53.1

Section 53 states that 'unless otherwise agreed by the parties, where the seat of the arbitration is in England and Wales or Northern Ireland, any award in the proceedings shall be treated as made there, regardless of where it was signed, despatched or delivered to any of the parties.' In other words, the seat determines where it was *made*, and where it was signed or sent is immaterial. This makes sense as an award will sometimes be signed in a country other than the one in which the hearing took place, eg, a hearing in London may well be attended by Swiss, German and French arbitrators, all of whom sign the award in their local offices.

53.2

This short but important section reverses the House of Lords decision (but not the result) in *Hiscox v Outhwaite (No 1)* [1991] 3 WLR 297. In brief, it was held that for the purposes of the New York Convention an award is 'made' at the place where it was signed and it was therefore desirable that it should be signed in the place in which the arbitration was held. This case illustrated the problems which could otherwise arise. While England was the seat of the arbitration, the arbitrator signed the award in Paris because he happened to be there when it was completed. It was held to be an award made outside England and therefore enforceable under the New York Convention, causing difficult questions on the right to appeal under the 1979 Act.

53.3

Section 53 is designed to avoid such problems. Its significance is that it determines the legal identity of an award, ie whether it is a domestic or an international one (see Part III of the Act, in particular s 100 and subsequent sections, which deal with recognition and enforcement of New York Convention awards).

Section 54: Date of award

54.1

Section 54(1) provides that 'unless otherwise agreed by the parties, the tribunal may decide what is to be taken as the date on which the award was made.' The dating of an award is an important matter since any interest awarded under s 49(4) on an award of money will run from the date of the award unless directed by the arbitrator or otherwise agreed by the parties.

54.2

Section 54(2) states that in the absence of such a decision, the date of the award shall be the date on which it is signed by the arbitrator or, where more than one arbitrator signs the award, by the last of them. This is the fall-back position. It is important for limitation periods. For example, time limits for challenging the award run from the date of the award (which we have seen is, in the absence of contrary agreement by the parties or directions by the arbitrator, the date on which the award is signed).

Section 55: Notification of award

55.1

By s 55(1) the parties are free to agree on the requirements as to notification of the award to the parties.

55.2

Section 55(2) provides: 'If there is no such agreement, the award shall be notified to the parties by service on them of copies of the award, which shall be done without delay after the award is made'. This is the fall-back provision where the parties have not agreed how the award should be notified. The words 'the parties' make it clear that all parties must be notified. This will prevent one party paying for the award, obtaining it and then sitting on it until the expiration of time limits for appeal or other challenge; something which apparently has occurred from time to time. The words 'without delay' are simple and mean that the parties should be sent the award as soon as possible after it has been made. They need to be able to avail themselves of the maximum time limits, for example, within which to appeal or challenge the award (see s 70(3), which restricts to 28 days the time available to make an application or appeal). The parties also might wish to apply for an award to be corrected under the provisions of s 57. Section 57(4) for example provides a time limit of 28 days from the date of the award for the parties to apply to the tribunal to correct the award or for an additional award to be made. Time limits, we shall see, can be extended under s 79.

55.3

Notification is to be by service. Service is dealt with in s 76, and as might be expected, the parties are free to make any agreement as to the manner of service, failing which default provisions are set down.

55.4

Section 55(3) provides that 'nothing in the section affects s 56.' As will be seen, s 56 gives power to withhold the award in case of non-payment. This provision makes it absolutely clear that s 55 is subject to the right of the tribunal to withhold the award where fees and expenses which have been incurred remain unpaid. But once the tribunal has been paid, it would be under a duty to notify all parties.

Section 56: Power to withhold award in case of non-payment

56.1

Section 56 supersedes with amendments the provisions of s 19 of the 1950 Act. It is a mandatory provision.

56.2

Section 56(1) provides that 'the tribunal may refuse to deliver an award to the parties except upon full payment of the fees and expenses of the arbitrators.'

56.3

The usual practice is for the parties to be informed that, on payment of the arbitrator's fees, the award is ready to be delivered, or alternatively collected. Either party, usually the claimant, then forwards a cheque or banker's draft, on receipt of which (or after a few days in order for the cheque to be cleared) the arbitrator sends off copies of the award to both parties or informs them that it is ready for collection. Whether the fees have been agreed or not it is usual for an arbitrator to encourage/ensure payment by exercising his right of lien over the award. He has probably spent days, weeks or even months, if the matter was a complicated one, in drafting an enforceable award. He will be reluctant to part with it without his fees in some way being protected. A lien is a right to keep possession of property until a debt due in respect of it is discharged, a common example being a garage's lien over a vehicle left at the garage in respect of repair work which has been carried out on it. Unless the car's owner pays the garage, he cannot take the car away. This is also the case with an award. As to the arbitrator's fees, however, it may be that the party seeking to secure the award considers that such fees and expenses which have now been asked are excessive. Yet the award will not be released by the arbitrator until this excessive amount is paid. Section 56(1) states the existing right at common law.

56.4

Under the previous law there were only limited powers to review an arbitrator's fees and expenses. Section 19(1) of the 1950 Act stated:

> 'If in any case an arbitrator or umpire refuses to deliver his award except on payment of the fees demanded by him, the High Court may, on an application for the purpose, order that the arbitrator or the umpire shall deliver the award to the applicant on payment into court by the applicant of the fees demanded, and further that the fees demanded shall be taxed by the taxing officer and that out of the money paid into court there shall be paid out to the arbitrator or umpire by way of fees such sums as may be found reasonable on taxation and that the balance of the money, if any, shall be paid out to the applicant.'

56.5

Section 56(2) provides a mechanism whereby the party can seek the assistance of the court if it considers that the arbitrator is asking too much for the release of its award. The party may apply to the court which may order that:

'(a) the tribunal shall deliver the award on the payment into court by the applicant of the fees and expenses demanded, or such lesser amount as the court may specify,

(b) the amount of the fees and expenses properly payable shall be determined by such means and upon such terms as the court may direct, and

(c) out of the money paid into court there shall be paid out such fees and expenses as may be found to be properly payable and the balance of the money (if any) shall be paid out to the applicant.'

When an application is made by a party it must give notice to the other side and to the tribunal.

56.6

Section 56(2), unlike s 19 of the 1950 Act, gives the court discretion ('may specify') to order that a lesser amount of money is to be paid. In s 56(2)(b) the words 'fees and expenses properly payable' mean that the assessment of the appropriate level of costs will be determined. The term which has been habitually used in the United Kingdom to describe this process is 'taxation', and it is bewildering both to foreigners and laymen, implying as it does something to do with the Inland Revenue and the raising of government money. The Act carefully avoids using this ambiguous term. What might constitute 'determined by such means and upon such terms' will be for the court to decide. Presumably in a really 'heavy' arbitration the court might conclude that the use of a Taxing Master of the High Court is inevitable, bearing in mind that such proceedings are costly, cumbersome and involve considerable delay. However, it may be that the court redirects the tribunal to assess and settle its own costs (for most awards would be framed, 'The arbitrator determines his costs at ...', implying that he has already carefully gone through all his time sheets, considered the extent to which some time was wasted (eg in looking up certain matters), considered that some time was more valuably spent than other and made appropriate deductions, rather like costing clerks in solicitors' offices). It may be that the court itself undertakes this task.

56.7

Section 56(3) states that 'the amount of fees and expenses properly payable is the amount the applicant is liable to pay under s 28 or any agreement relating to the payment of the arbitrators.' Section 28, it may be recalled, deals with the joint and several liability of the parties to pay the tribunal's fees and expenses. In other words, if the parties have agreed with the arbitrator to pay a certain sum, then that sum is the sum 'properly payable'. If they have not so agreed, then s 28 provides that they must pay 'such reasonable fees and expenses (if any) as are appropriate in the circumstances'. In maritime arbitrations it is extremely rare for there to be an agreement in advance as to the amount to be paid. Commodity arbitrators usually fix their own fees but at an agreed hourly rate and the particular commodity trade arbitration will then distribute the award (after having added its own expenses and fees for administering the arbitration). In the case of institutional arbitrations, schedules of fees and costs are normally provided with the rules. In arbitrations under the Rules of the International Chamber of Commerce (ICC) the fees payable to arbitrators are fixed by the International Court of Arbitration in Paris.

56.8

Section 56(4) provides that 'no application to the court may be made where there is any available arbitral process for appeal or review of the amount of fees or expenses demanded.' This subsection departs from the 1950 Act. No recourse to the court is possible if there is already an arbitral machinery for review or appeal of the fees or expenses demanded. This preserves the arbitration agreement relied upon.

56.9

Section 56(5) makes clear that 'arbitrators' in this section includes an arbitrator who has ceased to act and an umpire who has not replaced the other arbitrators, in other words one who has not been called upon to act.

56.10

Section 56(6) states that the above provisions also apply to any arbitral or other institution given powers by the parties in relation to the delivery of the award. References to fees and expenses include those of that institution. In other words, a similar right of lien in respect of institutions is introduced. The Chartered Institute of Arbitrators, for example, administers hundreds of different kinds of consumer arbitrations, for example financial services, travel, ones to do with claims against the Post Office and other services. The Institute negotiates fees with ABTA or FIMBRA, for example, and the claimants pay certain registration fees. The Institute takes the responsibility for delivering the award rather than leaving this to the arbitrator. Until the agreed fees are paid the awards are not sent out.

56.11

Section 56(7) states that the leave of the court is required for any appeal from a decision of the court under this section.

56.12

Section 56(8) provides that nothing in this section shall be construed as excluding an application under s 28 where payment has been made to the arbitrators in order to obtain an award. This is an important provision. It makes clear that if a party pays the fees in order to obtain the award, this will not affect its right to challenge those fees and expenses under s 28. Just because it has paid them in order to get hold of the award, which it might need to do quickly, particularly in view of the time limits for challenges and appeals under s 70(3), it will not lose this right. In other words, a party will always have the possibility of having those fees reviewed by the court even if they have already been paid.

Section 57: Correction of award or additional award

57.1

Section 57 corresponds to Article 33 of the Model Law. It supersedes ·ss 17 and 18(4) of the 1950 Act.

57.2

Section 57(1) states that the parties are free to agree on the powers of the tribunal to correct an award or make an additional award. Section 57(2) makes the usual provision that if the parties do not agree then the default procedure, set out in the following subsections, applies.

57.3

Section 57(3) states that the tribunal on its own initiative *or* on the application of a party may:

'(a) correct an award so as to remove any clerical mistake or error arising from an accidental slip or omission or clarify or remove any ambiguity in the award, *or*

(b) make an additional award in respect of any claim (including a claim for interest or costs) which was presented to the tribunal but was not dealt with in the award'.

It provides that these powers shall not be exercised without first giving the other parties an opportunity to make representations to the tribunal.

57.4

The award is the consummation of the arbitrator's work. It should be final, certain and clear. Unless the award is enforceable the arbitrator will have failed in his duty. If its terms are ambiguous, for example where it is unclear whether the relevant figures refer to loads, rather than tonnes, the courts have always tried to resolve such ambiguities in a way in which the award is upheld, rather than destroyed. Section 57(3)(a), a most useful provision, enables the tribunal to correct itself. The object is to give the tribunal the maximum opportunity to correct things which have gone wrong rather than cause the parties to go to the courts. Note that the tribunal may correct the matter on its own initiative, alternatively a party can apply to the tribunal.

57.5

The removal of clerical mistakes or errors etc was possible in the previous law. Section 17 of the 1950 Act stated, 'Unless a contrary intention is expressed in the arbitration agreement, the arbitrator or umpire shall have power to correct in any award any clerical mistake or error arising from any accidental slip or omission.' This means such matters as typing errors—'now' having been typed for 'not', negatives being omitted—errors of calculation which have arisen, even errors which have arisen as the result of a 'mental lapse' (*The Montan* [1985] 1 Lloyd's Rep 198). However, this is not wide enough to cover a change of mind, ie something the arbitrator particularly addressed in the award on which he now has different views. He cannot reconsider his award

(*Mutual Shipping Corp of New York v Bayshore Shipping Co of Monrovia* [1985] 1 All ER 520).

57.6

However, in addition to the preservation of the above rule, s 57(3) provides *new* powers. These are (*a*) 'clarify or remove any ambiguity in the award' or (*b*) 'make an additional award'. This is considerable widening, and it means that not only is the correction of an award possible, but any amiguities in it can be explained.

57.7

Section 57(3)(*b*) gives the tribunal the power to make an additional award where something which was agreed to be referred has been omitted from the award, for example, no provision has been made for costs.

57.8

Section 18(4) of the 1950 Act provided:

> 'If no provision is made by an award with respect to the costs of the reference any party to the reference may, within fourteen days of the publication of the award or such further time as the High Court or a judge thereof may direct, apply to the arbitrator for an order directing by and to whom those costs shall be paid, and thereupon the arbitrator shall, after hearing any party which may desire to be heard, amend his award by adding thereto such directions as he may think proper with respect to the payment of the costs of the reference.'

57.9

The new provision extends beyond the provision of costs since the words used are 'an additional award in respect of any claim (including a claim for for interest or costs)'. The section goes on to make it clear that these powers will not be exercisable by the tribunal unless the other parties have first been given the opportunity to make representations to the tribunal. This is clearly necessary in the interests of fairness.

57.10

Section 57(4) sets down time limits for making application for such corrections or additional awards. This is to avoid unnecessary lengthening of the reference and is in keeping with the philosophy of the Act. Unless there were some time limit, applications might be made long after the event. The period is within 28 days of the award or a longer period if the parties agree. Section 57(5) deals with the correction of the award and sets down a period of within 28 days from the date the tribunal received the application or, if it is the tribunal which makes the correction on its own initiative, within 28 days of the award. Section 57(6) deals with additional awards and the time limit is that it shall be made within 56 days of the date of the original award. The parties may also agree longer periods. Section 57(7) clarifies and makes certain that any correction of an award shall form part of the award.

57.11

Correction of an award may be made by way of an amending award, ie by an award so headed, and setting out the corrections that are to be made. It can also be effected by re-issuing the original award clearly marked 'amended', marking the corrections in some way, perhaps by striking through the original provisions and setting out the corrected provisions underlined or printed in red. Whatever method is used it is essential that the correction is clear, unambiguous and certain. The amended or corrected award should be made in the same way as the original, for example, if the arbitrator's signature has been witnessed in the original award it should also be witnessed in the amending or corrected award (though not necessarily by the same witness), and the date of correction should be stated.

Section 58: Effect of award

58.1

Section 58 restates s 16 of the 1950 Act. It provides that the award is final and binding on the parties and on any persons claiming through or under them. Section 58(2) makes it clear that this provision does not affect the right of a person to challenge the award by any available arbitral process of appeal or review or in accordance with Part I.

58.2

Section 16 of the 1950 Act said, 'Unless a contrary intention is expressed therein, every arbitration agreement shall, where such a provision is applicable to the reference, be deemed to contain a provision that the award to be made by the arbitrator or umpire shall be final and binding on the parties and the persons claiming under them respectively'. In other words, such a term is implied into the arbitration agreement unless a contrary intention is expressed. Note the language used, including the typical 'deeming' provision which foreigners had difficulties in comprehending. Compare and contrast this with the simple and lucid statement of the present law.

58.3

A decision made by an arbitrator, assuming its validity is not successfully attacked, is the equivalent of a decision by a court and conclusive as between the parties of the facts found by it. Thus the parties could not—and cannot—reopen the same issues in subsequent proceedings; they would be precluded from pursuing litigation, for example. However, the award is of no substantive or evidential effect against a third party (ie one which is neither a party nor anyone claiming through or under a party, for example an insurer; or indeed in any criminal matter).

58.4

In the Report by the DAC (February 1996), it was made clear that consideration had been given to the inclusion of a clause to cover this matter. However, such a course was not adopted as 'it would be very difficult to construct an acceptable provision and we are not persuaded that it is needed'.

Costs of the arbitration

The whole of this part of the Act, ie from and including ss 59–65, has no parallel in the Model Law, presumably because in civil law systems each party will normally pay its own costs and neither party is usually ordered to pay any part of the costs of the other party.

Section 59: Costs of the arbitration
59.1

Section 59 is new. It defines what is meant by 'costs'.

59.2

Section 59(1)(a) states that costs are to include 'the arbitrators' fees and expenses', often referred to as 'the costs of the award'. It allows the arbitrator, where he has power to direct that one party should pay the costs, or part of the costs, of the arbitration, to direct which party is to pay his own fees and expenses or in what proportion they should be divided between the parties. It is normal for the arbitrator to state the amount of his fees and expenses in the award. Note, however, the effect of s 64 below (recoverable fees and expenses of arbitrators). For the arbitrator's general entitlement as to fees see s 28 (joint and several liability of parties to arbitrators for fees and expenses). By s 37, it will be recalled, the arbitrator's expenses may include the fees of 'an expert, legal adviser or assessor' appointed by an arbitrator.

59.3

It is normal for an arbitrator to hold his award in reserve once made and signed, pending payment of his fees (and see s 56 which refers to his lien). In his award, therefore, he should first state which party is to be responsible for his fees and expenses and then provide that, if the other party has paid the whole or any part of those costs, the costs so paid shall be reimbursed by the responsible party, perhaps less any value added tax which the party which has paid can recover as input tax (VAT not normally being chargeable on reimbursements unless actually included in a tax invoice). A suggested form of wording is:

> The respondent shall pay [or the claimant shall pay 40 per cent and the respondent pay 60 per cent of] the costs of this Award which I determine to be the sum of £x including Value Added Tax. If the claimant has paid the whole or any part of this sum [or the sum payable by the respondent under this direction] the respondent shall forthwith reimburse to the claimant the amount so paid [less any Value Added Tax recoverable by the claimant from HM Customs and Excise].

The words in square brackets relating to VAT may be omitted if the claimant is clearly unable to recover VAT, for instance, where he is a private individual and the subject matter of the arbitration does not relate to any business activities for which he may be registered for VAT.

59.4

Section 59(1)(*b*) gives the arbitrator the power to direct which party shall pay 'the fees and expenses of any arbitral institution concerned'. Many institutions, such as the ICC and the LCIA, necessarily charge quite substantial fees for the administration of arbitrations under their rules, and this empowers the arbitrator to direct which party shall be responsible for payment of those fees and the institution's expenses or their repayment to the party which has already paid them. Most institutional rules contain similar provisions in any case, but the Act now makes the position clear in the rare cases where they do not.

59.5

Section 59(1)(c) empowers the arbitrator to direct which party is to pay 'the legal or other costs of the parties'. The phrase 'other costs' is important, particularly in view of the parties' rights to appoint non-legal representatives under s 36, although it would also cover other non-legal costs such as the costs of expert witnesses.

59.6

Section 59(2) makes it clear that costs include 'the costs of or incidental to any proceedings to determine the amount of the recoverable costs of the arbitration'. This makes it clear that, if the arbitrator determines the amount of costs in the arbitration to be paid by a party under s 63(3) (the recoverable costs of the arbitration), the power to award costs extends to the costs of the proceedings leading to that determination. While the provision appears to give the arbitrator the power to determine who should pay the costs if determination of the original costs is referred to the court under s 63(4) by the process known as 'taxation', it is suggested that this is not normally necessary. This is because the costs of taxation are almost invariably paid by the party seeking the taxation, ie, by the paying party. The arbitrator should follow the same principle if he determines the costs of the arbitration, except in exceptional circumstances.

Section 60: Agreement to pay costs in any event
60.1

Section 60 is mandatory. It follows s 18(3) of the 1950 Act with one important modification. It preserves the prohibition on parties agreeing to pay their own costs of the arbitration in any event before the dispute has arisen and extends the prohibition to an agreement by one party to pay the costs of the other party as well as an agreement simply to pay his own costs.

60.2

There was much discussion during the consultation period on the Bill as to whether this prohibition should be removed. Many of those consulted thought that to allow parties to agree to pay at least their own costs, win or lose, before any dispute had arisen, normally in the arbitration agreement itself, might encourage arbitration in this country. This was particularly the case for foreign parties from civil law jurisdictions who are unaccustomed to the whole concept of parties not paying their own costs in any event. However, it was very strongly pointed out by others, not least by one of the present authors, that generally to allow this could lead to substantial abuse, the very abuse in fact which the inclusion of the provision in the 1950 Act was intended to prevent. In the building field, for instance, small subcontractors are frequently dependent for much of their business on large contractors, many of whom have their own standard forms of subcontract. If the large contractors were able to include arbitration clauses which provided that the subcontractor would pay his own costs of an arbitration in any event, regrettable as it may be to have to say it, most of them would be in a position to exert unfair pressure. In short, they would be able to blackmail or hoodwink the smaller subcontractors into accepting such a clause as part of the price for getting what may be a very important job for them. This would effectively prevent a small subcontractor from ever starting an arbitration against a large contractor since he would have to pay his own costs, win or lose, and simply would not be able to afford to do so. This consideration of the possibility of abuse prevailed and the provision has therefore been retained and extended to fill a former lacuna in the law. There is, of course, nothing to prevent an agreement of this kind *after* a dispute has arisen.

Section 61: Award of costs

61.1

Section 61 repeats s 18(1) of the 1950 Act with important changes.

61.2

Section 61(1) states that subject to any agreement between the parties (except, of course, an agreement of the kind prohibited by s 60), arbitrators are given the powers to direct in an award that one party should pay the legal and other costs of the other party as well as his own costs, and pay the arbitrator's own fees and expenses, or that the parties should each pay a part of such costs in such proportions as the arbitrator may decide.

61.3

Section 61(2) contains an important limitation of the arbitrator's discretion by providing that, unless the parties agree otherwise, costs must 'follow the event', which in plain terms, means 'loser pays all'. 'Loser' in this context means the party which, after taking all claims and counterclaims into account, is finally directed to pay a sum of money to the other party. (In non-monetary awards, such as declaratory awards, it would mean the party which loses its case on the merits.) However, this limitation is modified by the provision that this need not apply 'where it appears to the tribunal that in the circumstances this is not appropriate in relation to the whole or part of the costs'. This enables an arbitrator, if he considers the circumstances justify it, to disregard the principle that 'loser pays all' and apportion the costs according to what he considers to be the merits of the case.

61.4

This provision puts into statutory form the position as it has long been thought to exist at common law. While the severity of the limitation on the arbitrator's discretion may appear to be substantially relaxed by the exception, that relaxation is probably not as great as it appears. There have been many cases over the years where arbitrators have been severely rapped over the knuckles by the courts for departing unjustifiably from the general rule that 'costs follow the event'. *Mustill & Boyd*, at pp 396–398 gives as reasons found to be justified:

- unsatisfactory conduct by the party in the course of the arbitration or unreasonable or obstructive conduct which has protracted the proceedings or increased the costs incurred by the other party;

- failure by the successful party on an issue or issues on which a large amount of time was spent;
- an offer by one party before or during the reference to compromise the dispute, which the other party has unreasonably failed to accept (this ground is further discussed below);
- extravagance in the conduct of the hearing, for example the employment of an excessive number of counsel or expert witnesses. (This would normally be taken into account in determining the amount of costs payable, rather than by a direction in the award on the issues. However, an arbitrator may wish to give effect to his opinion as to the conduct of the party concerned in his award rather than leaving it to the taxing master if the costs are determined by the court.)

61.5

Mustill & Boyd gives as examples of matters which have been found not to justify a departure from the general rule:

- a feeling on the part of the arbitrator that the conduct of the successful party before the commencement of the arbitration was immoral;
- the small size of the claim;
- the successful party taking a technical point of which the arbitrator disapproves.

61.6

An arbitrator may also be justified in apportioning responsibility for costs if there is a true counterclaim which has been, if only in part, also successful. By a true counterclaim we mean a counterclaim which deals with separate issues from the claim and is not simply a defence to it. A counterclaim is a cause of action which a defendant has against a plaintiff. It need have no particular connection with the plaintiff's cause of action. The defendant simply adds a counterclaim to his defence and this operates as a statement of claim against the plaintiff (to which the plaintiff will in time serve a defence to the counterclaim). An example of a counterclaim which is, in fact, a defence, is where a builder is claiming payment for work done and the building owner counterclaims for the cost of putting right defects, stating that he has deliberately withheld that amount from payments to the builder. This is in fact a defence to the claim by way of 'set-off', since it is the reason, or part of the reason, the building owner is advancing for not paying the builder his money. In such a case, if the award on the claim exceeds the award on the counterclaim, costs should follow the event, ie the respondent building owner should pay the costs of the arbitration.

61.7

The effect of offers of settlement needs further discussion. In general, if an offer of settlement has been made and rejected by the winning party during the arbitration, and the offer proves to be equal to or more than the amount actually awarded to the winning party, the winning party will be entitled to recover its costs only up to the date of the offer. Further, it will have to pay the losing party's costs thereafter on the basis that the costs of proceeding with the arbitration, instead of accepting the offer, have been wasted. This is not quite as simple a principle as it appears and what follows is a brief comment on the principles. For a very full and interesting passage on the effect of offers on costs see *Bernstein's Handbook*, pp 190–194.

61.8

In the past it was often the practice, where an offer of settlement had been made and rejected, for a copy of the offer and the rejection to be placed in a sealed envelope and handed to the arbitrator at the end of the hearing with a request that it be opened only after he had completed his award except as to costs. If on opening it the arbitrator found that the offer exceeded the award he would direct that the claimant's costs be paid up to the date of the offer and that the respondent should be paid his costs thereafter. This practice had the disadvantage of revealing to the arbitrator that an offer had been made, and the temptation to the arbitrator to take a peek before completing his award on the issues may sometimes have proved irresistible. The practice originated in the Lands Tribunal, but in their case the envelope would be handed to the Registrar and would not be brought to the tribunal's attention until after it had made its decision on the issues. (The practice may also be contrasted with a payment into court in litigation where, again, the judge will be unaware of the payment-in until after he has delivered his judgment on the issues.)

61.9

The 'sealed offer' procedure described above has now been largely superseded by what is usually, but not strictly correctly, called a '*Calderbank* offer', after the approval of a similar practice in the case of *Calderbank v Calderbank* [1975] 3 All ER 333, which was a matrimonial case. In this procedure an offer of settlement is made in the form of a letter, now usually endorsed 'without prejudice save as to costs'. This sets out the offer and goes on to say that if it is not accepted within a stated time it will be revealed to the arbitrator after he has completed and published his award on the issues. If the offer is not accepted and the arbitration proceeds to a hearing, the arbitrator is then asked at the conclusion of the hearing to reserve his award of costs for later submissions. If, in the event, the award equals or is less than the offer, the offer will then be revealed to the arbitrator who will be asked to take account of it in his award on costs. This still has the disadvantage that the arbitrator is aware that an offer has been made, but at least the amount of the offer is not placed in his hands and, as stated earlier in another context, no arbitrator worth his salt is going to be influenced in his decision on the issues simply by the knowledge that an offer of settlement has been made.

61.10

As with a sealed offer, there is still a disadvantage to the *Calderbank* offer when compared with a payment into court in litigation, and that is that it is not backed up by actual money. Further, there may be doubt as to the offerer's real ability to pay, had the offer been accepted.

61.11

To be properly considered, a *Calderbank* or sealed offer should not only be for the principal sum in settlement of the dispute, but should also offer to pay interest and costs up to the date of the offer. If it does not, the arbitrator may be faced with difficult calculations when comparing his actual award with what the offeree would have received, taking interest and costs up to the date of the offer into account. Arbitrators are well advised to make clear to the parties that they will not consider *Calderbank* or sealed offers unless they also contain offers to pay interest and costs up to the date of the offer.

61.12

The principle that a *Calderbank* or sealed offer should be disregarded by the arbitrator even if it falls only slightly short of the amount awarded appears to be firm; see, for example, Ralph Gibson J (reluctantly) in *Archital Luxfer v Boot Construction* [1981] 1 Lloyd's Rep 642, and Judge Diamond in *The Maria* [1992] 3 All ER 851. There appears to be a recent tendency slightly to erode this into a principle that the arbitrator should consider whether it was reasonable in all the circumstances for the offeree to reject the offer. However, arbitrators would be well advised to exercise caution in applying this modified principle until it has been more firmly approved by the courts.

61.13

In all cases where an arbitrator departs from the general principle that 'costs follow the event' he must clearly state his reasons for doing so in his award. In the past it has frequently been treated as 'misconduct' for an arbitrator to depart from the narrow application of the general principles, and awards have been set aside or remitted on that ground. In view of the terms of s 61(2) it may now be considered to be a possible error of law, and therefore appealable under s 69, for the arbitrator to depart from the principle unless there are very good reasons for that departure. Those reasons should therefore be set out under the general obligation to provide for reasons under s 52(4).

Section 62: Effect of agreement or award about costs

62.1

Section 62 states that, unless the parties otherwise agree, any costs recoverable under an agreement between them as to how the costs of the arbitration are to be borne, or any award allocating the costs of the arbitration between the parties, extend only to costs which are recoverable under s 63 . Parties may therefore agree between themselves that costs recoverable by one of them against the other, or by each of them against the other, may extend to costs which would not normally be recoverable under the terms of s 63 or may exclude costs which would have been recoverable under that section.

Section 63: The recoverable costs of the arbitration

63.1

Section 63 supersedes parts of s 18 of the 1950 Act.

63.2

Section 63(1) enables the parties to agree on what costs of the arbitration, as defined in s 59, are to be recoverable by one party from the other. This appears to duplicate to some extent s 62. There is the usual provision in s 63(2) for what costs are to be recoverable in default of the parties' agreement.

63.3

Section 63(3) gives the arbitrator the power to determine what the recoverable costs of the arbitration are, ie, in the old terminology to 'tax' the costs. Section 18(2) of the 1950 Act stated that 'any costs directed by an award to be paid shall, unless the award otherwise directs, be taxable in the High Court', while s 18(1) of the 1950 Act said that, unless the parties agreed otherwise, the arbitrator 'may tax or settle the amount of costs to be paid or any part thereof'. There were therefore two possible regimes, taxation in the High Court or by the arbitrator (who alternatively had the power to 'settle' the costs). The distinction between 'taxing' and 'settling' was obscure but was generally understood to allow an arbitrator to determine the amount of costs to be paid without being bound by the Supreme Court rules on taxation. Taxation would be in the High Court unless otherwise directed by the arbitrator, and it was generally understood that an arbitrator would only so direct if the parties had agreed that he would be empowered to tax or settle the costs either in the arbitration agreement, or in rules governing the arbitration, such as Article 16.2 of the Chartered Institute of Arbitrators' Rules 1988 and Article 18.2 of the LCIA Rules, or by *ad hoc* agreement during the arbitration.

63.4

The new provisions now assume that, unless the parties can agree the costs between themselves, the arbitrator will determine the costs to be paid by one party to the other, either in an award on the issues or in a subsequent award on costs alone following representations by the parties.

63.5

Section 63(3) also requires the tribunal to specify, firstly, 'the basis on which it has acted', ie, the criteria it has applied in determining the amount of recoverable costs. This will be particularly important if the arbitrator departs from the normal basis of determining costs as set out in s 63(5). Secondly, the arbitrator must specify 'the items of recoverable costs', such as the costs of legal or other expenses and the like, and of his own fees and expenses, and 'the amount referable to each', in particular, in view of s 64, the amount of his own costs.

63.6

Section 63(4) provides that, if the arbitrator does not determine the recoverable costs, any party can, upon notice to the other parties, apply to the court for determination. Note that by s 105 'the court' means the High Court or a county court. The court will by s 63(4)(a) 'determine the recoverable costs of the arbitration on such basis as it thinks fit'. This means that the court is *not* necessarily bound to determine the costs in the same way as if they were litigation costs taxed in the High Court under RSC Ord 62.

63.7

Section 63(4)(*b*) also empowers the court to 'order that [the recoverable costs] shall be determined by such means and upon such terms as it may specify'. This gives the court the power to order that the costs be determined by a Taxing Master in the High Court, in which case they would probably be taxed in the same way as litigation costs unless the court specifically ordered otherwise. They could be determined by a qualified costs clerk or even, where the recovering party has been represented by experts in a specialist field and not by lawyers, by an expert in the same field best able to judge whether the costs charged are reasonable.

63.8

Section 63(5) states the basis on which recoverable costs are to be determined unless the arbitrator or the court decides otherwise. In default of directions to the contrary, they are to be determined 'on the basis that there shall be allowed a reasonable amount in respect of all costs reasonably incurred' and that 'any doubt as to whether costs were reasonably incurred or were reasonable in amount shall be resolved in favour of the paying party'. This is essentially the 'standard basis' of costs as taxed in the High Court in litigation under RSC Ord 62. Note that the *paying* party is to be given the benefit of any doubt as to whether the costs were reasonably incurred or reasonable in amount. This will almost invariably mean that the receiving party will not recover the whole of its costs. For example, the arbitrator or the court may doubt that it was reasonable for counsel to attend a preliminary meeting; or for a senior partner of the firm of solicitors to be personally involved in inspecting documents; or for the receiving party's personnel to recover first-class train fares in attending a hearing. We are not, of course, suggesting that such costs should be disallowed in all cases. It will depend on the circumstances (for instance, in a dispute which has already been very hard-fought before arbitration even started, it may be perfectly reasonable for counsel to attend the preliminary meeting, particularly if counsel has also attended for the paying party). However, they are the sort of doubts which typically arise and the rule is that the paying party must have the benefit of such doubts following, of course, a reasonable opportunity for the receiving party to argue that the costs are reasonable in all the circumstances.

63.9

The alternative to the standard basis of costs is the indemnity basis. (These two bases, with some variations, used to be described as 'party and party' and 'solicitor and own client' costs, hence the reference to the latter in s 18(1) of the 1950 Act.) The essential difference between the two bases is that, on the indemnity basis, all doubts as to whether costs were reasonably incurred or reasonable in amount are to be determined in favour of the *receiving* party. This party is therefore more likely to receive, if not the whole, then at least a major part of its actual costs. This basis should only be applied in special cases and essentially as a punitive measure against the paying party, for instance where it is considered by the arbitrator that the behaviour of the paying party has been so unreasonable that the receiving party has been forced to incur costs which the standard basis might exclude and which the arbitrator considers he should recover.

63.10

The scale of costs to be applied would normally be stated by the arbitrator in his award allocating responsibility for costs under s 61. If the arbitrator does not state any specific basis, the criteria set out in s 63(5) will apply. It will certainly be very unusual for the court to determine the costs on any other basis without an indication from the arbitrator as to what other basis should be applied. The authors consider that the court is likely to exercise its discretion to disallow costs which, on a strict application of the criteria, would be allowable, rather than to increase the costs beyond what would be determined by the criteria.

63.11

It will still be very important for the arbitrator, if he departs from the normal scale of costs as defined in s 63(5), to state his reasons for doing so. Imposition of a punitive scale of costs without explanation might lead to an imputation of bias or serious irregularity, and a challenge to the award under s 68.

63.12

Section 63(6) makes the determination of the arbitrator's own fees and expenses subject to the provisions of s 64 (see below). If this were not the case the arbitrator could fix his own fees and expenses in his award on the amount of costs with no redress for the paying party if they were excessive.

63.13

Section 63(7) states that nothing in s 63 affects the rights of the arbitrator in respect of his fees and expenses under s 28 (joint and several liability of the parties), or those of experts, legal advisers and assessors under s 37(2) (fees and expenses of such people to be expenses of arbitrators). This will mean that, if the paying party fails to pay the fees and expenses of the arbitrator or of any expert, legal adviser or assessor, the fees and expenses concerned would be recoverable from the other party on the basis of its joint and several liability under s 28. Of course, in most cases the arbitrator will have secured his fees and expenses through his lien on his award under s 56 (power to withhold award in case of non-payment), but in some smaller arbitrations where the arbitrator waives that right the power to recover from the other party under this section could be useful.

63.14

Concern has been expressed in some quarters at the idea of arbitrators being given the responsibility for determining the amount of costs payable by one party to the other—in the old terminology, 'taxing' costs. The authors see no reason for such concern. Many arbitrators already 'tax' parties' costs, in many cases because it is quicker to get a taxation hearing before the arbitrator than before a taxing Master of the High Court, and we have heard of no disastrous consequences. It is surely no more difficult for an arbitrator to determine the costs payable by one party to the other than it is for him to determine the outcome of the substantive dispute. The procedure already often adopted is that the receiving party puts in its 'claim' in the form of a solicitor's bill of costs or some other form. The paying party is then invited to put in a written response setting out those items which it considers it should not have to pay or which, in its view, should be reduced with reasons for each. If the circumstances appear to require it, the receiving party may put in a written reply. The matter will often then proceed to a determination on the basis of the written submissions without a hearing. If a hearing is needed, it will proceed like the hearing of the substantive issues except that each item of costs claimed will be examined individually with the receiving party making submissions, the paying party making counter-submissions and the receiving party then having 'the last word'. The arbitrator may state his decision on each item orally as the hearing proceeds but may prefer to reserve his decisions for his written award. The arbitrator will in any case make a written award after the hearing stating the amount to be paid. It is no more difficult than that, and the authors are somewhat puzzled as to the reasons for the concern that the process is in some way too difficult for lay arbitrators to handle, particularly since the Act now sets out so clearly the criteria to be applied.

Section 64: Recoverable fees and expenses of arbitrators

64.1

This section is new. It has no parallel in the Model Law.

64.2

Section 64(1) confines the arbitrator's recoverable fees and expenses, unless otherwise agreed by the parties, to 'such reasonable fees and expenses as are appropriate in the circumstances.' By s 37(2) 'expenses' may include the fees and expenses of experts, legal advisers and assessors appointed by the arbitrator, so that by this section all such fees and expenses must have been reasonably incurred by the arbitrator and themselves be reasonable 'in all the circumstances'. By s 64(3) this is subject to any order of the court under s 24(4) or s 25(3)(*b*), ie, any order as to the arbitrator's entitlement to fees or expenses if he has been removed under s 24 or has resigned under s 25.

64.3

Secton 64(2) provides that any question as to the reasonableness of the arbitrator's fees and expenses which is not already before the court on an application under s 63(4), for the court to determine the arbitrator's fees and expenses as part of the recoverable costs of the arbitration if they have not already been determined by the arbitrator, may be determined by the court on the application of any party upon notice to the other parties. Such notice does not apparently have to be given to the arbitrator—which seems rather hard. Alternatively, the court may 'order that it be determined by such means and upon such terms as the court may specify' (see the comments on the similar provision in s 63(4)(*b*) above).

64.4

Section 64(4) provides that nothing in s 64 affects any rights an arbitrator may have to payment of his fees and expenses.

If the arbitrator has already agreed his fees and expenses, perhaps in his initial agreement with the parties setting out his terms, it would obviously not be right to allow the court in effect to rewrite that agreement. It is unusual, except in small simple arbitrations or where the arbitrator's entitlement to fees and expenses is determined by rules, for an arbitrator to agree a lump sum in advance. If, as will usually be the case, he has simply agreed hourly and daily rates for his fees and reimbursement of out-of-pocket expenses, the rates agreed will be applied by the court, but the hours and days spent may be subject to examination as to whether they were reasonable in all the circumstances, as will his expenses.

Section 65: Power to limit recoverable costs

65.1

This section is completely new and a substantial addition to the powers of arbitrators. It is another example of the radical thinking behind the Act.

65.2

Section 65(1) empowers the arbitrator, unless the parties have agreed otherwise, to limit the recoverable costs of the arbitration or any part of the arbitral proceedings to a fixed amount. As pointed out by the DAC in its Report (February 1996) reducing unnecessary expenditure is part of the arbitrator's duty under s 33 (avoidance of unnecessary delay and expense). This provision will help arbitrators, in appropriate cases, to limit the costs which will be recoverable by a party in the event of an award of costs in its favour to a specified amount. This will not prevent that party from running up costs in excess of the limit, but it will not be able to recover the excess from the other party. As the DAC says, 'this will have the added virtue of discouraging those who wish to use their financial muscle to intimidate their opponents into giving up through fear that by going on they might be subject to a costs order which they could not sustain'.

65.3

Section 65(2) sensibly provides that any direction for limitation of costs under s 65(1) may be made or may be varied at any stage during the arbitration. However, it must be made or varied 'sufficiently in advance of the incurring of costs to which it relates, or the taking of any steps in the proceedings which may be affected by it, for the limit to be taken into account'. It would be grossly unfair to make the order, or to vary it once made, without giving the party which may be adversely affected by the order or the variation of it, time to make arrangements to reduce the adverse effect.

65.4

The authors have known of cases in which similar arrangements have been made in the past, but the lack of any power in the arbitrator to make any such order without the agreement of both parties has made it rare and only done when it is in the interests of both parties to limit costs. This new provision, which gives the arbitrator the power unless the parties agree otherwise, will, no doubt be extremely helpful in reducing time and costs spent on arbitrations, particularly where there is an imbalance of financial strength between the parties. An arbitrator in a construction dispute between a large contractor and a small subcontractor, for example, may consider it only fair that the contractor's power to recover costs should be limited to what should reasonably be enough to enable him to fight the case properly. His power to intimidate the subcontractor by employing expensive counsel etc, which may not be justified by the size and complexity of the dispute, would thereby be removed. If the contractor still wants to employ expensive counsel he may do so, but he will not recover the excess cost. Arbitrators may also wish to make such orders even where there is no financial imbalance between the parties, simply to ensure that costs do not run away and that the arbitration is indeed conducted 'avoiding unnecessary delay or expense' (s 33(1)(*b*)).

65.5

Arbitrators should obviously be very careful in making such orders to ensure that unfairness to the more prosperous party does not result and that any limit fixed takes all the circumstances of the dispute into account. However, they should not hesitate to make such orders if the circumstances justify it in their view. It is suggested that such orders should only be made after proper consultation with the parties at an early stage and allowing both parties, but particularly the party likely to be most adversely affe cted by it, every opportunity to make representations as to what a reasonable limit should be.

Powers of the court in relation to award

Section 66: Enforcement of the award

66.1

This is one of the mandatory provisions listed in Sched 1. It replaces s 26 of the 1950 Act and reflects Article 35 of the Model Law.

66.2

Section 66(1) and (2) repeat almost verbatim s 26(1) of the 1950 Act. They provide that an award made pursuant to an arbitration agreement as defined in s 6 may, by leave of the court, be enforced in the same way that a judgment of the court would be enforced and that, where leave is given, judgment may be entered in the terms of the award. Note that the word 'may' still leaves the court with a discretion, although it is highly unlikely that leave will be refused or judgment will not be entered in terms of the award except in the cases listed in s 66(3) and (4). An application must be made to the court for leave to enforce the award and if the award is not then complied with, the remedies where a judgment of the court is not complied with will be available to the party seeking enforcement. While the section does not specifically repeat Article 35(2) of the Model Law regarding the documents to be submitted in support of an application for enforcement, it is fairly obvious that the court will have to be supplied with the award or a certified copy of it and a copy of the arbitration agreement.

66.3

Section 26(2) and (3) of the 1950 Act, which had been inserted by s 18(2) of the Administration of Justice Act 1977 and which referred to the position where the amount of the award came within the current limit of jurisdiction in the county court, have not been reproduced. By the definition in s 105(1) the term 'court', as we have seen, includes both the High Court and a county court.

66.4

Section 66(3) is new. It sets out the only situation in which the court must refuse leave to enforce an award, and that is where the person against whom it is sought to be enforced shows that the arbitrator lacked jurisdiction to make the award. Challenges to jurisdiction are dealt with in ss 30 to 32. Section 67 (challenging the award: substantive jurisdiction). Section 73 (loss of right to object) sets out the circumstances in which a party may lose the right to raise lack of jurisdiction as a reason for the court not to give leave to enforce the award against it. These are basically that the challenge to jurisdiction could have been, but for no good reason was not, raised by the party concerned at an earlier stage in the arbitration. This is more fully discussed in the commentary to s 73.

66.5

It is interesting to note that, when first presented in the House of Lords as a Bill, clause 66 contained two further grounds upon which a court would be compelled to refuse leave to enforce an award. The first was that the award 'is so defective in form or substance that it is incapable of enforcement'. Although this ground has now been deleted from the text, it is suggested that the court will certainly still refuse leave to enforce an award which is so defective, since to do so would simple waste the parties' time and money if an attempt were made to enforce it pursuant to leave. An award can be defective in a number of ways. It may be unintelligible, or directions it contains may not be clear or may be ambiguous, or it may not deal with matters which it was essential should be dealt with in order to make it enforceable (if it purports to deal with matters which were not referred to arbitration, leave would in any case be refused under s 66(3)). It may show that the arbitrator had not decided the dispute in accordance with the law chosen by the parties as applicable to the substance of their dispute or with such other considerations as they may have chosen under s 46(1). It may not comply with an agreement of the parties as to its form under s 52(1) or, failing such agreement, with the requirements set out in s 52(3) to (5) (relating to its being signed by all the arbitrators and stating the seat of the arbitration). It is an arbitrator's duty to ensure that the award does everything which it is required by the parties and by the Act to do and is set out in a properly intelligible manner. If it does not comply with these requirements, despite the absence of specific provisions in the Act, a court will almost certainly exercise its discretion under s 66(1) and refuse leave to enforce it.

66.6

The second ground previously given for the court not to have the power to give leave to enforce an award was that its enforcement would be contrary to public policy. This has now been transferred to s 81(1) (saving for certain matters governed by the common law) and is now commented upon in para 81.6

66.7

Section 66(4) makes it clear that the provisions of this section regarding enforcement do not affect the position where enforcement is sought under any other rule of law and, in particular, where it is sought under the Geneva or New York Conventions. See Part II of the 1950 Act (which has *not* been repealed—see s 99 and Sched 4 to this Act) and also see Part III (recognition and enforcement of certain foreign awards).

66.8

By s 2(2), s 66 applies wherever the seat of the arbitration is.

Section 67: Challenging the award: substantive jurisdiction

67.1

This section is new. It reflects in part Article 34 of the Model Law. It is one of the mandatory provisions listed in Sched 1. It is supplementary to the provisions regarding challenges to the arbitrator's jurisdiction set out in ss 30 to 32, and in particular to s 32 (determination of preliminary point of jurisdiction), and deals with the situation where the court has not already made a decision on a question of jurisdiction under s 32.

67.2

Section 67(1) provides that a party may, upon notice to the other parties and the arbitrator, apply to the court challenging the arbitrator's jurisdiction. Firstly, if the arbitrator has already made an award upholding his jurisdiction under s 31 (objection to substantive jurisdiction of tribunal) either as a specific award on the question of jurisdiction or in an award on the merits of the dispute, the challenge may be to that award. Secondly, if the arbitrator has *not* made a specific award as to the jurisdiction, or the question as to jurisdiction has not already been settled by the court under s 32, an award on the merits may be challenged by an allegation that the arbitrator did not have jurisdiction to make it. The section points out that the party concerned may have lost its right to challenge the arbitrator's jurisdiction by the operation of s 73. It also points out that its right to apply is also subject to restrictions set out in s 70(2) and (3). These provisions are dealt with below, but basically s 73 provides that if a party knows of some defect in jurisdiction and continues with the arbitration notwithstanding it will, subject to certain savings, forfeit its right to object. Equally, in brief, s 70(2) requires the applicant first to exhaust any arbitral process of appeal/review and s 70(3) imposes a time limit in which to make the application.

67.3

Because of the new provisions for early challenges to jurisdiction in ss 30 to 32, challenges to an award on the merits on grounds of lack of jurisdiction should in future be rare. However, there will always be cases where an award possibly deals with matters which a party is able to allege lay outside the arbitrator's jurisdiction and the party had no means of knowing in advance that it was going to do so. It may also be that the alleged lack of jurisdiction only became apparent when the reasons for the arbitrator's decision were set out in the award. However, we expect that the provisions of this section will more often be used to challenge an arbitrator's decision on the question of jurisdiction itself, either when set out in a specific award on that question under s 31(4)(a) or included in an award on the merits of the dispute under s 31(4)(b).

67.4

Section 67(2) enables the arbitrator to continue with the arbitration and he may make further awards while a decision of the court under s 67(1) is pending. This will apply when the arbitrator has made a decision on jurisdiction in a specific award on the question, or has made his decision in a partial award on the merits, under s 47, or has made a partial award on publication of which the question of juris-diction has arisen. This is a useful provision but, of course, the parties should always be consulted before the arbitrator continues with the arbitration once the question of jurisdic-tion has arisen. This is important since it may well go to the heart of the dispute and it may be in the parties' interests to adjourn the arbitration pending the court's decision.

67.5

Section 67(3) sets out the three courses of action the court may take on a challenge to the jurisdiction arising from an award. It may *confirm* the award, which it will obviously do if it determines that the arbitrator did have the degree of jurisdiction necessary, or if it considers that the question of jurisdiction ought not to affect the decisions set out in the award. Another option is to *vary* the award, perhaps by amending those parts of it which are affected by the lack of jurisdiction which it has found to exist (although it is diffi-cult to see how a decision of the arbitrator may be amended if he had no jurisdiction to make it in the first place). The third course of action which the court may take by s 67(3)(c), is that it may *set aside* the award in whole or in part, rendering it wholly or partly unenforceable.

67.6

Section 67(4) provides that leave of the court is required for any appeal to a higher court against its decisions under this section.

Section 68: Challenging the award: serious irregularity

68.1

Section 68 corresponds to Article 34 of the Model Law. It is one of the mandatory provisions listed in Sched 1. It re-places s 23(2) and (3) of the 1950 Act.

68.2

Section 68(1) states that a party 'may (upon notice to the other parties and to the tribunal) apply to the court chal-lenging an award on the grounds of serious irregularity af-fecting the tribunal, the proceedings or the award.' It adds that a party may lose the right to object (see s 73) and that the right to apply is subject to the restrictions in s 70(2) and

(3) (challenge or appeal and time limits). Section 68 defines a new concept which is 'serious irregularity'. Note that a distinction is drawn between challenges to the substantive jurisdiction (those matters set out in s 30, for example, whether the tribunal is properly constituted), and dealt with in s 67 above (challenging the award: substantive jurisdiction), and challenges in respect of 'serious irregularity' which is dealt with by s 68.

68.3

The new provision reflects the internationally accepted view that the court should be able to correct serious failure to comply with the due process of arbitral proceedings. It makes various changes to the law. The provision replaces the somewhat approbrious term 'misconduct' used (but undefined) in s 23(1) and (2) of the 1950 Act. It supersedes s 22 of the 1950 Act which said:

'(1) In all cases of reference to arbitration the High Court … may from time to time remit the matters referred, or any of them, to the reconsideration of the arbitrator or umpire.

(2) Where an award is remitted, the arbitrator or umpire shall, unless the order otherwise directs, make his award within 3 months after the date of the order.'

Section 68(1) deals with the situation where a party wishes to challenge an award on the basis that there has been a serious irregularity affecting the tribunal or the proceedings or the award. Compare and contrast this with a challenge on the merits, such as an appeal on a point of law, dealt with in s 69 which follows.

68.4

Section 68(2) defines 'serious irregularity' as

'an irregularity of one or more of the following kinds which the court considers has caused or will cause substantial injustice to the applicant—

(a) failure by the tribunal to comply with section 33 (general duty of tribunal);

(b) the tribunal exceeding its powers (otherwise than by exceeding its substantive jurisdiction: see section 67);

(c) failure by the tribunal to conduct the proceedings in accordance with the procedure agreed by the parties;

(d) failure by the tribunal to deal with all the issues that were put to it;

(e) any arbitral or other institution or person vested by the parties with powers in relation to the proceedings or the award exceeding its powers;

(f) uncertainty or ambiguity as to the effect of the award;

(g) the award being obtained by fraud or the award or the way in which it was procured being contrary to public policy;

(h) failure to comply with the requirements as to the form of the award; or

(i) any irregularity in the conduct of the proceedings or in the award which is admitted by the tribunal or by any arbitral or other institution or person vested by the parties with powers in relation to the proceedings or the award.'

This is a very helpful list of matters which could give rise to a successful challenge to an award, replacing the vague concept of 'misconduct' used in the 1950 Act.

68.5

As to s 68(2)(a), it will be remembered that the provisions of s 33(1)(a) constrain the tribunal mandatorily to act fairly and impartially. This reflects the rules of natural justice— the first being that the judge/arbitrator is unbiased and disinterested, and the second being that every party must be given a fair opportunity to present its case and to hear the case against it. As to s 68(2)(f), note the power in s 57(3)(a) to correct awards and in particular, that given to the arbitrator who may, on his own initiative, 'clarify or remove any ambiguity in the award'. Note also that it will not be enough to establish serious irregularity. In addition the court will have to be satisfied that it has caused, or will cause substantial injustice to the applicant. Thus *two* hurdles will have to be overcome.

68.6

Section 68(2) provides a closed list of grounds. These will not be extendable by the court. This is in contrast to the provisions of s 23(1) and (2) of the 1950 Act where, as mentioned above, no definition was provided. In *Bernstein's Handbook*, p 206, it says, 'The courts have always refused to give an exhaustive definition of what constitutes "misconduct": the word is used to cover a range extending from fraud or other grave malpractice at one extreme to a mere procedural error at the other'. There have been many cases on 'misconduct' and over recent years the courts have exercised their discretion generously. This might be said to call into question the finalilty of awards, and the intention of s 68 is to limit the circumstances in which the courts may act.

68.7

The term 'misconduct' gave rise to uncertainties abroad, and offence to arbitrators here, particularly when it was used not to describe moral turpitude, such as bribery or partiality, but when it involved mere procedural error. It was a chameleon word, not necessarily implying morally reprehensible conduct by the arbitrator, as it would seem to suggest, but more often referring to procedural unfairness or the mishandling of procedures, ie more of a technical nature and frequently indicating no degree of dishonesty. Cases where arbitrators were removed for misconduct include where actual bias was established, where the relationship between the arbitrator and the parties/subject matter of the dispute created a risk that the arbitrator had been or would be incapable of acting impartially; where, other than partiality, the conduct of the arbitrator was such that he was incapable of conducting the reference properly eg because of his inexperience (see *Bremer Handelsgesellschaft etc v Ets Soules* [1985] 2 Lloyd's Rep 199).

68.8

Section 68(3) states what options are open to the court if serious irregularity is found, in particular:

> '... the court may—
> (a) remit the award to the tribunal, in whole or in part, for reconsideration,
> (b) it may set aside the award in whole or in part, or
> (c) it may declare the award to be of no effect, in whole or in part.
> The court shall not exercise its power to set aside or to declare an award to be of no effect, in whole or in part, unless it is satisfied that it would be inappropriate to remit the matters in question to the tribunal for reconsideration.'

This provision underlines the reluctance of the court effectively to end the arbitration. It emphasises the philosophy of the Act which is to support the process.

68.9

These provisions offer far more flexibility than under the 1950 Act. They are also more logical in that they give the court power to declare the award to be of no effect. The previous phrase of 'setting aside' (s 23 of the 1950 Act) was inappropriate, even absurd, when referring to something which had no existence, such as an award made without jurisdiction. The options now offered are slanted towards remission rather than to the more drastic powers of setting aside or declaring the award to be of no effect, a further example of the philosophy of the Act which is to support arbitrations and to get them back on track where they have gone wrong.

68.10

Section 68(4) states that the leave of the court is required for any appeal from a decision of the court under this section.

68.11

In its Report (February 1996) the DAC said that s 68 'is really designed as a long stop, only available in extreme cases where the tribunal has gone so wrong in its conduct of the arbitration that justice calls out for it to be corrected'.

Section 69: Appeal on point of law

69.1

Section 69 replaces s 1 of the 1979 Act and incorporates the restrictions later placed upon the operation of that section by decisions of the House of Lords in, for example, *The Nema.*

69.2

Section 69(1) states that unless otherwise agreed by the parties, a party may appeal to the court on a question of law arising out of an award made in the proceedings. Notice must be given to the other parties and to the tribunal. Where the parties have made an agreement to dispense with reasons for the award, this will be considered to be an agreement to exclude the court's jurisdiction under this section.

69.3

This section is non-mandatory. Parties are free to enter into exclusion clauses as they were under the 1979 Act. (Note s 87 which deals with exclusion clauses in relation to domestic arbitration agreements. Also note, however, that the distinction between domestic and international arbitrations may be removed by order made under s 88 and may indeed already have been removed by the time the Act comes into force. See important note on p 243) However, there is one important change. Under the 1979 Act, parties to marine, commodity and insurance contracts were not free in their contracts to exclude the right of appeal to the courts. They were known as 'special category' disputes although the term was not defined. A 'domestic arbitration agreement' was defined in s 3(7) of the 1979 Act as one (*a*) which did not provide for arbitration outside the United Kingdom, and (*b*) did not have as a party when it was entered into either 'an individual who was a national/habitually resident of a state other than the United Kingdom or a body corporate either incorporated or with central management and control being exercised in a state other than the United Kingdom'. Non-domestic arbitrations are international arbitrations, and are treated differently.

69.4

The DAC had extensive consultation with users during the gestation of the Act. One of the many questions asked was whether the special categories should be abolished. There was a big difference between a specially drafted arbitration clause in a 'one off' contract such as a large building project, and arbitration under a printed form of contract, for example a charter party, where the parties gave no thought to the form of an exclusion clause. The Commercial Court Committee (the Donaldson Committee), under the chairmanship of Donaldson J as he then was, published its Report on Arbitration in July 1978, Cmnd 7284. It drew attention to the risk that contracting-out provisions might, as much by default as anything else, become standard terms. It felt, however, that contractual freedom should not be confined, that the existence of special categories diminished the attractions of English law and England as a forum to foreign users who might decide to go elsewhere for the resolution of their disputes, and that parties in disputes in activities which fell within the special categories were usually of equal bargaining power and tended to be experienced businessmen. There was no good reason to distinguish between disputes in this way. Section 4 of the 1979 Act specifically excluded the special categories of contract but also included a provision in s 4(3) that the Secretary of State could by order repeal the section. Thus it was clearly envisaged at the time that the differentiation of categories was temporary. Against this was a lack of evidence that such parties wanted the special categories abolished, and that inability to contract out was not a disincentive. Special categories of non-domestic arbitration agreements have now been swept away by the Act. This is considered to be a welcome change.

69.5

Section 69(2) states that an appeal shall not be brought under this section except (*a*) with the agreement of all the other parties to the proceedings *or* (*b*) with the leave of the court. The right to appeal is also subject to the restrictions in s 70(2) (appeal may not be brought until any available arbitral process of appeal or review first exhausted) and s 70(3) (must be brought within 28 days, etc). Section 69(2) then restates the previous law, subject to this further and new restriction.

69.6

The relevant part of s 1(2) of the 1979 Act stated:

> 'Subject to subsection (3) an appeal shall lie to the High Court on any question of law arising out of an award made on an arbitration agreement; and on the determination of such an appeal the High Court may by order
> (*a*) confirm, vary or set aside the award; or
> (*b*) remit the award to the reconsideration of the arbitrator or umpire together with the court's opinion on the question of law which was the subject of the appeal.'

Section 1(3) and (4) of the 1979 Act said that such an appeal may be brought with the consent of all the other parties to the reference or, subject to certain limitations, with leave of the court.

69.7

Section 69(3) states that leave to appeal shall only be given:

'... if the court is satisfied—
(a) that the determination of the question will substantially affect the rights of one or more of the parties,
(b) that the question is one which the tribunal was asked to determine,
(c) that, on the basis of the findings of fact in the award—
  (i) the decision of the tribunal on the question is obviously wrong, *or*
  (ii) the question is one of general public importance and the decision of the tribunal is at least open to serious doubt, *and*
(d) that, despite the agreement of the parties to resolve the matter by arbitration, it is just and proper in all the circumstances for the court to determine the question.'

Emphasis has been supplied to draw attention to the fact that *two* hurdles have to be overcome.

69.8

This provision restates the 1979 Act condition that 'the determination of the question of law concerned could substantially affect the rights of one or more of the parties to the arbitration agreement'. However, not only is s 69(3) more felicitously drafted but now the court must be definite that the question *'will'* substantially affect the rights of one or more of the parties. In addition, the court must now also be convinced that the tribunal has obviously reached the wrong conclusion or, in the alternative, that the question of law is one of general public importance and the decision reached by the tribunal is at least open to serious doubt. This new provision represents a codification of the *Nema* guidelines as they became known, which were set out in *Pioneer Shipping v BTP Tioxide, the Nema* [1982] AC 724; *Antaios Compania Naviera SA v Salen Rederierna* [1985] AC 191.

69.9

There is another important new pre-condition in this provision: 'that the question is one which the tribunal was asked to determine', ie the point of law must, before the appeal, have been raised before the tribunal. Apparently a regrettable common practice has been for lawyers to trawl through awards in an attempt to find any possible error of law in order to appeal an award. This led to delay and expense and was a contributory factor in diminishing the attraction of English arbitration in the eyes of foreign users. This provision is designed to prevent such practice.

69.10

Section 69(3)(*d*) adds the further requirement (since the previous conditions are set out and followed by 'and') that the court must now be satisfied that notwithstanding the agreement of the parties to arbitration as a method for resolving their dispute, it is 'just and proper in all the circumstances' for the court to determine the question of law. In other words, there are various difficult hurdles to get over and this should further reassure foreign users in particular.

69.11

Section 69(4) states that an application for leave to appeal under this section shall identify the question of law to be determined and state the grounds on which it is alleged that leave to appeal should be granted. This provision is new. It is intended to reduce time and increase efficiency by requiring these matters to be clearly set out in writing, as s 69(5) goes on to state that such an application shall be determined on documents alone, unless it appears to the court that a hearing is required. Applications for leave used to develop into long and expensive court hearings, a matter which was commented on in *The Nema*. The new provision is practical and sensible and will save time and costs.

69.12

Section 69(6) requires that leave of the court is a pre-requisite for any appeal from the court under this section to grant or refuse leave to appeal and s 69(7) lists the courses of action open to the court: it may:

'(*a*) confirm the award,
(*b*) vary the award,
(*c*) remit the award to the tribunal, in whole or in part, for reconsideration in the light of the court's determination, or
(*d*) set aside the award in whole or in part'.

Wherever possible the court is to remit the award rather than to set it aside. This is made clear by the words in s 69(7) which follow s 67(7)(*d*): 'The court shall not exercise its power to set aside an award, in whole or in part, unless it is satisfied that it would be inappropriate to remit the matters in question to the tribunal for reconsideration'. By this means the agreed procedures are preserved as far as possible.

69.13

Section 69(8) states that the decision of the court on an appeal under this section shall be treated as a judgment of the court for the purposes of a further appeal. However, it makes absolutely clear that no such appeal lies without leave of the court which shall not be given unless the court considers that the question is one of general importance or is one which for some other special reason should be considered by the Court of Appeal. Note the two conditions are alternatives. In the 1979 Act, s 1(7)(*a*) said, '... the High Court or the Court of Appeal gives leave ...'. The provision for the Court of Appeal to give leave is not included in s 69(8).

69.14

There were many who called for the abolition of any right of appeal on the substantive issues. As was stated in the Report (February 1996) of the DAC:

'These were based on the proposition that by agreeing to arbitrate their dispute, the parties were agreeing to abide by the decision of their chosen tribunal, not by the decision of the Court, so that whether or not a Court would reach the same conclusion was simply irrelevant. To substitute the decision of the Court on the substantive issues would be wholly to subvert the agreement the parties had made.'

The DAC most carefully considered these submissions as they considered those on evry aspect of the Act, and they decided that 'with the safeguards we propose, a limited right of appeal is consistent with the fact that the parties have chosen to arbitrate rather than litigate'. —And of course, the parties can always exclude the right to appeal.

69.15

In summary, the effect of s 69, is that the part of s 1 of the 1979 Act as relates to appeal on a point of law is superseded. The key common law developments based on s 1 of the 1979 Act have been codified, the 'special categories' have been abolished and the provisions have generally been drawn more narrowly, tightening the criteria which must be met before the court can grant leave to appeal, in order to restrict access to the court. The previous serious flaw in the arbitration process (ie that foreign users were unaware that the 1979 Act had been construed so as to limit appeals) has now been remedied by setting out clearly and simply those limitations. Note s 69 must be read in conjunction with ss 70 and 71.

69.16

It is, perhaps, a pity that the opportunity was not taken to make it clear that the parties' agreement to appeal under s 69(2)(a) will only be valid if reached *after* a dispute has arisen. This would remove what the authors consider to be an abuse of the appeal procedure now common in building disputes. The JCT Standard Forms of Building Contract contain a provision by which both parties give prior agreement to any question of law arising from an award being subject to appeal, thereby satisfying the requirement of s 69(2)(a) (s 1(3)(a) of the 1979 Act). The validity of this provision and its effectiveness to remove the need to apply for leave to appeal were upheld by Judge Humphrey Lloyd QC in *Vascroft (Contractors) Ltd v Seeboard plc* 1996 CILL 1127. The result of this provision in the JCT Forms has been a flood of appeals against arbitrators' awards in the Official Referees' courts, many of them with little merit, clogging up the machinery of the courts and leading to long delays in getting far more meritorious cases heard in them. It has also had the effect of discouraging parties from going to arbitration because of the virtual certainty in many cases that the matter will end up in court on appeal, whatever the arbitrator's decision. It is to be hoped that the JCT will shortly remove this undesirable provision from its standard terms.

Section 70: Challenge or appeal: supplementary provisions

70.1

This section is largely new. It has no parallel in the Model Law. As stated in s 70(1), it applies to applications or appeals under ss 67 (challenging the award: substantive jurisdiction), 68 (challenging the award: serious irregularity) and 69 (appeal on point of law). It is one of the sections listed as mandatory in Sched 1 except in relation to applications and appeals under s 69, since that section itself is not mandatory.

70.2

Section 70(2) states that an application or appeal under any of the sections listed cannot be brought until, firstly 'any available arbitral process of appeal or review' has been exhausted. This means, for example, that if there is any provision for appeal in, say, institutional rules such as those of GAFTA, recourse must be had to that process of appeal before an application or appeal may be made under any of the sections listed. It also means that if it had been possible for a question of jurisdiction to have been dealt with under s 31 (objection to substantive jurisdiction of tribunal) or s 32 (determination of preliminary point of jurisdiction) before any application challenging an award on grounds of lack of jurisdiction under s 67 (challenging the award: substantive jurisdiction), that application will be refused. See also commentary on s 42(3) (enforcement of peremptory orders of tribunal) which contains similar provisions.

70.3

Section 70(3) sets down a time limit within which applications or appeals under the affected sections may be brought. Formerly such time limits were not set out in the legislation but in the Rules of the Supreme Court (the *White Book*) and were generally 21 days from the date of the award. In the interests of making the Act a comprehensive statement of the law, a single time limit for all applications and appeals has now been stated in this section. The time limit has been extended to 28 days in all cases, and this is from the date of the award or from the date when the applicant was notified of the result of any arbitral process of appeal or review referred to in s 70(2). Under s 54 the date of the award, unless the parties agree otherwise, may be decided by the arbitrator or, in the absence of such decision, will be the date it was signed by the arbitrator or by the last arbitrator to sign, if there is more than one. Formerly there was no statutory provision as to the date of an award, and it was customary for arbitrators to sign and date the award on the day they notified the parties that the award was ready to be taken up. This could create substantial difficulties since the 21 days limit for lodging an application for leave to appeal or for applying for the award to be set aside or remitted to the arbitrator could well expire before either party had paid the arbitrator's fees and taken up the award, leaving the losing party with no redress. In the default situation, ie if the date of the award is the date of signing, and the arbitrator exercises his lien on the award until payment of his fees, as he is now given statutory authority to do by s 56 (power to withhold award in case of non-payment), this can still happen even though the losing party now has an additional seven days in which to make its application.

70.4

However, subject to the parties' agreement otherwise, it would seem that an arbitrator may now fix the date of the award at some date later than signing so as effectively to extend the period for applications. He might do this perhaps by dating it on the day it is to be taken up, rather than the date of notification to the parties that it is available. It is suggested, however, that any arbitrator having it in mind to do this should consult the parties beforehand.

70.5

Section 70(4) replaces s 1(5) and (6) of the 1979 Act. These provisions empowered the High Court to order an arbitrator to give reasons, or further reasons, for his award in relation to an appeal if no reasons or insufficient reasons were given. This was subject to one of the parties having requested the arbitrator to give reasons before the award was made unless there was some special reason why such a request was not made. There was no compulsion on an arbitrator to give reasons in his award even if requested to do so by one of the parties, unless the High Court ordered him to provide them under this provision. The 1979 Act has been repealed in full and s 52(4) now requires that an award contains reasons whether requested by the parties or not, unless all parties have agreed to dispense with them. Even so, if there is an application or appeal and the award does not set out the reasons for the award, or does not do so sufficiently for the purposes of the appeal, the court can order the arbitrator to produce reasons or such further reasons as it considers necessary for proper consideration of the application or appeal. However, this will not apply if the parties themselves have agreed to dispense with reasons under s 52(4) since by s 69(1) such an agreement is considered to be an agreement to exclude appeal. By s 87(1), however, such an agreement can only be made in a domestic arbitration as defined in s 85(2) if it is made after the dispute has arisen. Note this is correct at the time of writing. However, the distinction may be removed by order under the provisions of s 88 and may indeed have already been removed by the time the Act comes into force. See important note on p 243.

70.6

Section 70(5) states that where the court makes an order for reasons or further reasons to be provided under s 70(4) 'it may make such further order as it thinks fit with respect to any additional costs of the arbitration resulting from its order'. It may, for example, if it considers that the arbitrator was seriously at fault in not providing reasons or sufficient reasons, order that the arbitrator pay the additional costs of the arbitration which result, or at least that he should not be paid for producing the reasons or further reasons.

70.7

Section 70(6) empowers the court to order the applicant or appellant under ss 67 (challenging the award: substantive jurisdiction), 68 (challenging the award: serious irregularity) or 69 (appeal on a point of law), to provide security for the costs of the application or appeal and that the application or appeal will be dismissed if the order is not complied with. However, as with the arbitrator's power to order a claimant to provide security for the costs of the arbitration under s 38(3), the court may not order security to be provided on the ground that the applicant or appellant is an individual ordinarily resident *outside* the United Kingdom, or is a corporation or association incorporated or formed under the law of a country *outside* the United Kingdom, or whose central management or control is *outside* the United Kingdom.

70.8

Section 70(7) provides that the court may order any money payable under an award which is the subject of an application for leave or of an appeal, to be brought into court or otherwise secured until the application or appeal has been determined. It may also direct that the application or appeal be dismissed if the order is not complied with.

70.9

Section 70(8) provides that the court may attach conditions, similar to those set out in s 70(6) and (7) relating to security for costs or the bringing of money awarded into court, to any grant of leave to appeal without prejudice to the court's general rights to attach conditions to the grant of leave. All these conditions are obviously intended to discourage frivolous applications and appeals.

Section 71: Challenge or appeal: effect of order of court

71.1

Section 71 is mandatory to the extent of orders made under s 67, 68 or 69. It restates s 1(8) of the 1979 Act and a new power is provided. Sections 70 and 71 are linked, both dealing with challenges or appeals.

71.2

Section 71(1) provides that where the court makes an order under s 67 (challenging the award: substantive jurisdiction), s 68 (challenging the award: serious irregularity), or s 69 (appeal on point of law), the following provisions set out in s 71(2), (3) and (4) have effect.

71.3

Section 71(2) states that where the award is varied, the variation has effect as part of the award. This restates s 1(8) of the 1979 Act. This said, 'Where the award of an arbitrator or umpire is varied on appeal, the award as varied shall have effect (except for the purposes of this section) as if it were the award of the arbitrator or umpire'. This provision was necessary since the variation was in effect an intrusion by a non-contractual judge into a decision of a contractually appointed arbitrator. By using the term 'as if it were the award', this meant that, variation notwithstanding, a valid award emerged without the delay and cost associated with other remedial powers. It is in the interests of the public that disputes are resolved justly and efficiently and thus control of any form of private dispute resolution, such as arbitration, is necessary. While parties should be free to choose whatever means they feel appropriate to their dispute, yet the court should still be able to intervene to prevent abuse and unfairness, particularly where, in the event of a party refusing to comply with an award, the courts are asked to enforce it. The control of arbitration is exercised almost exclusively by the Commercial Court. However, such control must be exercised within clearly defined terms.

71.4

'A variation involves a partial setting aside. A remission involves a total setting aside because the award remitted has no validity unless and until it is confirmed by the arbitrator at a later date and so becomes to that extent a different award. In most cases he will make a new award in different terms.' (per Lord Donaldson MR in *Hiscox v Outhwaite (No 1)* [1991] 2 All ER 124).

The appellate power to order variation has been used when the legal error related to the proper basis for the calculation of damages (*Shipping Corporation of India v NBB* [1991] 1 Lloyd's Rep 77); to contractual payment entitlements (*Vagres Compania Maritime SA v Nissho-Iwai American Corporation* [1988] 2 Lloyd's Rep 330); and to the question of causation (*Paros Shipping Corporation v Nafta* [1987] 2 Lloyd's Rep 269). The part of the award which contains the error is first set aside and then the court substitutes its own solution for that of the tribunal. (For a detailed analysis of variation, remission and setting aside see pp 212–219 of *The Law and Practice Relating to Appeals from Arbitration Awards* by Professor D Rhidian Thomas.)

71.5

Section 71(3) provides that where the award is remitted to a tribunal, in whole or in part, for reconsideration, the tribunal shall make a fresh award in respect of the matters remitted within three months of the date of the order for remission or such longer or shorter period as the court may direct.

71.6

Remission means that the award will be sent back to the arbitrator for his reconsideration. The arbitrator must consider or reconsider matters which are drawn to his attention by the court. Remission may be appropriate where the arbitrator has made a legal error. It will not be ordered merely to give the arbitrator 'a second bite at the cherry'. It keeps the award alive. However, delay and additional expense are inevitable. '... There is no basis for remitting a matter to the arbitrator unless there is something further for the arbitrator to consider and upon which he should exercise his own judgment afresh', per Hobhouse J in *Islamic Republic of Iran Shipping Lines v Zannis etc* [1991] 2 Lloyd's Rep 265.

71.7

Setting aside an award is the most serious remedy open to the court. The result is that the arbitration has failed to produce a valid and binding award, thus the reference has been wasteful, costly and wholly ineffectual. The arbitrator has failed in his appointed task. The award is deprived of all effect. Not surprisingly, it is a remedy of last resort. Section 71(4) states that when the award is set aside, in whole or in part, the court may also order that any provision that an award is a condition precedent to the bringing of legal proceedings in respect of a matter to which the arbitration agreement applies, is of no effect as regards the subject matter of the award/relevant part of the award. This is a *Scott v Avery* clause, discussed earlier, and the provision gives the court a new power to order that this condition is of no effect when it sets the award aside.

Miscellaneous

Section 72: Saving for rights of person who takes no part in proceedings

72.1

This section is new. It has no parallel in the Model Law. It is one of the provisions listed in Sched 1 as mandatory.

72.2

The DAC describes this section in its Report (February 1996) as a 'vital provision'. It is designed to protect the rights of persons who dispute that they are properly joined in the proceedings or that the arbitrator has any jurisdiction with respect to them. Such a person must have the right simply not to take part in the proceedings, although by so doing he may at the end find that he is held to be a party to the proceedings and discover that an enforceable award has been made against him. As the DAC says, '... those who do decide to take part in arbitral proceedings in order to challenge the jurisdiction are, of course, in a different category, for then, having made that choice, such people can fairly and properly be required to abide by the time limits etc [that the Act provides for]'.

72.3

Section 72(1) provides that a person who is alleged to be a party to arbitral proceedings but who takes no part in them may question, first, whether there is a valid arbitration agreement; second, whether the tribunal is properly constituted; and third, what matters have been submitted to arbitration in accordance with the arbitration agreement. He may put these questions by proceedings in court for 'a declaration or injunction or other appropriate relief'. If successful, of course, he will be relieved of any obligation to take part in the arbitralproceedings and no enforceable award can be made against him.

72.4

Section 72(2) provides that such a person may also have the same rights to make an application to the court under s 67, challenging the award the arbitrator has made asserting that he has jurisdiction, or may make an application to the court under s 68 challenging any award on grounds of serious irregularity affecting him. The provisions of s 70(2) relating to prior exhaustion of any available process of appeal and any recourse to the arbitrator under s 57 for correction of an award or any additional award, do not apply to such applications.

Section 73: Loss of right to object
73.1

This provision is new. It mirrors in part Article 4 of the Model Law. It is a mandatory provision.

73.2

The provision seeks to prevent parties who have taken part

in arbitral proceedings from delaying any objections as to jurisdiction etc until a late stage in the arbitration for tactical advantage. For reasons which will be apparent from the commentary on s 72, it does not apply to persons alleged to be parties to arbitral proceedings but who take no part in them at all.

73.3

Section 73(1) applies where a party takes part in the proceedings without raising any objection:

(a)   that the arbitrator lacks substantive jurisdiction, or

(b)   that the proceedings have been improperly conducted, or

(c)   that there has been a failure to comply with the arbitration agreement or with any provision of Part I of the Act, or

(d)   that there has been any other irregularity affecting the arbitrator or the proceedings.

If the party does not raise any such objection forthwith or at the time when it could and should have done so in accordance with any time limits allowed by the arbitration agreement, the arbitrator or any provisions of Part I of the Act, it is debarred from raising them later. The party will be debarred from raising them either before the arbitrator or the court unless it can show that, at the time it took part or continued to take part, it did not know, and could not with reasonable diligence have discovered, the grounds for the objection.

73.4

Section 73(2) applies where the arbitrator has made a ruling that he has substantive jurisdiction under s 31 (objection to substantive jurisdiction of the tribunal). If a party which could have questioned the ruling either by way of any available arbitral process of appeal or review, such as any appeal procedure available under rules governing the arbitration, or by challenging the award under s 67 (challenging the award: substantive jurisdiction) and does not do so, or does not do so within the time limit set by the arbitration agreement or any provision of Part I of the Act, it may not object later to the arbitrator's ruling on any ground which was the subject of the ruling.

73.5

The whole substance of this section can be summed up in the phrase, 'Put up or shut up'. Such a provision has long been needed. There have been far too many cases in the past of parties to an arbitration delaying objections, which they could perfectly well have raised earlier, until a late stage in the proceedings. There have been cases when they have delayed such objections until an award has been made, for purely tactical advantage and to gain time, putting off the evil day when they would have to pay what they owe. This has often been done quite openly by a party stating that it 'will take part in the arbitration but without prejudice to his right to raise his objections on jurisdiction until after the award is made'. This gave it the opportunity to wait and see whether the award was in its favour before raising the objection. However, s 73 should very effectively put a stop to such abuses which have done nothing to advance the reputation of arbitration as an efficient and effective means of dispute resolution. The declared aim of the Act is to obtain the fair resolution of disputes by an impartial tribunal without unnecessary delay and expense and the above illustrates how innovatively the provisions have tried to achieve this.

Section 74: Immunity of arbitral institutions, &c

74.1

This section is new and has no parallel in the Model Law. It is one of the provisions listed in Sched 1 as mandatory.

74.2

Section 74 extends the immunity from suit given to arbitrators by s 29 to institutions or persons who appoint or nominate arbitrators under the terms of arbitration agreements or rules. There is a similar provision to that in s 29—'unless the act or omission is shown to have been in bad faith'. The word 'person' is necessary to cover cases where an individual, such as the president of an institution, is named rather than the institution itself. (See the commentary to s 16 where the distinction, if any, between 'appointment' and 'nomination' is explored.)

74.3

This provision is very necessary since, if the arbitrator is immune from suit, a party might otherwise be tempted to try to sue the institution or person which appointed him for making a negligent appointment. As the DAC pointed out in its Report (February 1996), many institutions who commonly are named as appointers of arbitrators 'do not in the nature of things have deep pockets' and many of them operate through volunteers. They would find it very difficult to finance a defence to any such action and insurance (as the number of cases increased), would become very expensive.

74.4

There is the further point that, without this protection, institutions would become very reluctant to accept the responsibility for appointing or nominating arbitrators and would themselves seek to impose conditions protecting themselves from liability. It is far more preferable to have a single statutory immunity than leave institutions to devise their own different (possibly idiosyncratic?) ways of protecting themselves. Fees charged by institutions would also be bound to increase sharply, to the detriment of many 'low cost' schemes for consumer protection, such as those set up and administered by the Chartered Institute of Arbitrators—and of course to the detriment of consumers for whom such schemes provide a service.

74.5

Section 74(1) gives an institution or person charged with the appointment or nomination of an arbitrator, immunity from suit for negligence in relation to the appointment or nomination. There is the usual exception to the immunity in cases of 'bad faith'. (See the commentary to s 29 for comment on the effect of the exclusion mentioned above.)

74.6

Section 74(2) makes the further provision that the institution or person who has appointed or nominated an arbitrator is not vicariously liable by reason of their having appointed or nominated him, for anything which that arbitrator does or omits to do 'in the discharge or purported discharge of his functions as arbitrator'. While it is likely that any attempt to sue an appointing authority for the action or inaction of the appointed arbitrator would probably fail in any case, it is as well to have this firm statutory authority.

74.7

It should be noted that the institution or person concerned is only immune from suit in relation to the appointment or nomination of an arbitrator. Where the institution or person also administers the arbitration by, for example, collecting together the statements of claim and defence and documentary evidence, and sending them to the arbitrator as, for instance, the Chartered Institute of Arbitrators does in its many consumer arbitration schemes, or the LCIA does to a lesser extent under its rules, they will still be liable for any negligence in the exercise of those functions.

74.8

Section 74(3) extends the immunity to employees or agents of the appointing institution or person. As both the authors can testify, persons charged with responsibility for appointing or nominating arbitrators on a fairly large scale rely heavily on the staff of the institution concerned to put forward suitable names. It goes without saying that they are always conscious of their own personal responsibility for making sure, within reason, that any person appointed or nominated is suitable for the job. The extension of immunity to members of staff who make the initial selections and suggestions is, in their view, both very necessary and welcome.

74.9

It may be thought that, since both authors have been in the position of being an appointing or nominating authority on many occasions during their terms of office, in their capacity as chairmen of the Chartered institute of Arbitrators, they would be bound to approve such a provision, ie 'they would say that, wouldn't they?' However, they have looked at the matter objectively and still think it is a sound and sensible idea.

Section 75: Charge to secure payment of solicitors' costs

75.1

This provision repeats and updates s 18(5) of the 1950 Act

which referred to s 69 of the Solicitors' Act 1932. It is a mandatory provision.

75.2

The section gives the court the same power to charge property which is the subject of arbitration proceedings to secure payment of solicitors' costs as it had in relation to court proceedings under s 73 of the Solicitors Act 1974 or Article 71H of the Solicitors (Northern Ireland) Order 1976. It is worth noting that only solicitors appear to have this special protection. Members of other professions who may act for and represent parties in arbitrations as provided for in s 36 (legal or other representation) will not have that protection, nor will counsel or experts retained by non-solicitors on their clients' behalf. (Counsel retained by solicitors have that protection, since their fees are included in bills of costs which their instructing solicitor will send to his client for payment.)

Supplementary

Section 76: Service of notices, &c

76.1

This section is new. It has no parallel in the Model Law.

76.2

It deals with the manner in which notices or other documents are to be given or served by one party to or on the other, or given by or to the arbitrator for the purposes of the arbitration. It does not apply to notices in legal proceedings arising from an arbitration, such as appeals, which are to be served in accordance with the normal requirements for service of documents in litigation. It will, therefore, not apply to notices in connection with legal proceedings arising from the arbitration proceedings which are required by the Act, such as the notices required to be given to the other parties and the arbitrator under ss 67(1) (challenging the award: substantive jurisdiction) and 68(1) (challenging the award: serious irregularity). Those will have to be given or served in accordance with rules of court. However, please see s 80 for further comment on this point.

76.3

Section 76(1) gives the parties power to agree between themselves how notices and other documents relating to the proceedings are required or authorised to be given or served 'in pursuance of the arbitration agreement or for the purposes of the arbitral proceedings'. Section 76(2) is the usual provision for what is to happen in default of agreement by the parties.

76.4

Section 76(3) provides that, in default of agreement, service or delivery may be effected 'by any effective means'. In essence this means that service can be effected by any means which will bring the notice or document to the attention of the addressee. For example, fax, e-mail or telex may be used as well as post, courier service etc. The effect of s 76(1) is that, by agreement, parties may exclude a particular method. They might agree, for instance, that fax or e-mail will not be used. Regarding e-mail, and without going into detailed technological explanation, this is basically communication between computers. Thus, while it will quite effectively draw the notice or document to the attention of the addressee, it is ephemeral unless it is printed out, or put onto a floppy disk by the recipient (or by the sender who then posts it as a 'hard copy'). It will disappear and be lost as soon as the screen is wiped. For that reason it is suggested that it should only ever be used as a back-up to service by other more permanent means.

76.5

Section 76(4) deals with service by post. Service will be treated as effective if it is done by means of ordinary pre-paid post. The document must be addressed:

> '(*a*) to the addressee's last known principal residence or, if he is or has been carrying on a trade, profession or business, his last known principal business address, or
>
> (*b*) where the addressee is a body corporate, to the body's registered or principal office.'

If these conditions are met the notice or document will be treated as effectively served even if the addressee does not in fact receive it. However, the sender would be well advised to retain some proof that the notice or other document was posted. This can be done by getting a receipt from the post office. However, by far the most effective means is to send the document by recorded delivery post with a request for notice of receipt. The DAC in its Report (February 1996) says that service by post 'can best be described as a "fail safe" method, which a party may employ if he wishes, for example if he is not sure that other methods will be effective'. Parties and arbitrators are therefore well advised to send notices and documents by post as well as by other means such as fax and e-mail, to be on the safe side. Documents sent by first class post are normally deemed to have been received on the second day after posting, excluding Sundays and bank holidays.

76.6

Section 76(5) confirms that these provisions do not apply to service of documents for the purposes of legal proceedings. Provision for these is made by rules of court.

76.7

Section 76(6) provides that references in Part I of the Act to notices and documents include any form of communication in writing. By s 5(6) 'in writing' includes recording by any means (see the commentary on that section).

Section 77: Powers of court in relation to service of documents

77.1

Section 77 is new. It has no parallel in the Model Law.

77.2

It is intended to allow the court to support the arbitral process by providing means of ensuring service where difficulties arise which an arbitrator would have no powers to deal with. The arbitration process could therefore be delayed or even frustrated by a reluctant party determined to avoid service. As the DAC said in its Report (February 1996):

'In the nature of human affairs, it is sadly the case that potential respondents to arbitration proceedings quite often go to considerable lengths to avoid service and thus to achieve this state of affairs, by making normal methods difficult or even impossible to use effectively. This [section] should, in appropriate cases, help to deal with such cases.'

77.3

Section 77(1) states that the section applies 'where service of a document on a person in the manner agreed by the parties, or in accordance with provisions of section 76 having effect in default of agreement, is not reasonably practical'.

77.4

Section 77(2) states that 'unless agreed by the parties, the court may make such order as it thinks fit—(a) for service in such manner as the court may direct, or (b) dispensing with service of the document'. The provisions for agreement of the parties is unlikely to arise since, if there is any chance of agreement, the need for court intervention is unlikely to be required. Effectively the court may take over and use its own means of ensuring that service is effected properly. If that fails or appears unlikely to be successful, it can simply dispense with the need for service and allow the party seeking the order to continue with the arbitration without the notice or other documents having been served.

77.5

Section 77(3) provides that any party to an arbitration may apply for an order under this section 'but only after exhausting any available arbitral process for resolving the matter'. Institutional rules applicable to the arbitration may provide for what is to be done if service is not possible by normal means. Also, a party which has tried one means of service under s 76 that has failed (other than post, provided that proof of posting is available), must exhaust all other possibilities before applying to the court.

77.6

Section 77(4) provides that leave of the court is required for any appeal against a decision of the court under this section.

Section 78: Reckoning periods of time

78.1

This section is new. It has no parallel in the Model Law.

78.2

Section 78(1) provides that the parties are free to agree on the method of reckoning periods of time. For example, they may, for their own reasons, agree that periods of days should include Sundays but exclude certain days such as Jewish or any other religious holidays. The section also covers periods of time applicable under Part I of the Act. See, however, s 80(5) in relation to service of notices etc in legal proceedings related to arbitration, such as challenges to the award under ss 67 and 68, and appeals under s 69.

78.3

Section 78(2) provides that, if there is no agreement between the parties, periods of time are to be reckoned in accordance with the following provisions. Section 78(3) provides that if something is required to be done 'within a specified period after or from a specified date, the period begins immediately after that date'. Thus, if the period is 24 days, the first of those days is the day immediately after the starting date.

78.4

Section 78(4) provides that where a number of clear days is specified after a specified date, at least that number of days must intervene between the specified date and the concluding date. If the period is 14 clear days, the first day will be the day immediately after the starting date and the last day will be the day after the 14th day from that first day.

78.5

Section 78(5) provides that where a period of seven days or less is specified and that period includes a Saturday, Sunday or public holiday, those days shall be *excluded*. 'Public holiday' is such a holiday 'in the place where anything which has to be done within the period falls to be done'. If that is England, Wales or Northern Ireland it means 'Christmas Day, Good Friday or a day which under the Banking and Financial Dealings Act 1971 is a bank holiday'. To give some examples, in 1996 with Good Friday falling on 5 April and Easter Monday (both bank holidays) falling on 8 April, periods of time starting on 1 April expired as follows:

- a period of seven days expired on Friday, 12 April (excluding Good Friday, Saturday, Sunday and Easter Monday);

- a period of eight days expired on Tuesday, 9 April (because no days were excluded by s 78(5), the period being longer than seven days);
- a period of 14 days expired on Monday, 15 April;
- a period of 14 clear days expired on Tuesday, 16 April.

Of course the answer where the period is seven days would be different if whatever was to be done were to be done in a country in which Good Friday and Easter Monday were not public holidays. For example, in France Good Friday is not a holiday but Easter Monday is. In that case the period of seven days would have expired on Thursday, 11 April.

78.6

All this may appear complicated. However, its merit is that it is clear, which previously it was not. None the less, parties and arbitrators should take care to ensure that difficulties do not arise from the fact that Saturdays, Sundays and, particularly, public holidays are not excluded from periods of more than seven days; for instance, that the period does not expire on a public holiday. All this can be avoided, of course, if the parties agree under s 78(1) that all periods shall be stated in working days. If they do this then automatically Saturdays, Sundays and public holidays are excluded.

Section 79: Power of court to extend time limits relating to arbitral proceedings

79.1

Section 79 supersedes s 13(2) of the 1950 Act. It has no parallel in the Model Law.

79.2

Section 79(1) gives the court power, unless the parties agree otherwise, to extend any time limit agreed by the parties or specified in any provision in Part I of the Act, other than time limits to which s 12 (power of court to extend time for beginning arbitral proceedings, &c) applies. Time limits may be agreed by the parties in the arbitration agreement itself, in rules applicable to the arbitration or in subsequent agreements during the proceedings. Time limits set out in Part I of the Act include, for example, time limits for making applications for leave to appeal under s 70(3) (challenge or appeal:

supplementary provisions). Any such time limits, including any time limit within which an award is to be made, may now be extended by the court, but subject to the stringent conditions set out below.

79.3

Section 13(2) of the 1950 Act stated, 'The time, if any, limited for making an award, whether under this Act or otherwise, may from time to time be enlarged by order of the High Court ... whether that time has expired or not'. In short, the previous law only empowered the court to extend a time limit for the making of an award. Section 79 enlarges this to a power to extend any time limits other than those for commencing arbitration proceedings, which are dealt with in s 12.

79.4

Section 79(2) provides that an application to the court for an order under this section may be made (*a*) by any party to the arbitration proceedings, upon notice to the other parties and the arbitrator, or (*b*) by the arbitrator himself upon notice to the parties. An arbitrator may well find, for instance, that for perfectly good reasons, such as illness within his family, he cannot produce his award within a time limit set. His first recourse would be to the parties, of course, asking them to agree an extended time. However, if they refuse he may apply to the court under this section, giving notice to the parties that he is doing so.

79.5

Section 79(3) states that the court shall not exercise its powers to extend any time limit unless it is satisfied, '(*a*) that any available recourse to the tribunal, or to any arbitral or other institution or person vested by the parties with power in that regard, has first been exhausted'. This common condition for application to the courts is scattered throughout the Act and is commented on. The second, and most important condition is, by s 79(3)(*b*), that the court must be satisfied 'that a substantial injustice would otherwise be done'.

79.6

Section 79(4) provides that the court may exercise its power under this section whether or not the time limit has already expired. It may therefore extend a time limit even though it has already expired and the party or the arbitrator is already in default. Of course, if the application is made after the time limit has expired it may be thought that it would be more likely to succeed, since whatever was to be done within the time limit now cannot be done. The risk of substantial injustice will therefore be increased. However, the court is unlikely to be sympathetic if it considers that a party or the arbitrator has deliberately delayed an application in order to achieve precisely that effect.

79.7

Section 79(5) empowers the court to attach such conditions to an order under this section as it thinks fit. It may, for instance, order that the costs of the application be paid by the applicant, even—possibly—if the applicant is the arbitrator.

79.8

Section 79(6) provides that the leave of the court is required for any appeal against any decision of the court under s 79.

79.9

Time limits set by the Act have been most carefully considered and a court will only extend them if they consider that not to do so would result in substantial injustice in the special circumstances of the case. Where the parties have agreed time limits they should be held to their bargain, again unless substantial injustice would otherwise be done because of special circumstances. (They could, of course, mutually agree to alter such limits, in the same way as solicitors often tolerate applications for extensions of time from the other side, recognising that they, too, might want an extension in the future.) Arbitrators, having accepted the appointment in the knowledge that applicable rules apply strict time limits for their actions, or having agreed to time limits set by the parties, should be held to them except in exceptional circumstances. It should be noted that s 1 emphasises the resolution of disputes 'without delay'; that s 33(1)(*b*) refers to the adoption of arbitral proceedings which avoid 'unnecessary delay'; that s 40(1) puts a duty on the parties 'for the proper and expeditious conduct of the arbitral proceedings', which includes s 40(2)(*a*) 'complying without delay' to certain matters; and that s 40(2)(*b*) again emphasises the taking of necessary steps 'without delay'. It should also be noted that serious irregularity under s 68 includes failure of the tribunal to comply with s 33. Throughout the Act is the clear message: that to encourage and promote arbitration and to obtain the fair resolution of disputes by an impartial tribunal it is essential to eradicate as much as possible the twin evils of unnecessary delay and expense. It will be rare for the court to intervene by granting extensions of time, but the Act provides for it in exceptional cases. Further, the strictness of the rules now arguably makes it more likely that users will appreciate the need to comply.

Section 80: Notice and other requirements in connection with legal proceedings

80.1

Section 80 is new. It has no parallel in the Model Law.

80.2

It lays down provisions for notices etc required to be given by the applicant to other parties or to the arbitrator in legal proceedings in connection with arbitration proceedings. Section 80(1) states that references to notices in the affected sections are to 'such notice of the originating process as is required by rules of court and do not impose any separate requirement'.

80.3

Section 80(2) states that rules of court shall be made requiring such notice to be given as is indicated by any provision in Part I of the Act, and setting out conditions as to the manner, form and content of such notices. The new rules are not available at the time of writing. However, it is expected that they will be carefully framed so as to comply with the spirit as well as the letter of the Act.

80.4

Section 80(3) provides that where notice is to be given to the tribunal, it is to be given to all the arbitrators where there is more than one. If the tribunal is incomplete the notice must be given to the arbitrators who have been appointed at the relevant time.

80.5

Section 80(4) makes it clear that where there is a reference to making an application or appeal to the court within a time limit, as for example in s 70(3) (challenge or appeal: supplementary provisions), that reference is to 'the issue within that period of the appropriate originating process in accordance with rules of court', eg an originating summons.

80.6

Section 80(5) states that where a provision of Part I of the Act requires an application or appeal to be made to the court within a specified period, the rules of court relating to the reckoning of periods, and not the provisions of s 78 of the Act (reckoning periods of time), will apply to such applications. The rules of court will also determine the consequences of not taking a step within the period prescribed by the rules.

80.7

Section 80(6) states that provision may be made by rules of court amending the provisions of Part I of the Act with respect to the time within which any application or appeal to the court must be made, so as to keep the provisions of Part I of the Act as to arbitration and legal proceedings in step with rules of court generally. This gives power for rules of court effectively to amend the Act. This provision is obviously a prudent one to have been inserted. However, as rules of court develop, particularly since recent changes have been very much for the better and still further radical improvements will almost certainly result from Lord Woolf's examination into 'access to justice', the authors think it unlikely that this provision will have any significant effect in the near future.

80.8

Section 80(7) simply preserves the generality of the power to make rules of court.

80.9

Sections in the Act which are affected by the provisions of s 80 are:

- 9(1) (application for stay of legal proceedings);
- 12(2) (application to extend time for beginning arbitral proceedings);
- 18(2) (application on failure of appointment procedure);
- 21(5) (application for umpire);
- 24(1) (application for the removal of an arbitrator);
- 25(3) (application by the arbitrator for relief in connection with his resignation);
- 28(2) (application in connection with the amount of an arbitrator's fees and expenses);
- 32(1) (application for determination of a question as to the arbitrator's substantive jurisdiction);
- 42(2) (application for enforcement of peremptory orders);
- 44(4) (application for the exercise of court powers in support of arbitral proceedings);
- 45(1) (application for determination of preliminary point of law);
- 50(2) (application for an order extending time for making award);
- 56(2) (application relating to arbitrator's refusal to deliver his award pending payment of fees);
- 63(4) (application for determination of the costs of the arbitration);
- 64(2) (application regarding determination of reasonable fees and expenses of the arbitrator);
- 67(1) (application challenging an award on ground of lack of substantive jurisdiction);
- 68(1) (application challenging an award on grounds of serious irregularity);
- 69(1) (application for appeal on point of law); and
- 79(2) (application to extend time limits generally).

80.10

The Notes on Clauses circulated to the House of Lords for its consideration of the Bill stated that this provision 'is included for user friendliness, and is not intended as a substitute for familiarisation with the relevant rules of court'. Often, of course, such applications will be made through solicitors who will be familiar with the relevant rules of court or will make themselves familiar with any new rules made as a consequence of this provision. However, it is to be hoped that guidance will readily be available for parties and arbitrators who may wish to make such applications in person.

Section 81: Saving for certain matters governed by common law

81.1

Section 81 saves certain matters governed by common law.

81.2

Section 81(1) provides that nothing in Part I of the Act 'shall be construed as excluding the operation of any rule of law consistent with the provisions of this Part'.

81.3

Common law is capable of continuity of growth and development because of our doctrine of precedent. Over the centuries an enormous body of case law has built up. It was clearly impossible, and undesirable, for the Act to cover every conceivable aspect of the law of arbitration. This section, therefore, preserves those aspects of common law which are not inconsistent with the Act. The more important principles of common law, such as the *Nema* guidelines, have been included in the Act.

81.4

Section 81(1) goes on to give three particular examples of rules of law which are preserved. The first is where the dispute involves 'matters which are not capable of settlement by arbitration'. Clearly if a dispute involves a matter which is not capable of being resolved by arbitration (it is difficult to think of examples of such disputes, but they must exist) the rights of the parties to an arbitration agreement to have that dispute settled by other means must be preserved.

81.5

The second example is 'the effect of an oral arbitration agreement'. While the Act governs only arbitration agreements in writing, it is still possible for binding arbitration agreements to be made orally. The difference is that if they are oral agreements they will simply not be governed by any provisions of the Act. While, therefore, it is not possible to enforce an award made pursuant to an oral agreement by the operation of s 66, it will still be possible to seek enforcement as a matter of contract. A party, having contracted orally to submit a dispute to arbitration, possibly as part of a larger oral contract, could be held to its contract as a matter of common law and be made to abide by the award. It is also possible, of course, to enforce the oral arbitration agreement itself if one of the parties tries to refer a dispute covered by it to litigation, although again, it would be as a matter of contract and not by the operation of s 9.

81.6

The third example is 'the refusal of recognition or enforcement of an arbitral award on grounds of public policy'. When the Act was introduced in the House of Lords as a Bill this appeared in s 66 (enforcement of an award) as a ground on which a court must refuse leave to enforce, but this section now makes it clear that an award may not even be recognised (eg under the New York Convention), far less enforced, if it contravenes public policy. This may be because it seeks to enforce an illegal contract, such as an agreement relating to trade with a country against which there is an enforceable trade embargo, for example, in the past, Southern Rhodesia, or now, Iraq. It may be because it ought not to be enforced for other reasons of public policy, for example if it contains an order that certain matters be revealed by one party to another which ought not be revealed in the interests of public policy, such as trade or State secrets.

81.7

Section 81(2) makes it clear that the repeal of the 1979 Act, (which itself contained the repeal of ss 1 and 21 of the 1950 Act giving the court power to set aside or remit an award for error of law on its face, and abolished the special case procedure) does not revive the power to set aside or remit through any principle of common law.

Section 82: Minor definitions

82.1

Setion 82(1) sets out certain definitions. While some are self-explanatory, others deserve further comment.

82.2

'Available arbitral process' which appears in a number of sections which require their exhaustion before an application can be made to the court, is defined as including 'any process of appeal to or review by an arbitral or other institution or person vested by the parties with powers in relation to that matter'. For example, the arbitration rules of GAFTA have a comprehensive provision for appeals against awards under the GAFTA arbitration scheme. Parties submitting to arbitration under this scheme have therefore agreed to submit appeals to the tribunal set up under the scheme. Recourse must be made to this tribunal before any appeal can be lodged under s 69. Any appeal to the court would then, in effect, be an appeal against the decision of the GAFTA appeal tribunal.

82.3

'Claimant' is defined as including a counterclaimant. It is very important to realise that courses of action available to claimants under the Act, such as applications for security for costs under s 38(3) (general powers exercisable by the tribunal), are also available to counterclaimants.

82.4

'Dispute' is defined as including any 'difference'. The 1950 Act used the term 'difference' throughout and this has now been changed to 'dispute'. As is noted above, there is a possibility that some distinction might be drawn between the two terms and thus the definition makes it clear that there is no such distinction.

82.5

'Question of law' is defined as including any question of law in Northern Ireland when the applicable court is there. For historical reasons the 1950 and 1979 Acts did *not* apply to Northern Ireland, where arbitration law until the passing of this Act was governed by the Arbitration Act (Northern Ireland) 1937. This was essentially the same as the 1950 Act but remained unamended by the 1979 Act or any other amendments to either Act made in other legislation, such as the introduction of ss 13A and 19A into the 1950 Act. This, in the experience of one of the authors, was the cause of much confusion when someone used to arbitration in England was required to carry out an arbitration in Northern Ireland. Northern Ireland now has the *same* arbitral regime as England and Wales.

82.6

Section 82(2) contains the very necessary provision that any reference in the Act to a party to an arbitration agreement includes any party claiming under or through a party to the agreement. 'Name borrowing' arbitrations are common in the construction industry, where standard forms of sub contract often contain provisions entitling the subcontractor to use the main contractor's name to pursue a dispute with the building owner. This provision confirms that in such arbitrations the subcontractor is to be regarded as if he were a party to the main contract arbitration agreement.

Section 83: Index of defined expressions: Part I

83.1

This section lists a number of expressions used throughout Part I of the Act and sets out where their definitions are to be found. It requires no commentary.

Section 84: Transitional provisions

84.1

Section 84 states that Part I of the Act will apply to all arbitrations commenced *after* the date on which the Part is to come into force in accordance with an order made under the provisions of s 109. It will then be subject to any transitional provisions contained in that order as provided in s 109(2).

Chapter 5

Part II—Other Provisions Relating to Arbitration

Domestic arbitration agreements

[*Important.* At the time of writing (Spring 1996), the authors have been informed that an order repealing the whole or a significant part of ss 85 to 88 may be made before the Act comes into force, subject to consultations currently in progress. It is therefore possible that the existing distinction between domestic and international arbitrations preserved in these sections will be removed and that these sections will never actually come into force under this Act.]

Sections 85 to 88 under this heading set out certain modifications to the provisions of Part I of the Act which relate to domestic, as opposed to international, arbitration agreements. Considerable pressure was exercised in some quarters to remove the distinctions between domestic and international arbitrations and in the committee stage of the Bill's consideration in the House of Lords, Lord Hacking moved an amendment which would have deleted these sections of the Bill. He objected to the different treatment applied to domestic and international arbitrations. 'The distinction only came about when we put into force in the UK the New York Convention on Recognition and Enforcement of Foreign Arbitral Awards in 1958', he said and added that he could not see 'the logic of that distinction with one set of rights for one category of parties and another set of rights for another category of parties' (*Hansard* 18 January 1996, p 771). That amendment was withdrawn on the government's assurance that the matter would be reconsidered and on the basis that s 88 provides for reconsideration of the matter at some future time. The DAC in its Report (February 1996) also made clear its opinion that the distinctions no longer serve any useful purpose. However, it came down (only just) in favour of retaining them for the time being while making provisions for their easy amendment or repeal. This is particularly necessary as there is the possibility of conflict with European law in that the provisions make distinctions between the treatment of nationals of the United Kingdom and those of other countries which, if applied to nationals of member states of the European Union, might be ruled *ultra vires*.

The distinction in the law applicable as between domestic and international arbitrations first came about, as Lord Hacking said, in the 1975 Act which enacted into English law the provisions of the New York Convention on the Recognition and Enforcement of Foreign Arbitral Awards, and then related only to the circumstances in which a court could refuse to enforce an arbitration agreement by granting a stay of litigation proceedings (see s 9). The New York Convention removed almost entirely the discretion of national courts as to whether a stay should be granted or not. This removal of discretion was enacted in s 1 of the 1975 Act. The whole of the 1975 Act has been repealed. Section 9 of the present Act now reflects the position as it was under s 1 of the 1975 Act but s 86 of this Part restores the court's discretion in respect of arbitrations pursuant to domestic arbitration agreements—although not to the extent provided in the 1950 Act. (The whole of Part II of the 1950 Act remains in force.)

A further distinction between domestic and international arbitrations was brought about in the 1979 Act in relation to agreements to exclude the right to appeal to the court on a point of law arising out of an award and to refer to the court questions of law arising during the course of an arbitration under ss 1 and 2, respectively, of that Act. Section 3(7) of the 1979 Act provided that, in domestic arbitration agreements, exclusion agreements would only be effective if entered into after the arbitration had commenced. The corollary was, of course, that in international arbitrations they could be entered into at any time. This distinction is also reaffirmed by s 87 of this Act. However, the further limitation of exclusion clauses to those made after the arbitration had begun in arbitration agreements in what were described as the 'special categories' set out in s 4 of the 1979 Act (see s 69), ie questions or claims falling within the Admiralty jurisdiction of the High Court and disputes arising out of contracts of insurance and commodity contracts, have not been repeated.

Section 85: Modification of Part I in relation to domestic arbitration agreement

85.1

Section 85(1) provides that the provisions of Part I are to be modified in accordance with the following sections.

85.2

Section 85(2) defines a domestic arbitration agreement as one in which:

'... none of the parties is
(a) an individual who is a national of, or habitually resident in, a state other than the United Kingdom, or
(b) a body corporate which is incorporated in, or whose central control and management is exercised in, a state other than the United Kingdom,
and under which the seat of the arbitration (if the seat has been designated or determined) is in the United Kingdom.'

This repeats the definition in s 1(4) of the 1975 Act, repeated also in s 3(7) of the 1979 Act, the only difference *now* being the requirement that the seat of the arbitration should be in the United Kingdom. Previously the requirement was that the arbitration agreement should not provide 'for arbitration in a State other than the United Kingdom'. This is not a difference of great practical significance.

85.3

Note that arbitrations where a party is a person resident in, or a company whose base of operations is in, Scotland, but where the seat of arbitration is in England, Wales or Northern Ireland, is a domestic arbitration agreement even though Scotland has a totally different system of arbitration law from that which now applies in the rest of the United Kingdom.

85.4

Section 85(3) simply confirms, as it falls in Part II of the Act, that the definitions of 'arbitration agreement' and 'seat' in this section are the same as that set out in s 3 in Part I.

Section 86: Staying of legal proceedings

86.1

Section 86(1) states that the provision of s 9(4) that the court shall grant a stay only if 'satisfied that the arbitration agreement is null and void, inoperative, or incapable of being performed' does *not* apply to a domestic arbitration agreement. Section 86(2) then reinstates that condition for granting a stay but goes on to empower the court *not* to grant a stay if satisfied '(*b*) that there are other sufficient grounds for not requiring the parties to abide by the arbitration agreement'. Section 86(3) then goes on to state that the court may treat as a 'sufficient ground' 'the fact that the applicant is or was at any material time not ready and willing to do all things necessary for the proper conduct of the arbitration or of any other dispute resolution procedures required to be exhausted before resorting to arbitration'.

86.2

In summary this provision restores, to some extent, the court's discretion when considering whether to grant a stay of litigation in favour of arbitration which it formerly had in *all* arbitrations under s 4(1) of the 1950 Act but which was removed in respect of non-domestic arbitrations by s 1 of the 1975 Act.

86.3

Section 86(1) to (3) now brings in the provision regarding the arbitration agreement being 'null and void, inoperative, or incapable of being performed' which did not appear in s 4(1) of the 1950 Act. The court *shall* grant a stay in that event. It has no discretion, except of course, insofar as the decision whether the arbitration agreement meets those criteria is in itself discretionary. The other significant difference is that the 1950 Act said that the court *may* grant a stay 'if satisfied that there is *no* sufficient reason why the matter should *not* be referred [to arbitration] in accordance with the agreement, and that the applicant was, at the time when the proceedings were commenced, and still remains, ready and willing to do all things necessary to the proper conduct of the arbitration'.

86.4

The emphasis is now reversed. The court *shall* grant a stay *unless* satisfied that there *are* sufficient grounds for *not* requiring the parties to abide by the arbitration agreement, including the consideration of whether the applicant is, or was at the relevant time, *not* ready and willing to do what is necessary for the conduct of the arbitration. In other words, the court is obliged to grant a stay unless those criteria are met instead of having a discretion to grant a stay if they were *not* met. There is also the additional consideration of whether the applicant is, or was not, ready and willing to do all things necessary for the proper conduct of 'any other dispute resolution procedures required to be exhausted before resorting to arbitration'. This is to provide for cases where, for example, the parties have agreed to try conciliation, or where there is to be some kind of adjudication, before embarking on arbitration.

86.5

Section 86(4) states, 'for the purposes of this section the question whether an arbitration agreement is a domestic arbitration agreement shall be determined by reference to the facts at the time the legal proceedings are commenced'. Parties' circumstances change and a party which was not a national of or resident in the United Kingdom at the time of the arbitration agreement may now be a national or resident at the time the application is made. If that is the case the agreement is now considered to be 'domestic'. This is in line with s 1(4) of the 1975 Act, which stated that the criteria were to be those 'at the time the proceedings are commenced'. (However, compare and contrast this provision with that in s 87(3). The relevant time there is the time of the agreement *not* the time the arbitration commences.)

Section 87: Effectiveness of agreement to exclude court's jurisdiction

87.1

Section 87 restates the law in s 3 of the 1979 Act.

87.2

Section 87(1) provides that an agreement to exclude the jurisdiction of the court under ss 45 (determination of preliminary point of law) and 69 (appeal on a point of law), in a domestic arbitration agreement as defined in s 85 'is not effective unless entered into *after* the commencement of the arbitral proceedings in which the question arises or the award is made'. Section 87(2) states that 'for this purpose the commencement of the arbitral proceedings has the same meaning as in Part I' (see commentary on s 14 in Chapter 4). This provision is necessary as it falls in Part II of the Act. Any provisions in Part I which are also applicable in Part II have to be restated.

87.3

Section 87(3) states that, '[f]or the purposes of this section the question whether an arbitration agreement is a domestic arbitration agreement shall be determined by reference to facts at the time the agreement is entered into'. Note that the question is whether the criteria apply at the time of the arbitration agreement, *not* at the time the arbitration commences. This is in contrast to the similar provision in s 86(4).

Section 88: Power to repeal or amend ss 85–87

88.1

Section 88(1) gives the Secretary of State for Trade and Industry (also, at the time of writing, described as the President of the Board of Trade), power by order to repeal or amend ss 85 to 87. By s 88(3) any such orders are to be made by statutory instrument and shall not be made unless a draft of the order has been laid before, and approved by, both Houses of Parliament. By s 88(2) it may also contain 'such supplementary, incidental and transitional provisions as appear to the Secretary of State to be appropriate'. As stated previously, the survival of these provisions is in some doubt and the authors would not be surprised to see the distinction between domestic and international arbitrations as set out in ss 87 and 88 removed before too long. They have outlived their purpose and serve only to confuse the law.

Consumer arbitration agreements

This part of the Act replaces the Consumer Arbitration Agreements Act 1988 (the 1988 Act) which has been repealed in its entirety. The 1988 Act was introduced in order to correct what was seen as a degree of unfairness to 'consumers' resulting from the incorporation of arbitration clauses in traders' standard conditions. In the mid-1980s there had been a well-publicised case in which a customer of a removal firm suffered damage to his furniture during a removal. He tried to sue the removal firm in the county court but was prevented from doing so by the firm which successfully applied for a stay of the litigation on the grounds that its standard terms of contract contained an arbitration clause. The customer decided that he could not afford to take the matter to arbitration as he could not get legal aid to pay for employing lawyers to conduct his case (he was presumably afraid that, if he did not employ lawyers, the removal firm would, to his disadvantage).

Following pressure from the Consumers' Association among others, the 1988 Act, originally introduced in the House of Commons as a Private Member's Bill by Mr James Pawsey MP, was passed. Essentially, its purpose was to state that an arbitration agreement in a consumer contract, ie a contract between a person acting as a consumer and a supplier of goods and/or services, would not be binding on the consumer provided that the sum in dispute did not exceed the limit for claims in the county court. If, after the dispute arose, he chose to avail himself of arbitration, say under the ABTA Scheme, then once he agreed to have the dispute resolved by this method he had effectively relinquished his right to litigate.

Unfortunately the 1988 Act was not the model of clarity that the present Act is. In particular, it contained a number of cross-references to other legislation, for example the Unfair Contract Terms Act 1977 (also not an Act easy to understand). It also referred to other provisions which made it very difficult to know what types of contract were or were not covered by it. It was possible to argue, for example, that it did not cover contracts for building works because of a provision that it applied only where 'the goods passing under or in pursuance of the contract are of a type ordinarily supplied for private use and consumption', or to contracts which had been let by competitive tender, because of the provision that 'on a sale by auction or by competitive tender the buyer is not in any circumstances to be regarded as entering into the contract as a consumer'.

On 1 July 1995 the position was further complicated by the coming into force of the Unfair Contract Terms in Consumer Contracts Regulations 1994 (SI No 3159) ('the Regulations') which had been introduced in compliance with EEC Council Directive 93/13/EEC. The essence of the Regulations is contained in reg 5 which states:

> '5(1) An unfair term in a contract concluded with a consumer by a seller or supplier shall not be binding on the consumer.
> (2) The contract shall continue to bind the parties if it is capable of continuing in existence without the unfair term.'

'Consumer' is defined as 'a natural person who, in making a contract to which these Regulations apply, is acting for purposes outside his business'. Regulation 3(1) says that 'these Regulations apply to any term in a contract concluded between a seller or supplier and a consumer where the said term has not been individually negotiated'.

Regulation 4 runs as follows:

> '4(1) In these Regulations, subject to paragraphs (2) and (3) below, 'unfair term' means any term which contrary to the requirement of good faith causes a significant imbalance in the parties' rights and obligations under the contract to the detriment of the consumer.
> (2) An assessment of the unfair nature of a term shall be made taking into account the nature of the goods or services for which the contract was concluded and referring, as at the time of the conclusion of the contract, to all circumstances attending the conclusion of the contract or of another contract on which it is dependent.
> (3) In determining whether a term satisfies the requirement of good faith, regard shall be had in particular to matters specified in Schedule 2 to these Regulations.
> (4) Schedule 3 to these Regulations contains an indicative and non-exhaustive list of the terms which may be regarded as unfair.'

Schedule 2 is headed 'Assessment of good faith' and runs as follows.

'In making an assessment of good faith, regard shall be had in particular to—

(a) the strength of the bargaining positions of the parties;

(b) whether the consumer had an inducement to agree to the term;

(c) whether the goods or services were sold or supplied to the special order of the consumer, and

(d) the extent to which the seller or supplier has dealt fairly and equitably with the consumer.'

Schedule 3 is headed 'Indicative and illustrated list of terms which *may* [authors' emphasis] be regarded as unfair'. Included among them is:

'(q) Excluding or hindering the consumer's right to take legal action or exercise any other legal remedy, particularly by requiring the consumer to take disputes exclusively to arbitration *not covered by legal provisions*, [authors' emphasis] unduly restricting the evidence available to him or imposing on him a burden of proof which, according to the applicable law, should lie with another party to the contract.'

Some puzzlement has been caused as to the exact meaning of the phrase 'not covered by legal provisions', which comes straight out of the English version of the EEC Directive. Would an arbitration covered by existing legislation be considered to be 'covered by legal provisions'?

To sum up, therefore, an arbitration clause in a trader's terms would be deemed to be unfair and therefore unenforceable against a consumer. However, the consumer would have to take action to resist arbitration and show that the clause was unfair and the trader would have a possible defence by seeking to demonstrate that the clause was not unfair in all the circumstances, given the criteria laid down in reg 4(2). This is in marked contrast to the position under the 1988 Act where an arbitration clause would simply be unenforceable and the consumer could safely commence litigation, secure in the knowledge that, if the trader tried to obtain a stay in favour of arbitration, he would undoubtedly fail. However, the consumer's right to ignore the arbitration clause in this way was limited, depending upon the type of contract in ways which were difficult to interpret. There were therefore two slightly different regimes affecting clauses in consumer contracts.

This has now been corrected. The 1988 Act is repealed and ss 89, 90 and 91 of this Act now, with certain necessary limitations, simply make arbitration clauses in consumer contracts unenforceable against the consumer by reference to the Regulations. The effect is therefore basically the same as the intended effect of the 1988 Act, but expressed in much simpler terms and with wider application.

Section 89: Application of unfair terms regulations to consumer arbitration agreements

89.1

Section 89(1) states that ss 90 and 91 extend the application of the Regulations in relation to a term which constitutes an arbitration agreement. An 'arbitration agreement' is defined as 'an agreement to submit to arbitration present or future disputes or differences (whether or not contractual)' which is essentially the general definition contained in s 6(1) in Part I of the Act. Section 89(2) makes it clear that the term 'the Regulations' includes any regulations amending or replacing them in the future.

89.2

Section 89(3) states that ss 90 and 91 apply 'whatever the law applicable to the arbitration agreement'. This means that the protection afforded to the consumer by these sections extends to consumers wherever they may be and whatever law applies to the agreement. Consumers in other states in the European Union, or in any other country, are therefore afforded the same protection as citizens of the United Kingdom if an arbitration agreement is sought to be enforced against them in the United Kingdom, even though the arbitration agreement may not be governed by the law of England and Wales, Scotland or Northern Ireland.

Section 90: Regulations apply where consumer is a legal person

90.1

As stated above, the Regulations define a consumer as 'a natural person who ... is acting for purposes outside his business'. This is the definition contained in the English version of the EEC Directive. Section 90 states that 'natural person' for these purposes includes a 'legal person', ie anyone who comes within the legal definition of 'a person', and could therefore include a firm/company provided that it is acting 'for purposes outside [its] business'.

Section 91: Arbitration agreement unfair where modest amount sought

91.1

Section 91(1) provides that a term which constitutes an arbitration agreement is unfair for the purposes of the Regulations provided that the claim being made is for money which does not exceed an amount to be specified by an order made under s 91(2) to (5). At the time of writing the order has still to be issued but it is thought likely to be the equivalent of the limit of claims in the county court.

91.2

Section 91(2) to (5) deals with the orders to be made defining the monetary limit under s 91(1). Section 91(2) states that 'Orders under this section may make different provision for different cases and for different purposes'. The orders for England and Wales and Scotland are to be made by the Secretary of State with the concurrence of the Lord Chancellor and the Lord Advocate respectively. Those for Northern Ireland are to be made by the Department of Economic Development for Northern Ireland with the concurrence of the Lord Chancellor. In each case the order is to be made by statutory instrument, or for Northern Ireland by statutory rule, subject to annulment by a resolution of both Houses of Parliament (in Northern Ireland it will be by negative resolution under s 41(6) of the Interpretation Act (Northern Ireland) 1954 which has the same effect).

In summary, an arbitration clause in a contract for the supply of goods and services will be unenforceable against the consumer provided that his claim does not exceed the limit to be set by order. If the supplier tries to obtain a stay of litigation started by the consumer, his application will not be entertained by the court. However, although not specifically stated (as it was under the 1988 Act), the authors believe there is little doubt that a consumer who has himself started an arbitration, or who has taken a step in an arbitration commenced by the supplier, such as putting in a defence, will be held to have waived his rights under these provisions. In the second case, however, he might be able to say that he put in his defence in ignorance of those rights and should therefore be entitled still to assert them.

Small claims arbitration in the county court

Section 92: Exclusion of Part I in relation to small claims arbitration in the county court

92.1

Section 92 makes it clear that the provisions of Part I have no application to small claims arbitration in the county court which are dealt with under s 64 of the County Courts Act 1984 and under the rules contained in the *County Court Practice* (the *Green Book*), in particular under CCR Ord 19. It is an informal proceeding where claims are for less than £3,000. No solicitors' charges are allowed, thus the majority of clients are not legally represented. It is an entirely separate regime and the previous legislation which dealt with arbitration, for example the 1950 Act, had no application.

Appointment of judges as arbitrators

Section 93: Appointment of judges as arbitrators

93.1

Section 93(1) provides that 'a judge of the Commercial Court or an official referee may, if in all the circumstances he thinks fit, accept appointment as a sole arbitrator or umpire by or as by virtue of an arbitration agreement'. The previous restriction that a judge of the Commercial Court could only accept an appointment when the dispute was of a commercial nature has not been reproduced. Official referees are to be treated on the same basis as judges.

93.2

Section 93(2) states that a judge of the Commercial Court shall not do so without permission of the Lord Chief Justice. This reflects the fact that while such judges are frequently asked, and would be pleased, to sit as arbitrators, yet such is the heavy pressure of their court commitment that permission would be necessary before they could be freed.

In the DAC Report (February 1996) it was said, 'We are told that the problem is particularly acute in the field of patents and the like, where the parties are anxious to arbitrate but where the only acceptable arbitrators are judges.'

93.3

Section 93(3) provides that an official referee also requires the permission of the Lord Chief Justice before he can accept an appointment as an arbitrator.

93.4

Sections 93(4) and (5) deals with fees payable and provide definitions of 'arbitration agreement' and 'official referee'.

93.5

Section 93(6) provides that Part I of the Act applies 'to arbitration before a person appointed under this section with the modifications specified in Schedule 2'.

93.6

These provisions restate the provisions of s 4(1)–(3) of the Administration of Justice Act 1970 (judges) and s 11 of the 1950 Act, as substituted by s 99 of the Courts and Legal Services Act 1990 (official referees).

Statutory arbitrations

Sections 94 to 98 deal with the application of the provisions of Part I of the Act to statutory arbitrations, ie, arbitrations which parties are obliged to enter into by statute and which therefore do *not* arise from arbitration agreements. An example of such is under s 76 of the Friendly Societies Act 1974; another is under the Housing Act 1957. Such Acts provide for certain kinds of disputes, say between a society and a branch, or in relation to a claim for compensation, to be resolved by a process referred to as 'arbitration' but which is covered by procedural codes and rules under the relevant statute. These have been treated in the previous legislation as though they were arbitrations pursuant to an arbitration agreement.

Essentially the new provisions re-enact s 31 of the 1950 Act but they substantially expand on that section to be more explanatory and comprehensive. Arbitrations under the Agricultural Holdings Act 1986 are expressly excluded from the operation of this Act by s 84 of that Act (the Agricultural Holdings Act) as now amended. (See Sched 3 to this Act: '46. In section 84(1) of the Agricultural Holdings Act 1986 (provisions relating to arbitration), for "the Arbitration Act 1950" substitute "Part I of the Arbitration Act 1996"').

Section 94: Application of Part I to statutory arbitrations

94.1

Section 94(1) states that the provisions of Part I apply to statutory arbitrations whether the Act in question was passed before or after this Act came into operation, but subject to the adaptations and exclusions set out in ss 95 to 98.

94.2

Section 94(2) states that the provisions of Part I do not apply if their application is inconsistent with the relevant Act under which the arbitration arises or to any rules or procedures authorised or recognised by the relevant Act. In other words, the provisions of any Act under which a statutory arbitration arises override the provisions of this Act where they are inconsistent with, or exclude, them.

94.3

Section 94(3) is a technical provision making it clear that references to 'enactment', ie to an Act from which a statutory arbitration arises, includes reference to any subordinate legislation within the meaning of the Interpretation Act 1978 or the Interpretation Act (Northern Ireland) 1954.

Section 95: General adaptation of provisions in relation to statutory arbitrations

95.1

Section 95(1) states that the provisions of Part I apply to a statutory arbitration

'(a) as if the arbitration were pursuant to an arbitration agreement and as if the enactment were that agreement, and

(b) as if the persons by and against whom a claim subject to

arbitration in pursuance of the enactment may be or has
been made were parties to that agreement.'

In other words, all the provisions of Part I of this Act will
apply as if the Act concerned were an arbitration agreement
and as if anyone able to pursue a claim or against whom a
claim may be pursued under the Act concerned were a party
to that arbitration agreement. This, of course, is subject to
the provision of s 94(2) giving the Act under which the arbitration arises precedence over this Act so far as it conflicts
with it or excludes it.

Section 96: Specific adaptations of provisions in relation to statutory arbitrations

96.1

Section 96 sets out certain necessary adaptations to the
provisions of Part I in relation to statutory arbitrations.

96.2

Section 96(2) provides that in s 30(1) (competence of tribunal to rule on its own jurisdiction), para (*a*), the question as
to whether there is a valid arbitration agreement shall be
construed as a question of whether the relevant Act applies
to the dispute or difference. The tribunal will have the same
power to rule on that matter as it would have if the validity
of an arbitration agreement were in question.

96.3

Section 96(3) provides that s 35 (consolidation of proceedings and concurrent hearings) 'applies only so as to
authorise the consolidation of proceedings, or concurrent
hearings in proceedings, under the same enactment'. In other
words, the parties will have the power to agree on consolidation of proceedings or to concurrent hearings, or to confer
power on the arbitrator to order them, *as if* the arbitration
were not a statutory arbitration but an arbitration entered
into in the usual manner by agreement between the parties.
However, this will only be the case to the extent that the
proceedings that they wish to consolidate/hold concurrently
arise under the same enactment. The parties therefore cannot agree to do so where the arbitrations, however closely
related, arise under different statutes.

96.4

Section 96(4) states that 'Section 46 (rules applicable to substance of dispute) applies with the omission of [46](1)(*b*) (determination in accordance with considerations agreed by the parties)'. The parties will therefore only have the power under s 46(1)(*a*) to choose the law applicable to the dispute. They will not be able to give the arbitrator power to decide the dispute in accordance with any other considerations such as 'rules of trade' or 'by considerations of fair play'.

Section 97: Provisions excluded from applying to statutory arbitrations

97.1

Section 97 sets out certain provisions in Part I which necessarily do not apply to statutory arbitrations. Section 8 (whether agreement discharged by death of a party) does *not* apply, so that a statutory arbitration cannot be pursued against the personal representatives of a party following his death unless the relevant enactment authorises such a practice. Section 12 (power of court to extend time for beginning arbitral proceedings, &c) does *not* apply, so that the court has no power to extend a time limit for commencing a statutory arbitration. Sections 9(5), 10(2) and 71(4) (restrictions on the effect of a provision that an award is a condition precedent to the right to bring legal proceedings) do *not* apply. The court will therefore have *no* power to direct that a provision relating to a statutory arbitration making an award a condition precedent to legal proceedings will not apply where a stay of litigation is refused under s 9, or where a court does not order that relief sought by way of interpleader is to be determined by arbitration in accordance with the enactment, or where a court sets aside an award in a statutory arbitration or declares it to be of no effect.

97.2

In its Report (February 1996) the DAC referred to ss 94 to 98 (96 to 100 in the Report) and said, 'These provisions adapt Part I to statutory arbitrations. This exercise is not within our remit and we have played no part in it'. Section 79 (general power to extend time limits) has not been included in s 97. Is this, the authors wonder, a deliberate omission of the draftsmen?

Section 98: Power to make further provision by regulations

98.1

Section 98(1) gives the Secretary of State power to 'make provision by regulations for adapting or excluding any provision of Part I in relation to statutory arbitrations in general or statutory arbitrations of any particular description'. Section 98(2) states that 'the power is exercisable whether the enactment concerned is passed or made before or after the commencement of this Act'. Section 98(3) provides that '[r]egulations under this section shall be made by statutory instrument which shall be subject to annulment in pursuance of a resolution of either House of Parliament'. Note that the Secretary of State will *not* have to lay any such regulation before both Houses of Parliament and obtain their approval as is the case for regulations made under s 88(3) (power to repeal or amend ss 85 to 87 relating to domestic as opposed to international arbitration agreements).

Chapter 6

Part III—Recognition and Enforcement of Certain Foreign Awards

The purpose of this part of the Act is to re-enact the substance of those provisions relating to the recognition and enforcement of foreign awards under Part II of the Arbitration Act 1950 (which implemented the United Kingdom's treaty obligations under the 1927 Geneva Convention) and under the Arbitration Act 1975 (which gave effect to obligations under the 1958 New York Convention).

Enforcement of Geneva Convention awards

Section 99: Continuation of Part II of the Arbitration Act 1950

99.1

Section 99 provides for the continuation in force of Part II of the Arbitration Act 1950 in relation to the enforcement of foreign awards which are not also New York Convention awards.

99.2

The Geneva Convention only remains in force as between those contracting states which did not subsequently become party to the New York Convention. Since nearly all parties to the Geneva Convention are now parties to the New York Convention (the only one left, so far as we know, being Mauritius) few awards will fall to be dealt with under the provisions of Part II of the 1950 Act which have been re-enacted here. Such awards will in effect form a residuary category of arbitral awards which, over time, will dwindle in number and eventually cease to exist altogether. At that time, Part II of the 1950 Act and this section can be repealed as spent enactments.

99.3

Because of the limited relevance of Part II of the 1950 Act, the present section merely confirms the continued application of that Part, rather than attempt to restate or reinterpret the abstruse language in which it is drafted.

99.4

In brief, Part II of the 1950 Act contains provisions which:

- define the foreign awards to which Part II of the 1950 Act applies (s 35);
- describe the way in which such awards shall be enforceable (s 36);
- lay down the conditions for such enforceability (s 37);
- state the evidence which must be produced before an award can be enforced (s 38);
- define the meaning of 'final award' (s 39);
- set out various savings for other rights (s 40); and
- extend the application of Part II of the 1950 Act to Scotland and Northern Ireland.

Recognition and enforcement of New York Convention awards

Section 100: New York Convention awards

100.1

Section 100(1) defines a 'New York Convention award' as an award made, in pursuance of an arbitration agreement, in the territory of any states (other than the United Kingdom) which are party to the New York Convention. As such, this definition is drafted in the same terms as 'Convention Award' is defined in the 1975 Act.

100.2

Section 100(2) defines what is meant by an 'arbitration agreement' under this part of the Act and removes some of the anomalies which arose under the equivalent provision in the 1975 Act (see in particular the case of *Hiscox v Outhwaite* referred to in the commentary to s 53 in Part I). The definition of an arbitration agreement is now generally consistent with that in s 5 which applies to arbitrations having their seat in the United Kingdom. Section 100(2)(*a*) states that 'arbitration agreement' means 'an arbitration agreement in writing', and the subsection then goes on to define 'in writing' as having the same meaning as in Part I. In total, then, this definition is now consistent with that in s 5. Section 100(2)(*b*) then says that 'an award shall be treated as made at the seat of the arbitration, regardless of where it was signed, despatched or delivered to any of the parties'. This repeats s 53 *apart* from the words 'unless otherwise agreed by the parties' which appear in that section, and states that the term 'seat of the arbitration' has the same meaning as in Part I, ie in s 3.

100.3

Section 100(3) confers power on Her Majesty by Order in Council to declare that a particular state is a party to the New York Convention. The section then goes beyond the terms of the corresponding provision in s 7(2) of the 1975 Act by providing that such a state may *also* be declared to be a party to the Convention in respect of any specified territory. This extension brings the legislation into line with art XI of the Convention which allows an acceding state to declare that the Convention shall extend to all or any of the territories for the international relations of which it is responsible. So long as the relevant Order is in force, it shall be conclusive evidence of the fact that the state in question is a party either in respect of itself or any specified territory for which it is responsible.

100.4

Section 100(4) confirms that the 'New York Convention' means the Convention on the Recognition and Enforcement of Foreign Arbitral Awards adopted by the United Nations Conference on International Commercial Arbitration on 10 June 1958. This replicates the corresponding provision in s 7(1) of the 1975 Act.

Section 101: Recognition and enforcement of awards

101.1

The wording of s 101(1) has its origins in s 3(2) of the 1975 Act. It provides that a New York Convention award shall be recognised as binding on the persons between whom it was made, and may accordingly be relied on by such persons by way of defence, set off or otherwise in any legal proceedings in England and Wales or Northern Ireland. The difference between this section and its predecessor in the 1975 Act lies in the fact that under this section, a New York Convention award must be recognised without separately looking at the question of its enforceability.

101.2

Section 101(2) and (3) substantially repeats the provisions of s 3(1) of the 1975 Act but contain no cross-references to Part I of the present Act. Section 101(2) provides that a New York Convention award may, by leave of the court, be enforced in the same manner as a judgment or order of the court to the same effect. Section 101(3) provides that where such leave is given, judgment may be entered in the terms set out in the award.

101.3

It will be noted that the definition of 'the court', by section 105(1), includes a county court. It is understood that there is no present intention that any action with regard to the enforcement of foreign awards will be referable to a county court, but it was considered that in the interests of flexibility the possibility should not be entirely excluded for the future.

Section 102: Evidence to be produced by party seeking recognition or enforcement

102.1

Section 102 sets out the documentary evidential requirements which a party seeking to enforce a New York Convention award must produce. Section 102(1) states that such a party must produce both the duly authenticated original award and the original arbitration agreement. A certified copy will serve as a sufficient substitute for either document. The term 'duly authenticated' relating to an original award presumably means that it must be signed, dated and have whatever else needs to be done to it to render it enforceable in the country in which it was made.

102.2

Section 102(2) reproduces s 4(c) of the 1975 Act in that it requires translation of an award or agreement in a foreign language. Such a translation must be certified by an official or sworn translator or by a diplomatic or consular agent.

Section 103: Refusal of recognition or enforcement

103.1

Section 103 implements arts V and VI of the New York Convention. Its basic premise is that a party seeking recognition or enforcement of a New York Convention award must have its application granted unless one or more of the circumstances set out in this section apply. In such a case the court may refuse to recognise or enforce the award. The circumstances described largely follow those set out in s 5(1) to (3) of the 1975 Act, save that they apply not only to the enforcement of awards, but also to their recognition. As such, the change from the wording of the previous legislation merely represents a polishing of the drafting and no substantial change is intended. Under the 1975 Act the presumed intention of a party coming to court was to enforce an award, and recognition is, therefore, recognition of an award which is enforceable. The present Act gives equal weight to the objective of recognition of the award on the one hand, and its enforcement on the other. It is implicit in the drafting that recognition can be an objective in its own right and is not necessarily a precursor to enforcement.

103.2

Section 103(1) states that '[r]ecognition or enforcement of a New York Convention award shall not be refused except in the following cases', which are then set out in the following subsections. Except as provided in those subsections, therefore, the court will have no discretion but to enforce the award provided that it is a New York Convention award within the definition set out in s 100. Contrast this with the general discretion given to the court as to the enforcement of awards under Part I of the Act as set out in s 66.

103.3

If the person against whom the award is invoked wishes to defeat the other party's application, he must prove at least one of the matters described in para (*a*) to (*f*) of s 103(2). These deal with incapacity; invalidity; lack of proper notice or inability to present a case; award differing from terms of submission to arbitration or being outside its scope; unlawful composition of arbitral tribunal, or procedure being in breach of contractual terms or unlawful; and an award not being binding on the parties, or having been suspended or set aside.

103.4

Section 103(3) gives the court discretion to refuse to enforce an award if it is 'in respect of a matter which is not capable of settlement by arbitration, or if it would be contrary to public policy to recognise or enforce the award'. The first part of this provision, relating to matters which are 'not capable of settlement by arbitration', is not strictly in compliance with the Convention. Article II 1 of the Convention only requires a state, and therefore a court, to recognise an arbitration agreement, and therefore enforce an award under it, which concerns 'a subject-matter capable of settlement by arbitration'. Since s 103(3) gives the court a discretion to refuse to enforce an award on this ground, it is theoretically possible that the court might decline to exercise that discretion in a particular case and enforce an award which, under the Convention, was not strictly referable to it in the first place. However, it is thought that this would be highly unlikely.

103.5

Section 103(4) permits a court to practice a certain amount of discretion in deciding to what extent it will recognise or enforce an award. If an award purports to decide matters which were not submitted to arbitration as well as those which were properly so submitted, it can recognise or enforce to the extent of those which were properly submitted, provided that they can be separated from those which exceeded the jurisdiction of the tribunal. This section follows the wording of s 5(4) of the 1975 Act.

103.6

Section 103(5) follows s 5(5) of the 1975 Act. It permits a court to adjourn a decision on the recognition or enforcement of an award where that award has been challenged in the courts of the country whose laws govern it. The party claiming recognition or enforcement may also apply to the court for an order requiring the other party to give suitable security for costs.

Section 104: Saving for other bases of recognition or enforcement

104.1

As in s 6 of the 1975 Act, s 104 preserves the rights of a party to rely upon or enforce a New York Convention award at common law or under s 66 of the Act.

Chapter 7

Part IV—General Provisions

Section 105: Meaning of 'the court': jurisdiction of High Court and county court

105.1

This section, inserted at Committee stage in the House of Commons, gives the Lord Chancellor power to order that certain matters referable to 'the court' throughout the Act may be referred to a county court rather than to the High Court. This is to be done by statutory instrument subject only to annulment by a resolution of either House of Parliament, so that for all intents and purposes the Lord Chancellor's decisions on the matter are likely to be regarded as final. The matter has been dealt with in this way since it was understood that it would not be possible for the necessary Rules of Court to be drafted and put into effect in time for the intended coming into force of the Act on 1 January 1997.

105.2

At the time of writing no order under this section has yet been promulgated, but it appears likely that when made it will ensure that applications to be made to, and actions to be taken by, 'the court' under the Act will, within certain limits yet to be defined, be dealt with in a county court rather than in the High Court, and may specify that only certain of the county courts should have jurisdiction. Until the order is issued, all such applications and actions will have to be made to, and be taken by, the High Court.

Section 106: Crown application

106.1

Section 106(1) provides that Part I of the Act applies to any arbitration agreement to which the Queen, either in right of the Crown or of the Duchy of Lancaster, or the Duke of Cornwall, ie the Prince of Wales, is a party.

106.2

Section 106(2) provides that when the Queen is a party otherwise than in right of the Crown, she shall be represented by the Chancellor of the Duchy or his appointee, or such person as the Queen may appoint.

106.3

Section 106(3) provides for the representation of the Duke of Cornwall when he is a party to an arbitration agreement. Section 106(4) states that references to a party/parties shall be construed according to s 106(2) and (3), ie to the persons representing the Queen or the Duke of Cornwall.

106.4

Part I of the Act binds the Crown. It is in much the same terms as the previous provision in s 30 of the 1950 Act. Section 30 stated, 'This part of this Act ... shall apply to any arbitration to which his Majesty, either in right of the Crown or of the Duchy of Lancaster or otherwise, or the Duke of Cornwall, is a party'. Note, however, that it has been expanded so as to provide for the case where the Queen is party to an arbitration agreement otherwise than in right of the Crown.

106.5

One of the authors is informed that many disputes which arise in connection with the Queen either in right of the Crown or otherwise, say, for example, relating to tenancies, employment contracts etc, are resolved by arbitration. This illustrates one of the great advantages of arbitration over litigation—privacy. If a problem has arisen on a royal estate concerning certain contract terms, for example, it is much better to have a private hearing which results in a final and binding award, away from media intervention.

Section 107: Consequential amendments and repeals

107.1

Section 107 is self-explanatory and simply states that consequential amendments to various statutes which provide in some way for arbitration, and repeals, are made by virtue of the Act. The amendments are set out in Sched 3 and the repeals are set out in Sched 4.

Section 108: Extent

108.1

Section 108(1) provides that the Act extends to England and Wales and, save as to exceptions set down in s 108(2,) to Northern Ireland. Section 108(2), excludes from Northern Ireland certain provisions which re-enact existing provisions applying to England and Wales only. The following relevant provisions of Part II are s 92 (exclusion of Part I in relation to small claims arbitration in the county court), and s 93 and Sched 2 which relate to the appointment of judges as arbitrators.

108.2

Section 108(3) and (4) apply to Scotland. Sections 89 to 91 relating to consumer arbitration agreements extend to Scotland, since it was considered invidious to exclude consumers in Scotland from the protection which they afford. Schedules 3 and 4 (consequential amendments and repeals) extend to Scotland so far as they relate to enactments which so extend, but the repeal of the Arbitration Act 1975 only extends to England, Wales and Northern Ireland.

108.3

The United Nations became involved in international arbitration as far back as 1958. In 1985 it published a Model Law for international commercial arbitration. Several countries adopted this. They tended to be those countries (for example Australia, Bulgaria, Canada) which had not developed a comprehensive body of arbitration laws, unlike England and Wales. It will be recalled that the DAC under the chairmanship of Lord Mustill in 1989 recommended that the UNCITRAL Model Law should not be adopted by the United Kingdom. However, it was adopted by Scotland. Thus the new provisions reflect that Scotland has separate legislation on arbitration.

Section 109: Commencement

109.1

Section 109(1) provides that the Secretary of State has a flexibility to order when the Act, or parts of it, are to come into force. He may, by s 109(2), make orders containing transitional provisions.

Section 110: Short title

110.1

Section 110 declares that the short title is the Arbitration Act 1996.

Chapter 8

Schedules

There are four Schedules to the Act. Schedule 1 sets out the mandatory provisions of Part I of the Act. This has already been referred to earlier in the text, in particular relating to s 4. Schedule 2 will be dealt with in more detail below. Schedule 3 lists the various amendments to be made to other Acts consequent upon enactment of the Act. These range from the Merchant Shipping Act 1894 to the Industrial Tribunal Act 1996. Most of the amendments are minor, for example, 'for "The Arbitration Act (Northern Ireland) 1937" substitute "Part I of the Arbitration Act 1996".' Some (for example, concerning The Insolvency Act 1986, where an insertion is made relating to arbitration agreements to which a bankrupt is a party) are more extensive. There are some 62 consequential amendments. Schedule 4 lists various Acts/Parts of Acts/Orders which are repealed by the Act. Some 47 Acts of Parliament or Orders are repealed in whole or in part. Of particular interest are the following:

(a)   the Arbitration Act (Northern Ireland) 1937—the whole Act is repealed;

(b)   the Arbitration Act 1950; Part I is repealed as is s 42(3) (this relates to the application of Part II of the 1950 Act to Northern Ireland)—note, however, that the whole of Part II which relates to the enforcement of certain foreign awards and the schedules which set out the Geneva and New York Conventions is still in force;

(c)   the Arbitration Act 1975—the whole Act is repealed;

(d)   the Arbitration Act 1979—the whole Act is repealed;

(e)   the Consumer Arbitration Agreements Act 1988—the whole Act is repealed.

Section 107(1) and (2), it may be recalled, are the relevant provisions which deal with the question of amendments and repeals.

Schedule 2—Modifications of Part I in relation to judge-arbitrators

It may be recalled that s 93 provides for the appointment of judges as arbitrators. Section 93(6) states that the provisions of Part I apply to arbitration before a person appointed under this section with the modifications specified in Sched 2. In other words, there are modifications where the arbitrator is a Commercial Court judge or official referee. The previous provisions were embodied in s 4(4) and (5) and Sched 3 to the Administration of Justice Act 1970. These have been superseded, as s 4 of, and Sched 3 to, the 1970 Act have been repealed.

It is unnecessary to go through the Schedule in any detail since it is written with the clarity and 'user-friendliness' which is such a distinguishing feature of the Act. The provisions of Sched 2 cover arbitrator's fees, exercise of court powers in support of the arbitration, extension of time for making an award, withholding the award in case of non-payment, correction of the award or additional award, costs, enforcement of the award, solicitors' costs, powers of the court in relation to service of documents and powers of the court to extend time limits relating to arbitral proceedings. A few examples of the schedule's provisions will suffice:

(1) Instead of applying to the court under s 28(2) for the adjustment of an arbitrator's fees, a party may ask the judge-arbitrator to do this.

(2) The powers of the court in support of the arbitration which are set out in ss 42–44 can be exercised by the High Court and also by the judge-arbitrator.

Section 56 confers on a tribunal a lien on its award to secure payment of its fees and for taxation of the fees demanded. Instead of applying to the court for payment of the fees and expenses into court, the application can be made to the judge-arbitrator who will be responsible for ordering what should happen.

Conclusion

This, then, is the Arbitration Act 1996. In concluding this study, in the authors' view, the Act represents a revolution in the whole approach to arbitration in England, Wales and Northern Ireland which should lead to its becoming again what it used to be and should be—a quick, efficient and cost-effective method of resolving disputes. It is hoped that the commentary may be of some help to parties, their advisers and to arbitrators, at home and abroad, as to how we see the Act working in practice, and may, to a modest extent, help to achieve the aim of those who drafted it.

Appendices

Appendix 1

Arbitration Act 1996

ARRANGEMENT OF SECTIONS

Part I   Arbitration pursuant to an arbitration agreement

Introductory

The arbitration agreement

Stay of legal proceedings

Commencement of arbitral proceedings

The arbitral tribunal

279

Jurisdiction of the arbitral tribunal

The arbitral proceedings

Powers of court in relation to arbitral proceedings

The award

Part II   Other provisions relating to arbitration

Domestic arbitration agreements

Consumer arbitration agreements

Small claims arbitration in the county court

Appointment of judges as arbitrators

Statutory arbitrations

Part III   Recognition and enforcement of certain foreign awards

Enforcement of Geneva Convention awards

Recognition and enforcement of New York Convention awards

An Act to restate and improve the law relating to arbitration pursuant to an arbitration agreement; to make other provision relating to arbitration and arbitration awards; and for connected purposes.

[17th June 1996]

Be it enacted by the Queen's most Excellent Majesty, by and with the advice and consent of the Lords Spiritual and Temporal, and Commons, in this present Parliament assembled, and by the authority of the same, as follows:—

Part I Arbitration pursuant to an arbitration agreement

Introductory

1 General principles

The provisions of this Part are founded on the following principles, and shall be construed accordingly—

(*a*) the object of arbitration is to obtain the fair resolution of disputes by an impartial tribunal without unnecessary delay or expense;

(*b*) the parties should be free to agree how their disputes are resolved, subject only to such safeguards as are necessary in the public interest;

283

(c) in matters governed by this Part the court should not intervene except as provided by this Part.

2 Scope of application of provisions

(1) The provisions of this Part apply where the seat of the arbitration is in England and Wales or Northern Ireland.

(2) The following sections apply even if the seat of the arbitration is outside England and Wales or Northern Ireland or no seat has been designated or determined—

(a) sections 9 to 11 (stay of legal proceedings, &c); and
(b) section 66 (enforcement of arbitral awards).

(3) The powers conferred by the following sections apply even if the seat of the arbitration is outside England and Wales or Northern Ireland or no seat has been designated or determined—

(a) section 43 (securing the attendance of witnesses), and
(b) section 44 (court powers exercisable in support of arbitral proceedings);

but the court may refuse to exercise any such power if, in the opinion of the court, the fact that the seat of the arbitration is outside England and Wales or Northern Ireland, or that when designated or determined the seat is likely to be outside England and Wales or Northern Ireland, makes it inappropriate to do so.

(4) The court may exercise a power conferred by any provision of this Part not mentioned in subsection (2) or (3) for the purpose of supporting the arbitral process where—

(a) no seat of the arbitration has been designated or determined, and
(b) by reason of a connection with England and Wales or Northern Ireland the court is satisfied that it is appropriate to do so.

(5) Section 7 (separability of arbitration agreement) and section 8 (death of a party) apply where the law applicable to the arbitration agreement is the law of England and Wales or Northern Ireland even if the seat of the arbitration is outside England and Wales or Northern Ireland or has not been designated or determined.

3 The seat of the arbitration

In this Part 'the seat of the arbitration' means the juridical seat of the arbitration designated—

(a) by the parties to the arbitration agreement, or
(b) by any arbitral or other institution or person vested by the parties with powers in that regard, or
(c) by the arbitral tribunal if so authorised by the parties,

or determined, in the absence of any such designation, having regard to the parties' agreement and all the relevant circumstances.

4 Mandatory and non-mandatory provisions

(1) The mandatory provisions of this Part are listed in Schedule 1 and have effect notwithstanding any agreement to the contrary.

(2) The other provisions of this Part (the 'non-mandatory provisions') allow the parties to make their own arrangements by agreement but provide rules which apply in the absence of such agreement.

(3) The parties may make such arrangements by agreeing to the application of institutional rules or providing any other means by which a matter may be decided.

(4) It is immaterial whether or not the law applicable to the parties' agreement is the law of England and Wales or, as the case may be, Northern Ireland.

(5) The choice of a law other than the law of England and Wales or Northern Ireland as the applicable law in respect of a matter provided for by a non-mandatory provision of this Part is equivalent to an agreement making provision about that matter.

For this purpose an applicable law determined in accordance with the parties' agreement, or which is objectively determined in the absence of any express or implied choice, shall be treated as chosen by the parties.

5 Agreements to be in writing

(1) The provisions of this Part apply only where the arbitration agreement is in writing, and any other agreement between the parties as to any matter is effective for the purposes of this Part only if in writing.

The expressions 'agreement', 'agree' and 'agreed' shall be construed accordingly.

(2) There is an agreement in writing—

(a) if the agreement is made in writing (whether or not it is signed by the parties),

(b) if the agreement is made by exchange of communications in writing, or

(c) if the agreement is evidenced in writing.

(3) Where parties agree otherwise than in writing by reference to terms which are in writing, they make an agreement in writing.

(4) An agreement is evidenced in writing if an agreement made otherwise than in writing is recorded by one of the parties, or by a third party, with the authority of the parties to the agreement.

(5) An exchange of written submissions in arbitral or legal proceedings in which the existence of an agreement otherwise than in writing is alleged by one party against another party and not denied by the other party in his response constitutes as between those parties an agreement in writing to the effect alleged.

(6) References in this Part to anything being written or in writing include its being recorded by any means.

The arbitration agreement

6 Definition of arbitration agreement

(1) In this Part an 'arbitration agreement' means an agreement to submit to arbitration present or future disputes (whether they are contractual or not).

(2) The reference in an agreement to a written form of arbitration clause or to a document containing an arbitration clause constitutes an arbitration agreement if the reference is such as to make that clause part of the agreement.

7 Separability of arbitration agreement

Unless otherwise agreed by the parties, an arbitration agreement which forms or was intended to form part of another agreement (whether or not in writing) shall not be regarded as invalid, non-existent or ineffective because that other agreement is invalid, or did not come into existence or has become ineffective, and it shall for that purpose be treated as a distinct agreement.

8 Whether agreement discharged by death of a party

(1) Unless otherwise agreed by the parties, an arbitration agreement is not discharged by the death of a party and may be enforced by or against the personal representatives of that party.

(2) Subsection (1) does not affect the operation of any enactment or rule of law by virtue of which a substantive right or obligation is extinguished by death.

Stay of legal proceedings

9 Stay of legal proceedings

(1) A party to an arbitration agreement against whom legal proceedings are brought (whether by way of claim or counterclaim) in respect of a matter which under the agreement is to be referred to arbitration may (upon notice to the other parties to the proceedings) apply to the court in which the proceedings have been brought to stay the proceedings so far as they concern that matter.

(2) An application may be made notwithstanding that the matter is to be referred to arbitration only after the exhaustion of other dispute resolution procedures.

(3) An application may not be made by a person before taking the appropriate procedural step (if any) to acknowledge the legal proceedings against him or after he has taken any step in those proceedings to answer the substantive claim.

(4) On an application under this section the court shall grant a stay unless satisfied that the arbitration agreement is null and void, inoperative, or incapable of being performed.

(5) If the court refuses to stay the legal proceedings, any provision that an award is a condition precedent to the bringing of legal proceedings in respect of any matter is of no effect in relation to those proceedings.

10 Reference of interpleader issue to arbitration

(1) Where in legal proceedings relief by way of interpleader is granted and any issue between the claimants is one in respect of which there is an arbitration agreement between them, the court granting the relief shall direct that the issue be determined in accordance with the agreement unless the circumstances are such that proceedings brought by a claimant in respect of the matter would not be stayed.

(2) Where subsection (1) applies but the court does not direct that the issue be determined in accordance with the arbitration agreement, any provision that an award is a condition precedent to the bringing of legal proceedings in respect of any matter shall not affect the determination of that issue by the court.

11 Retention of security where Admiralty proceedings stayed

(1) Where Admiralty proceedings are stayed on the ground that the dispute in question should be submitted to arbitration, the court granting the stay may, if in those proceedings property has been arrested or bail or other security has been given to prevent or obtain release from arrest—

    (a)   order that the property arrested be retained as security for the satisfaction of any award given in the arbitration in respect of that dispute, or

    (b)   order that the stay of those proceedings be conditional on the provision of equivalent security for the satisfaction of any such award.

(2) Subject to any provision made by rules of court and to any necessary modifications, the same law and practice shall apply in relation to property retained in pursuance of an order as would apply if it were held for the purposes of proceedings in the court making the order.

Commencement of arbitral proceedings

12 Power of court to extend time for beginning arbitral proceedings, &c

(1) Where an arbitration agreement to refer future disputes to arbitration provides that a claim shall be barred, or the claimant's right extinguished, unless the claimant takes within a time fixed by the agreement some step—

    (a)   to begin arbitral proceedings, or

    (b)   to begin other dispute resolution procedures which must be exhausted before arbitral proceedings can be begun,

the court may by order extend the time for taking that step.

(2) Any party to the arbitration agreement may apply for such an order (upon notice to the other parties), but only after a claim has arisen and after exhausting any available arbitral process for obtaining an extension of time.

(3) The court shall make an order only if satisfied—

    (*a*)   that the circumstances are such as were outside the reasonable contemplation of the parties when they agreed the provision in question, and that it would be just to extend the time, or

    (*b*)   that the conduct of one party makes it unjust to hold the other party to the strict terms of the provision in question.

(4) The court may extend the time for such period and on such terms as it thinks fit, and may do so whether or not the time previously fixed (by agreement or by a previous order) has expired.

(5) An order under this section does not affect the operation of the Limitation Acts (see section 13).

(6) The leave of the court is required for any appeal from a decision of the court under this section.

13   Application of Limitation Acts

(1) The Limitation Acts apply to arbitral proceedings as they apply to legal proceedings.

(2) The court may order that in computing the time prescribed by the Limitation Acts for the commencement of proceedings (including arbitral proceedings) in respect of a dispute which was the subject matter—

    (*a*)   of an award which the court orders to be set aside or declares to be of no effect, or

    (*b*)   of the affected part of an award which the court orders to be set aside in part, or declares to be in part of no effect,

the period between the commencement of the arbitration and the date of the order referred to in paragraph (*a*) or (*b*) shall be excluded.

(3) In determining for the purposes of the Limitation Acts when a cause of action accrued, any provision that an award is a condition precedent to the bringing of legal proceedings in respect of a matter to which an arbitration agreement applies shall be disregarded.

(4) In this Part 'the Limitation Acts' means—

    (*a*)   in England and Wales, the Limitation Act 1980, the Foreign Limitation Periods Act 1984 and any other enactment (whenever passed) relating to the limitation of actions;

    (*b*)   in Northern Ireland, the Limitation (Northern Ireland) Order 1989, the Foreign Limitation Periods (Northern Ireland) Order 1985 and any other enactment (whenever passed) relating to the limitation of actions.

14   Commencement of arbitral proceeding.

(1) The parties are free to agree when arbitral proceedings are to be regarded as commenced for the purposes of this Part and for the purposes of the Limitation Acts.

(2) If there is no such agreement the following provisions apply.

(3) Where the arbitrator is named or designated in the arbitration agree-

ment, arbitral proceedings are commenced in respect of a matter when one party serves on the other party or parties a notice in writing requiring him or them to submit that matter to the person so named or designated.

(4) Where the arbitrator or arbitrators are to be appointed by the parties, arbitral proceedings are commenced in respect of a matter when one party serves on the other party or parties notice in writing requiring him or them to appoint an arbitrator or to agree to the appointment of an arbitrator in respect of that matter.

(5) Where the arbitrator or arbitrators are to be appointed by a person other than a party to the proceedings, arbitral proceedings are commenced in respect of a matter when one party gives notice in writing to that person requesting him to make the appointment in respect of that matter.

The arbitral tribunal

15 The arbitral tribunal

(1) The parties are free to agree on the number of arbitrators to form the tribunal and whether there is to be a chairman or umpire.

(2) Unless otherwise agreed by the parties, an agreement that the number of arbitrators shall be two or any other even number shall be understood as requiring the appointment of an additional arbitrator as chairman of the tribunal.

(3) If there is no agreement as to the number of arbitrators, the tribunal shall consist of a sole arbitrator.

16 Procedure for appointment of arbitrators

(1) The parties are free to agree on the procedure for appointing the arbitrator or arbitrators, including the procedure for appointing any chairman or umpire.

(2) If or to the extent that there is no such agreement, the following provisions apply.

(3) If the tribunal is to consist of a sole arbitrator, the parties shall jointly appoint the arbitrator not later than 28 days after service of a request in writing by either party to do so.

(4) If the tribunal is to consist of two arbitrators, each party shall appoint one arbitrator not later than 14 days after service of a request in writing by either party to do so.

(5) If the tribunal is to consist of three arbitrators—

    (a)   each party shall appoint one arbitrator not later than 14 days after service of a request in writing by either party to do so, and

    (b)   the two so appointed shall forthwith appoint a third arbitrator as the chairman of the tribunal.

(6) If the tribunal is to consist of two arbitrators and an umpire—

    (a)   each party shall appoint one arbitrator not later than 14 days

(b)   after service of a request in writing by either party to do so, and the two so appointed may appoint an umpire at any time after they themselves are appointed and shall do so before any substantive hearing or forthwith if they cannot agree on a matter relating to the arbitration.

(7) In any other case (in particular, if there are more than two parties) section 18 applies as in the case of a failure of the agreed appointment procedure.

17   Power in case of default to appoint sole arbitrator

(1) Unless the parties otherwise agree, where each of two parties to an arbitration agreement is to appoint an arbitrator and one party ('the party in default') refuses to do so, or fails to do so within the time specified, the other party, having duly appointed his arbitrator, may give notice in writing to the party in default that he proposes to appoint his arbitrator to act as sole arbitrator.

(2) If the party in default does not within 7 clear days of that notice being given—

(a)   make the required appointment, and
(b)   notify the other party that he has done so,

the other party may appoint his arbitrator as sole arbitrator whose award shall be binding on both parties as if he had been so appointed by agreement.

(3) Where a sole arbitrator has been appointed under subsection (2), the party in default may (upon notice to the appointing party) apply to the court which may set aside the appointment.

(4) The leave of the court is required for any appeal from a decision of the court under this section.

18   Failure of appointment procedure

(1) The parties are free to agree what is to happen in the event of a failure of the procedure for the appointment of the arbitral tribunal.

There is no failure if an appointment is duly made under section 17 (power in case of default to appoint sole arbitrator), unless that appointment is set aside.

(2) If or to the extent that there is no such agreement any party to the arbitration agreement may (upon notice to the other parties) apply to the court to exercise its powers under this section.

(3) Those powers are—

(a)   to give directions as to the making of any necessary appointments;
(b)   to direct that the tribunal shall be constituted by such appointments (or any one or more of them) as have been made;
(c)   to revoke any appointments already made;
(d)   to make any necessary appointments itself.

(4) An appointment made by the court under this section has effect as if made with the agreement of the parties.

(5) The leave of the court is required for any appeal from a decision of the court under this section.

19 Court to have regard to agreed qualifications

In deciding whether to exercise, and in considering how to exercise, any of its powers under section 16 (procedure for appointment of arbitrators) or section 18 (failure of appointment procedure), the court shall have due regard to any agreement of the parties as to the qualifications required of the arbitrators.

20 Chairman

(1) Where the parties have agreed that there is to be a chairman, they are free to agree what the functions of the chairman are to be in relation to the making of decisions, orders and awards.

(2) If or to the extent that there is no such agreement, the following provisions apply.

(3) Decisions, orders and awards shall be made by all or a majority of the arbitrators (including the chairman).

(4) The view of the chairman shall prevail in relation to a decision, order or award in respect of which there is neither unanimity nor a majority under subsection (3).

21 Umpire

(1) Where the parties have agreed that there is to be an umpire, they are free to agree what the functions of the umpire are to be, and in particular—

  (a) whether he is to attend the proceedings, and

  (b) when he is to replace the other arbitrators as the tribunal with power to make decisions, orders and awards.

(2) If or to the extent that there is no such agreement, the following provisions apply.

(3) The umpire shall attend the proceedings and be supplied with the same documents and other materials as are supplied to the other arbitrators.

(4) Decisions, orders and awards shall be made by the other arbitrators unless and until they cannot agree on a matter relating to the arbitration.

In that event they shall forthwith give notice in writing to the parties and the umpire, whereupon the umpire shall replace them as the tribunal with power to make decisions, orders and awards as if he were sole arbitrator.

(5) If the arbitrators cannot agree but fail to give notice of that fact, or if any of them fails to join in the giving of notice, any party to the arbitral proceedings may (upon notice to the other parties and to the tribunal) apply to the court which may order that the umpire shall replace the

other arbitrators as the tribunal with power to make decisions, orders and awards as if he were sole arbitrator.

(6) The leave of the court is required for any appeal from a decision of the court under this section.

22 Decision-making where no chairman or umpire

(1) Where the parties agree that there shall be two or more arbitrators with no chairman or umpire, the parties are free to agree how the tribunal is to make decisions, orders and awards.

(2) If there is no such agreement, decisions, orders and awards shall be made by all or a majority of the arbitrators.

23 Revocation of arbitrator's authority

(1) The parties are free to agree in what circumstances the authority of an arbitrator may be revoked.

(2) If or to the extent that there is no such agreement the following provisions apply.

(3) The authority of an arbitrator may not be revoked except—

(a)   by the parties acting jointly, or

(b)   by an arbitral or other institution or person vested by the parties with powers in that regard.

(4) Revocation of the authority of an arbitrator by the parties acting jointly must be agreed in writing unless the parties also agree (whether or not in writing) to terminate the arbitration agreement.

(5) Nothing in this section affects the power of the court—

(a)   to revoke an appointment under section 18 (powers exercisable in case of failure of appointment procedure), or

(b)   to remove an arbitrator on the grounds specified in section 24.

24 Power of court to remove arbitrator

(1) A party to arbitral proceedings may (upon notice to the other parties, to the arbitrator concerned and to any other arbitrator) apply to the court to remove an arbitrator on any of the following grounds—

(a)   that circumstances exist that give rise to justifiable doubts as to his impartiality;

(b)   that he does not possess the qualifications required by the arbitration agreement;

(c)   that he is physically or mentally incapable of conducting the proceedings or there are justifiable doubts as to his capacity to do so;

(d)   that he has refused or failed—

(i)   properly to conduct the proceedings, or

(ii)   to use all reasonable despatch in conducting the proceedings or making an award,

and that substantial injustice has been or will be caused to the applicant.

(2) If there is an arbitral or other institution or person vested by the

parties with power to remove an arbitrator, the court shall not exercise its power of removal unless satisfied that the applicant has first exhausted any available recourse to that institution or person.

(3) The arbitral tribunal may continue the arbitral proceedings and make an award while an application to the court under this section is pending.

(4) Where the court removes an arbitrator, it may make such order as it thinks fit with respect to his entitlement (if any) to fees or expenses, or the repayment of any fees or expenses already paid.

(5) The arbitrator concerned is entitled to appear and be heard by the court before it makes any order under this section.

(6) The leave of the court is required for any appeal from a decision of the court under this section.

25 Resignation of arbitrator

(1) The parties are free to agree with an arbitrator as to the consequences of his resignation as regards—

(a)   his entitlement (if any) to fees or expenses, and

(b)   any liability thereby incurred by him.

(2) If or to the extent that there is no such agreement the following provisions apply.

(3) An arbitrator who resigns his appointment may (upon notice to the parties) apply to the court—

(a)   to grant him relief from any liability thereby incurred by him, and

(b)   to make such order as it thinks fit with respect to his entitlement (if any) to fees or expenses or the repayment of any fees or expenses already paid.

(4) If the court is satisfied that in all the circumstances it was reasonable for the arbitrator to resign, it may grant such relief as is mentioned in subsection (3)(a) on such terms as it thinks fit.

(5) The leave of the court is required for any appeal from a decision of the court under this section.

26 Death of arbitrator or person appointing him

(1) The authority of an arbitrator is personal and ceases on his death.

(2) Unless otherwise agreed by the parties, the death of the person by whom an arbitrator was appointed does not revoke the arbitrator's authority.

27 Filling of vacancy, &c

(1) Where an arbitrator ceases to hold office, the parties are free to agree—

(a)   whether and if so how the vacancy is to be filled,

(b)   whether and if so to what extent the previous proceedings should stand, and

(c)   what effect (if any) his ceasing to hold office has on any appointment made by him (alone or jointly).

293

(2) If or to the extent that there is no such agreement, the following provisions apply.

(3) The provisions of sections 16 (procedure for appointment of arbitrators) and 18 (failure of appointment procedure) apply in relation to the filling of the vacancy as in relation to an original appointment.

(4) The tribunal (when reconstituted) shall determine whether and if so to what extent the previous proceedings should stand.

This does not affect any right of a party to challenge those proceedings on any ground which had arisen before the arbitrator ceased to hold office.

(5) His ceasing to hold office does not affect any appointment by him (alone or jointly) of another arbitrator, in particular any appointment of a chairman or umpire.

28 Joint and several liability of parties to arbitrators for fees and expenses

(1) The parties are jointly and severally liabie to pay to the arbitrators such reasonable fees and expenses (if any) as are appropriate in the circumstances.

(2) Any party may apply to the court (upon notice to the other parties and to the arbitrators) which may order that the amount of the arbitrators' fees and expenses shall be considered and adjusted by such means and upon such terms as it may direct.

(3) If the application is made after any amount has been paid to the arbitrators by way of fees or expenses, the court may order the repayment of such amount (if any) as is shown to be excessive, but shall not do so unless it is shown that it is reasonable in the circumstances to order repayment.

(4) The above provisions have effect subject to any order of the court under section 24(4) or 25(3)(*b*) (order as to entitlement to fees or expenses in case of removal or resignation of arbitrator).

(5) Nothing in this section affects any liability of a party to any other party to pay all or any of the costs of the arbitration (see sections 59 to 65) or any contractual right of an arbitrator to payment of his fees and expenses.

(6) In this section references to arbitrators include an arbitrator who has ceased to act and an umpire who has not replaced the other arbitrators.

29 Immunity of arbitrator

(1) An arbitrator is not liable for anything done or omitted in the discharge or purported discharge of his functions as arbitrator unless the act or omission is shown to have been in bad faith.

(2) Subsection (1) applies to an employee or agent of an arbitrator as it applies to the arbitrator himself.

(3) This section does not affect any liability incurred by an arbitrator by reason of his resigning (but see section 25).

Jurisdiction of the arbitral tribunal

30 Competence of tribunal to rule on its own jurisdiction

(1) Unless otherwise agreed by the parties, the arbitral tribunal may rule on its own substantive jurisdiction, that is, as to—

- (a) whether there is a valid arbitration agreement,
- (b) whether the tribunal is properly constituted, and
- (c) what matters have been submitted to arbitration in accordance with the arbitration agreement.

(2) Any such ruling may be challenged by any available arbitral process of appeal or review or in accordance with the provisions of this Part.

31 Objection to substantive jurisdiction of tribunal

(1) An objection that the arbitral tribunal lacks substantive jurisdiction at the outset of the proceedings must be raised by a party not later than the time he takes the first step in the proceedings to contest the merits of any matter in relation to which he challenges the tribunal's jurisdiction.

A party is not precluded from raising such an objection by the fact that he has appointed or participated in the appointment of an arbitrator.

(2) Any objection during the course of the arbitral proceedings that the arbitral tribunal is exceeding its substantive jurisdiction must be made as soon as possible after the matter alleged to be beyond its jurisdiction is raised.

(3) The arbitral tribunal may admit an objection later than the time specified in subsection (1) or (2) if it considers the delay justified.

(4) Where an objection is duly taken to the tribunal's substantive jurisdiction and the tribunal has power to rule on its own jurisdiction, it may—

- (a) rule on the matter in an award as to jurisdiction, or
- (b) deal with the objection in its award on the merits.

If the parties agree which of these courses the tribunal should take, the tribunal shall proceed accordingly.

(5) The tribunal may in any case, and shall if the parties so agree, stay proceedings whilst an application is made to the court under section 32 (determination of preliminary point of jurisdiction).

32 Determination of preliminary point of jurisdiction

(1) The court may, on the application of a party to arbitral proceedings (upon notice to the other parties), determine any question as to the substantive jurisdiction of the tribunal.

A party may lose the right to object (see section 73).

(2) An application under this section shall not be considered unless—

- (a) it is made with the agreement in writing of all the other parties to the proceedings, or

(*b*) it is made with the permission of the tribunal and the court is satisfied—
  (i) that the determination of the question is likely to produce substantial savings in costs,
  (ii) that the application was made without delay, and
  (iii) that there is good reason why the matter should be decided by the court.

(3) An application under this section, unless made with the agreement of all the other parties to the proceedings, shall state the grounds on which it is said that the matter should be decided by the court.

(4) Unless otherwise agreed by the parties, the arbitral tribunal may continue the arbitral proceedings and make an award while an application to the court under this section is pending.

(5) Unless the court gives leave, no appeal lies from a decision of the court whether the conditions specified in subsection (2) are met.

(6) The decision of the court on the question of jurisdiction shall be treated as a judgment of the court for the purposes of an appeal.

But no appeal lies without the leave of the court which shall not be given unless the court considers that the question involves a point of law which is one of general importance or is one which for some other special reason should be considered by the Court of Appeal.

The arbitral proceedings

33 General duty of the tribunal
(1) The tribunal shall—
  (*a*) act fairly and impartially as between the parties, giving each party a reasonable opportunity of putting his case and dealing with that of his opponent, and
  (*b*) adopt procedures suitable to the circumstances of the particular case, avoiding unnecessary delay or expense, so as to provide a fair means for the resolution of the matters falling to be determined.

(2) The tribunal shall comply with that general duty in conducting the arbitral proceedings, in its decisions on matters of procedure and evidence and in the exercise of all other powers conferred on it.

34 Procedural and evidential matters
(1) It shall be for the tribunal to decide all procedural and evidential matters, subject to the right of the parties to agree any matter.
(2) Procedural and evidential matters include—

  (*a*) when and where any part of the proceedings is to be held;
  (*b*) the language or languages to be used in the proceedings and whether translations of any relevant documents are to be supplied;
  (*c*) whether any and if so what form of written statements of claim and defence are to be used, when these should be sup-

plied and the extent to which such statements can be later amended;

(d)   whether any and if so which documents or classes of documents should be disclosed between and produced by the parties and at what stage;

(e)   whether any and if so what questions should be put to and answered by the respective parties and when and in what form this should be done;

(f)   whether to apply strict rules of evidence (or any other rules) as to the admissibility, relevance or weight of any material (oral, written or other) sought to be tendered on any matters of fact or opinion, and the time, manner and form in which such material should be exchanged and presented;

(g)   whether and to what extent the tribunal should itself take the initiative in ascertaining the facts and the law;

(h)   whether and to what extent there should be oral or written evidence or submissions.

(3) The tribunal may fix the time within which any directions given by it are to be complied with, and may if it thinks fit extend the time so fixed (whether or not it has expired).

35 Consolidation of proceedings and concurrent hearings

(1) The parties are free to agree—

(a)   that the arbitral proceedings shall be consolidated with other arbitral proceedings, or

(b)   that concurrent hearings shall be held,

on such terms as may be agreed.

(2) Unless the parties agree to confer such power on the tribunal, the tribunal has no power to order consolidation of proceedings or concurrent hearings.

36 Legal or other representation

Unless otherwise agreed by the parties, a party to arbitral proceedings may be represented in the proceedings by a lawyer or other person chosen by him.

37 Power to appoint experts, legal advisers or assessors

(1) Unless otherwise agreed by the parties—

(a)   the tribunal may—

(i)   appoint experts or legal advisers to report to it and the parties, or

(ii)   appoint assessors to assist it on technical matters,

and may allow any such expert, legal adviser or assessor to attend the proceedings; and

(b)   the parties shall be given a reasonable opportunity to comment on any information, opinion or advice offered by any such person.

(2) The fees and expenses of an expert, legal adviser or assessor appointed by the tribunal for which the arbitrators are liable are expenses of   the
arbitrators for the purposes of this Part.

38 General powers exercisable by the tribunal
(1) The parties are free to agree on the powers exercisable by the arbitral tribunal for the purposes of and in relation to the proceedings.

(2) Unless otherwise agreed by the parties the tribunal has the following powers.

(3) The tribunal may order a claimant to provide security for the costs of the arbitration.

This power shall not be exercised on the ground that the claimant is—

(a)   an individual ordinarily resident outside the United Kingdom, or

(b)   a corporation or association incorporated or formed under the law of a country outside the United Kingdom, or whose central management and control is exercised outside the United Kingdom.

(4) The tribunal may give directions in relation to any property which is the subject of the proceedings or as to which any question arises in the proceedings, and which is owned by or is in the possession of a party to the proceedings—

(a)   for the inspection, photographing, preservation, custody or detention of the property by the tribunal, an expert or a party, or

(b)   ordering that samples be taken from, or any observation be made of or experiment conducted upon, the property.

(5) The tribunal may direct that a party or witness shall be examined on oath or affirmation, and may for that purpose administer any necessary oath or take any necessary affirmation.

(6) The tribunal may give directions to a party for the preservation for the purposes of the proceedings of any evidence in his custody or control.

39 Power to make provisional awards
(1) The parties are free to agree that the tribunal shall have power to order on a provisional basis any relief which it would have power to grant in a final award.

(2) This includes, for instance, making—

(a)   a provisional order for the payment of money or the disposition of property as between the parties, or

(b)   an order to make an interim payment on account of the costs of the arbitration.

(3) Any such order shall be subject to the tribunal's final adjudication; and the tribunal's final award, on the merits or as to costs, shall take account of any such order.

(4) Unless the parties agree to confer such power on the tribunal, the tribunal has no such power.

This does not affect its powers under section 47 (awards on different issues, &c).

40 General duty of parties

(1) The parties shall do all things necessary for the proper and expeditious conduct of the arbitral proceedings.

(2) This includes—

> (a) complying without delay with any determination of the tribunal as to procedural or evidential matters, or with any order or directions of the tribunal, and
>
> (b) where appropriate, taking without delay any necessary steps to obtain a decision of the court on a preliminary question of jurisdiction or law (see sections 32 and 45).

41 Powers of tribunal in case of party's default

(1) The parties are free to agree on the powers of the tribunal in case of a party's failure to do something necessary for the proper and expeditious conduct of the arbitration.

(2) Unless otherwise agreed by the parties, the following provisions apply.

(3) If the tribunal is satisfied that there has been inordinate and inexcusable delay on the part of the claimant in pursuing his claim and that the delay—

> (a) gives rise, or is likely to give rise, to a substantial risk that it is not possible to have a fair resolution of the issues in that claim, or
>
> (b) has caused, or is likely to cause, serious prejudice to the respondent,

the tribunal may make an award dismissing the claim.

(4) If without showing sufficient cause a party—

> (a) fails to attend or be represented at an oral hearing of which due notice was given, or
>
> (b) where matters are to be dealt with in writing, fails after due notice to submit written evidence or make written submissions,

the tribunal may continue the proceedings in the absence of that party or, as the case may be, without any written evidence or submissions on his behalf, and may make an award on the basis of the evidence before it.

(5) If without showing sufficient cause a party fails to comply with any order or directions of the tribunal, the tribunal may make a peremptory order to the same effect, prescribing such time for compliance with it as the tribunal considers appropriate.

(6) If a claimant fails to comply with a peremptory order of the tribunal

to provide security for costs, the tribunal may make an award dismissing his claim.

(7) If a party fails to comply with any other kind of peremptory order, then, without prejudice to section 42 (enforcement by court of tribunal's peremptory orders), the tribunal may do any of the following—

    (*a*)   direct that the party in default shall not be entitled to rely upon any allegation or material which was the subject matter of the order:

    (*b*)   draw such adverse inferences from the act of non-compliance as the circumstances justify;

    (*c*)   proceed to an award on the basis of such materials as have been properly provided to it;

    (*d*)   make such order as it thinks fit as to the payment of costs of the arbitration incurred in consequence of the non-compliance.

Powers of court in relation to arbitral proceedings

42 Enforcement of peremptory orders of tribunal

(1) Unless otherwise agreed by the parties, the court may make an order requiring a party to comply with a peremptory order made by the tribunal.

(2) An application for an order under this section may be made—

    (*a*)   by the tribunal (upon notice to the parties),

    (*b*)   by a party to the arbitral proceedings with the permission of the tribunal (and upon notice to the other parties), or

    (*c*)   where the parties have agreed that the powers of the court under this section shall be available.

(3) The court shall not act unless it is satisfied that the applicant has exhausted any available arbitral process in respect of failure to comply with the tribunal's order.

(4) No order shall be made under this section unless the court is satisfied that the person to whom the tribunal's order was directed has failed to comply with it within the time prescribed in the order or, if no time was prescribed, within a reasonable time.

(5) The leave of the court is required for any appeal from a decision of the court under this section.

43 Securing the attendance of witnesses

(1) A party to arbitral proceedings may use the same court procedures as are available in relation to legal proceedings to secure the attendance before the tribunal of a witness in order to give oral testimony or to produce documents or other material evidence.

(2) This may only be done with the permission of the tribunal or the agreement of the other parties.

(3) The court procedures may only be used if—

(a)   the witness is in the United Kingdom, and
(b)   the arbitral proceedings are being conducted in England and Wales or, as the case may be, Northern Ireland.

(4) A person shall not be compelled by virtue of this section to produce any document or other material evidence which he could not be compelled to produce in legal proceedings.

44 Court powers exercisable in support of arbitral proceedings

(1) Unless otherwise agreed by the parties, the court has for the purposes of and in relation to arbitral proceedings the same power of making orders about the matters listed below as it has for the purposes of and in relation to legal proceedings.

(2) Those matters are—

(a)   the taking of the evidence of witnesses;
(b)   the preservation of evidence;
(c)   making orders relating to property which is the subject of the proceedings or as to which any question arises in the proceedings—
   (i)   for the inspection, photographing, preservation, custody or detention of the property, or
   (ii)   ordering that samples be taken from, or any observation be made of or experiment conducted upon, the property;
   and for that purpose authorising any person to enter any premises in the possession or control of a party to the arbitration;
(d)   the sale of any goods the subject of the proceedings;
(e)   the granting of an interim injunction or the appointment of a receiver.

(3) If the case is one of urgency, the court may, on the application of a party or proposed party to the arbitral proceedings, make such orders as it thinks necessary for the purpose of preserving evidence or assets.

(4) If the case is not one of urgency, the court shall act only on the application of a party to the arbitral proceedings (upon notice to the other parties and to the tribunal) made with the permission of the tribunal or the agreement in writing of the other parties.

(5) In any case the court shall act only if or to the extent that the arbitral tribunal, and any arbitral or other institution or person vested by the parties with power in that regard, has no power or is unable for the time being to act effectively.

(6) If the court so orders, an order made by it under this section shall cease to have effect in whole or in part on the order of the tribunal or of any such arbitral or other institution or person having power to act in relation to the subject-matter of the order.

(7) The leave of the court is required for any appeal from a decision of the court under this section.

45 Determination of preliminary point of law

(1) Unless otherwise agreed by the parties, the court may on the application of a party to arbitral proceedings (upon notice to the other parties) determine any question of law arising in the course of the proceedings which the court is satisfied substantially affects the rights of one or more of the parties.

An agreement to dispense with reasons for the tribunal's award shall be considered an agreement to exclude the court's jurisdiction under this section.

(2) An application under this section shall not be considered unless—

    (*a*)   it is made with the agreement of all the other parties to the proceedings, or

    (*b*)   it is made with the permission of the tribunal and the court is satisfied—

        (i)   that the determination of the question is likely to produce substantial savings in costs, and

        (ii)   that the application was made without delay.

(3) The application shall identify the question of law to be determined and, unless made with the agreement of all the other parties to the proceedings, shall state the grounds on which it is said that the question should be decided by the court.

(4) Unless otherwise agreed by the parties, the arbitral tribunal may continue the arbitral proceedings and make an award while an application to the court under this section is pending.

(5) Unless the court gives leave, no appeal lies from a decision of the court whether the conditions specified in subsection (2) are met.

(6) The decision of the court on the question of law shall be treated as a judgment of the court for the purposes of an appeal.

But no appeal lies without the leave of the court which shall not be given unless the court considers that the question is one of general importance, or is one which for some other special reason should be considered by the Court of Appeal.

The award

46 Rules applicable to substance of dispute

(1) The arbitral tribunal shall decide the dispute—

    (*a*)   in accordance with the law chosen by the parties as applicable to the substance of the dispute, or

    (*b*)   if the parties so agree, in accordance with such other considerations as are agreed by them or determined by the tribunal.

(2) For this purpose the choice of the laws of a country shall be understood to refer to the substantive laws of that country and not its conflict of laws rules.

(3) If or to the extent that there is no such choice or agreement, the tribu-

nal shall apply the law determined by the conflict of laws rules which it considers applicable.

47 Awards on different issues, &c

(1) Unless otherwise agreed by the parties, the tribunal may make more than one award at different times on different aspects of the matters to be determined.

(2) The tribunal may, in particular, make an award relating—

(a) to an issue affecting the whole claim, or

(b) to a part only of the claims or cross-claims submitted to it for decision.

(3) If the tribunal does so, it shall specify in its award the issue, or the claim or part of a claim, which is the subject matter of the award.

48 Remedies

(1) The parties are free to agree on the powers exercisable by the arbitral tribunal as regards remedies.

(2) Unless otherwise agreed by the parties, the tribunal has the following powers.

(3) The tribunal may make a declaration as to any matter to be determined in the proceedings.

(4) The tribunal may order the payment of a sum of money, in any currency.

(5) The tribunal has the same powers as the court—

(a) to order a party to do or refrain from doing anything;

(b) to order specific performance of a contract (other than a contract relating to land);

(c) to order the rectification, setting aside or cancellation of a deed or other document.

49 Interest

(1) The parties are free to agree on the powers of the tribunal as regards the award of interest.

(2) Unless otherwise agreed by the parties the following provisions apply.

(3) The tribunal may award simple or compound interest from such dates, at such rates and with such rests as it considers meets the justice of the case—

(a) on the whole or part of any amount awarded by the tribunal, in respect of any period up to the date of the award;

(b) on the whole or part of any amount claimed in the arbitration and outstanding at the commencement of the arbitral proceedings but paid before the award was made, in respect of any period up to the date of payment.

(4) The tribunal may award simple or compound interest from the date of the award (or any later date) until payment, at such rates and with

such rests as it considers meets the justice of the case, on the outstanding amount of any award (including any award of interest under subsection (3) and any award as to costs).

(5) References in this section to an amount awarded by the tribunal include an amount payable in consequence of a declaratory award by the tribunal.

(6) The above provisions do not affect any other power of the tribunal to award interest.

50 Extension of time for making award

(1) Where the time for making an award is limited by or in pursuance of the arbitration agreement, then, unless otherwise agreed by the parties, the court may in accordance with the following provisions by order extend that time.

(2) An application for an order under this section may be made—

(a)   by the tribunal (upon notice to the parties), or

(b)   by any party to the proceedings (upon notice to the tribunal and the other parties),

but only after exhausting any available arbitral process for obtaining an extension of time.

(3) The court shall only make an order if satisfied that a substantial injustice would otherwise be done.

(4) The court may extend the time for such period and on such terms as it thinks fit, and may do so whether or not the time previously fixed (by or under the agreement or by a previous order) has expired.

(5) The leave of the court is required for any appeal from a decision of the court under this section.

51 Settlement

(1) If during arbitral proceedings the parties settle the dispute, the following provisions apply unless otherwise agreed by the parties.

(2) The tribunal shall terminate the substantive proceedings and, if so requested by the parties and not objected to by the tribunal, shall record the settlement in the form of an agreed award.

(3) An agreed award shall state that it is an award of the tribunal and shall have the same status and effect as any other award on the merits of the case.

(4) The following provisions of this Part relating to awards (sections 52 to 58) apply to an agreed award.

(5) Unless the parties have also settled the matter of the payment of the costs of the arbitration, the provisions of this Part relating to costs (sections 59 to 65) continue to apply.

52 Form of award

(1) The parties are free to agree on the form of an award.

(2) If or to the extent that there is no such agreement, the following provisions apply.

(3) The award shall be in writing signed by all the arbitrators or all those assenting to the award.

(4) The award shall contain the reasons for the award unless it is an agreed award or the parties have agreed to dispense with reasons.

(5) The award shall state the seat of the arbitration and the date when the award is made.

53 Place where award treated as made

Unless otherwise agreed by the parties, where the seat of the arbitration is in England and Wales or Northern Ireland, any award in the proceedings shall be treated as made there, regardless of where it was signed, despatched or delivered to any of the parties.

54 Date of award

(1) Unless otherwise agreed by the parties, the tribunal may decide what is to be taken to be the date on which the award was made.

(2) In the absence of any such decision, the date of the award shall be taken to be the date on which it is signed by the arbitrator or, where more than one arbitrator signs the award, by the last of them.

55 Notification of award

(1) The parties are free to agree on the requirements as to notification of the award to the parties.

(2) If there is no such agreement, the award shall be notified to the parties by service on them of copies of the award, which shall be done without delay after the award is made.

(3) Nothing in this section affects section 56 (power to withhold award in case of non-payment).

56 Power to withhold award in case of non-payment

(1) The tribunal may refuse to deliver an award to the parties except upon full payment of the fees and expenses of the arbitrators.

(2) If the tribunal refuses on that ground to deliver an award, a party to the arbitral proceedings may (upon notice to the other parties and the tribunal) apply to the court, which may order that—

(a) the tribunal shall deliver the award on the payment into court by the applicant of the fees and expenses demanded, or such lesser amount as the court may specify,

(b) the amount of the fees and expenses properly payable shall be determined by such means and upon such terms as the court may direct, and

(c) out of the money paid into court there shall be paid out such fees and expenses as may be found to be properly payable and the balance of the money (if any) shall be paid out to the applicant.

(3) For this purpose the amount of fees and expenses properly payable is the amount the applicant is liable to pay under section 28 or any agreement relating to the payment of the arbitrators.

(4) No application to the court may be made where there is any available arbitral process for appeal or review of the amount of the fees or expenses demanded.

(5) References in this section to arbitrators include an arbitrator who has ceased to act and an umpire who has not replaced the other arbitrators.

(6) The above provisions of this section also apply in relation to any arbitral or other institution or person vested by the parties with powers in relation to the delivery of the tribunal's award.

As they so apply, the references to the fees and expenses of the arbitrators shall be construed as including the fees and expenses of that institution or person.

(7) The leave of the court is required for any appeal from a decision of the court under this section.

(8) Nothing in this section shall be construed as excluding an application under section 28 where payment has been made to the arbitrators in order to obtain the award.

57 Correction of award or additional award

(1) The parties are free to agree on the powers of the tribunal to correct an award or make an additional award.

(2) If or to the extent there is no such agreement, the following provisions apply.

(3) The tribunal may on its own initiative or on the application of a party—

    (*a*)   correct an award so as to remove any clerical mistake or error arising from an accidental slip or omission or clarify or remove any ambiguity in the award, or

    (*b*)   make an additional award in respect of any claim (including a claim for interest or costs) which was presented to the tribunal but was not dealt with in the award.

These powers shall not be exercised without first affording the other parties a reasonable opportunity to make representations to the tribunal.

(4) Any application for the exercise of those powers must be made within 28 days of the date of the award or such longer period as the parties may agree.

(5) Any correction of an award shall be made within 28 days of the date the application was received by the tribunal or, where the correction is made by the tribunal on its own initiative, within 28 days of the date of the award or, in either case, such longer period as the parties may agree.

(6) Any additional award shall be made within 56 days of the date of the original award or such longer period as the parties may agree.

(7) Any correction of an award shall form part of the award.

58 Effect of award

(1) Unless otherwise agreed by the parties, an award made by the tribunal pursuant to an arbitration agreement is final and binding both on the par-

ties and on any persons claiming through or under them.

(2) This does not affect the right of a person to challenge the award by any available arbitral process of appeal or review or in accordance with the provisions of this Part.

Costs of the arbitration

59 Costs of the arbitration

(1) References in this Part to the costs of the arbitration are to—

(a) the arbitrators' fees and expenses,

(b) the fees and expenses of any arbitral institution concerned, and

(c) the legal or other costs of the parties.

(2) Any such reference includes the costs of or incidental to any proceedings to determine the amount of the recoverable costs of the arbitration (see section 63).

60 Agreement to pay costs in any event

An agreement which has the effect that a party is to pay the whole or part of the costs of the arbitration in any event is only valid if made after the dispute in question has arisen.

61 Award of costs

(1) The tribunal may make an award allocating the costs of the arbitration as between the parties, subject to any agreement of the parties.

(2) Unless the parties otherwise agree, the tribunal shall award costs on the general principle that costs should follow the event except where it appears to the tribunal that in the circumstances this is not appropriate in relation to the whole or part of the costs.

62 Effect of agreement or award about costs

Unless the parties otherwise agree, any obligation under an agreement between them as to how the costs of the arbitration are to be borne, or under an award allocating the costs of the arbitration, extends only to such costs as are recoverable.

63 The recoverable costs of the arbitration

(1) The parties are free to agree what costs of the arbitration are recoverable.

(2) If or to the extent there is no such agreement, the following provisions apply.

(3) The tribunal may determine by award the recoverable costs of the arbitration on such basis as it thinks fit.

If it does so, it shall specify—

(a) the basis on which it has acted, and

(b) the items of recoverable costs and the amount referable to each.

(4) If the tribunal does not determine the recoverable costs of the

arbitration, any party to the arbitral proceedings may apply to the court (upon notice to the other parties) which may—

    (*a*)   determine the recoverable costs of the arbitration on such basis as it thinks fit, or

    (*b*)   order that they shall be determined by such means and upon such terms as it may specify.

(5) Unless the tribunal or the court determines otherwise—

    (*a*)   the recoverable costs of the arbitration shall be determined on the basis that there shall be allowed a reasonable amount in respect of all costs reasonably incurred, and

    (*b*)   any doubt as to whether costs were reasonably incurred or were reasonable in amount shall be resolved in favour of the paying party.

(6) The above provisions have effect subject to section 64 (recoverable fees and expenses of arbitrators).

(7) Nothing in this section affects any right of the arbitrators, any expert, legal adviser or assessor appointed by the tribunal, or any arbitral institution, to payment of their fees and expenses.

64   Recoverable fees and expenses of arbitrators

(1) Unless otherwise agreed by the parties, the recoverable costs of the arbitration shall include in respect of the fees and expenses of the arbitrators only such reasonable fees and expenses as are appropriate in the circumstances.

(2) If there is any question as to what reasonable fees and expenses are appropriate in the circumstances, and the matter is not already before the court on an application under section 63(4), the court may on the application of any party (upon notice to the other parties)—

    (*a*)   determine the matter, or

    (*b*)   order that it be determined by such means and upon such terms as the court may specify.

(3) Subsection (1) has effect subject to any order of the court under section 24(4) or 25(3)(*b*) (order as to entitlement to fees or expenses in case of removal or resignation of arbitrator).

(4) Nothing in this section affects any right of the arbitrator to payment of his fees and expenses.

65   Power to limit recoverable costs

(1) Unless otherwise agreed by the parties, the tribunal may direct that the recoverable costs of the arbitration, or of any part of the arbitral proceedings, shall be limited to a specified amount.

(2) Any direction may be made or varied at any stage, but this must be done sufficiently in advance of the incurring of costs to which it relates, or the taking of any steps in the proceedings which may be affected by it, for the limit to be taken into account.

Powers of the court in relation to award

66 Enforcement of the award

(1) An award made by the tribunal pursuant to an arbitration agreement may, by leave of the court, be enforced in the same manner as a judgment or order of the court to the same effect.

(2) Where leave is so given, judgment may be entered in terms of the award.

(3) Leave to enforce an award shall not be given where, or to the extent that, the person against whom it is sought to be enforced shows that the tribunal lacked substantive jurisdiction to make the award.

The right to raise such an objection may have been lost (see section 73).

(4) Nothing in this section affects the recognition or enforcement of an award under any other enactment or rule of law, in particular under Part II of the Arbitration Act 1950 (enforcement of awards under Geneva Convention) or the provisions of Part III of this Act relating to the recognition and enforcement of awards under the New York Convention or by an action on the award.

67 Challenging the award: substantive jurisdiction

(1) A party to arbitral proceedings may (upon notice to the other parties and to the tribunal) apply to the court—

(a) challenging any award of the arbitral tribunal as to its substantive jurisdiction; or

(b) for an order declaring an award made by the tribunal on the merits to be of no effect, in whole or in part, because the tribunal did not have substantive jurisdiction.

A party may lose the right to object (see section 73) and the right to apply is subject to the restrictions in section 70(2) and (3).

(2) The arbitral tribunal may continue the arbitral proceedings and make a further award while an application to the court under this section is pending in relation to an award as to jurisdiction.

(3) On an application under this section challenging an award of the arbitral tribunal as to its substantive jurisdiction, the court may by order—

(a) confirm the award,

(b) vary the award, or

(c) set aside the award in whole or in part.

(4) The leave of the court is required for any appeal from a decision of the court under this section.

68 Challenging the award: serious irregularity

(1) A party to arbitral proceedings may (upon notice to the other parties and to the tribunal) apply to the court challenging an award in the proceedings on the ground of serious irregularity affecting the tribunal, the proceedings or the award.

A party may lose the right to object (see section 73) and the right to apply is subject to the restrictions in section 70(2) and (3).

(2) Serious irregularity means an irregularity of one or more of the following kinds which the court considers has caused or will cause substantial injustice to the applicant—

(a) failure by the tribunal to comply with section 33 (general duty of tribunal);

(b) the tribunal exceeding its powers (otherwise than by exceeding its substantive jurisdiction: see section 67);

(c) failure by the tribunal to conduct the proceedings in accordance with the procedure agreed by the parties;

(d) failure by the tribunal to deal with all the issues that were put to it;

(e) any arbitral or other institution or person vested by the parties with powers in relation to the proceedings or the award exceeding its powers;

(f) uncertainty or ambiguity as to the effect of the award;

(g) the award being obtained by fraud or the award or the way in which it was procured being contrary to public policy;

(h) failure to comply with the requirements as to the form of the award; or

(i) any irregularity in the conduct of the proceedings or in the award which is admitted by the tribunal or by any arbitral or other institution or person vested by the parties with powers in relation to the proceedings or the award.

(3) If there is shown to be serious irregularity affecting the tribunal, the proceedings or the award, the court may—

(a) remit the award to the tribunal, in whole or in part, for reconsideration,

(b) set the award aside in whole or in part, or

(c) declare the award to be of no effect, in whole or in part.

The court shall not exercise its power to set aside or to declare an award to be of no effect, in whole or in part, unless it is satisfied that it would be inappropriate to remit the matters in question to the tribunal for reconsideration.

(4) The leave of the court is required for any appeal from a decision of the court under this section.

69 Appeal on point of law

(1) Unless otherwise agreed by the parties, a party to arbitral proceedings may (upon notice to the other parties and to the tribunal) appeal to the court on a question of law arising out of an award made in the proceedings.

An agreement to dispense with reasons for the tribunal's award shall be considered an agreement to exclude the court's jurisdiction under this section.

(2) An appeal shall not be brought under this section except—

(a)   with the agreement of all the other parties to the proceedings, or

(b)   with the leave of the court.

The right to appeal is also subject to the restrictions in section 70(2) and (3).

(3) Leave to appeal shall be given only if the court is satisfied—

(a)   that the determination of the question will substantially affect the rights of one or more of the parties,

(b)   that the question is one which the tribunal was asked to determine,

(c)   that, on the basis of the findings of fact in the award—

   (i)   the decision of the tribunal on the question is obviously wrong, or

   (ii)   the question is one of general public importance and the decision of the tribunal is at least open to serious doubt, and

(d)   that, despite the agreement of the parties to resolve the matter by arbitration, it is just and proper in all the circumstances for the court to determine the question.

(4) An application for leave to appeal under this section shall identify the question of law to be determined and state the grounds on which it is alleged that leave to appeal should be granted.

(5) The court shall determine an application for leave to appeal under this section without a hearing unless it appears to the court that a hearing is required.

(6) The leave of the court is required for any appeal from a decision of the court under this section to grant or refuse leave to appeal.

(7) On an appeal under this section the court may by order—

(a)   confirm the award,

(b)   vary the award,

(c)   remit the award to the tribunal, in whole or in part, for reconsideration in the light of the court's determination, or

(d)   set aside the award in whole or in part.

The court shall not exercise its power to set aside an award, in whole or in part, unless it is satisfied that it would be inappropriate to remit the matters in question to the tribunal for reconsideration.

(8) The decision of the court on an appeal under this section shall be treated as a judgment of the court for the purposes of a further appeal.

But no such appeal lies without the leave of the court which shall not be given unless the court considers that the question is one of general importance or is one which for some other special reason should be considered by the Court of Appeal.

70   Challenge or appeal: supplementary provisions

(1) The following provisions apply to an application or appeal under sec-

tion 67, 68 or 69.

(2) An application or appeal may not be brought if the applicant or appellant has not first exhausted—

(a)   any available arbitral process of appeal or review, and

(b)   any available recourse under section 57 (correction of award or additional award).

(3) Any application or appeal must be brought within 28 days of the date of the award or, if there has been any arbitral process of appeal or review, of the date when the applicant or appellant was notified of the result of that process.

(4) If on an application or appeal it appears to the court that the award—

(a)   does not contain the tribunal's reasons, or

(b)   does not set out the tribunal's reasons in sufficient detail to enable the court properly to consider the application or appeal,

the court may order the tribunal to state the reasons for its award in sufficient detail for that purpose.

(5) Where the court makes an order under subsection (4), it may make such further order as it thinks fit with respect to any additional costs of the arbitration resulting from its order.

(6) The court may order the applicant or appellant to provide security for the costs of the application or appeal, and may direct that the application or appeal be dismissed if the order is not complied with.

The power to order security for costs shall not be exercised on the ground that the applicant or appellant is—

(a)   an individual ordinarily resident outside the United Kingdom, or

(b)   a corporation or association incorporated or formed under the law of a country outside the United Kingdom, or whose central management and control is exercised outside the United Kingdom.

(7) The court may order that any money payable under the award shall be brought into court or otherwise secured pending the determination of the application or appeal, and may direct that the application or appeal be dismissed if the order is not complied with.

(8) The court may grant leave to appeal subject to conditions to the same or similar effect as an order under subsection (6) or (7).

This does not affect the general discretion of the court to grant leave subject to conditions.

71   Challenge or appeal: effect of order of court

(1) The following provisions have effect where the court makes an order under section 67, 68 or 69 with respect to an award.

(2) Where the award is varied, the variation has effect as part of the tribunal's award.

(3) Where the award is remitted to the tribunal, in whole or in part, for reconsideration, the tribunal shall make a fresh award in respect of the matters remitted within three months of the date of the order for remission or such longer or shorter period as the court may direct.

(4) Where the award is set aside or declared to be of no effect, in whole or in part, the court may also order that any provision that an award is a condition precedent to the bringing of legal proceedings in respect of a matter to which the arbitration agreement applies, is of no effect as regards the subject matter of the award or, as the case may be, the relevant part of the award.

Miscellaneous

72 Saving for rights of person who takes no part in proceedings

(1) A person alleged to be a party to arbitral proceedings but who takes no part in the proceedings may question—

- (a) whether there is a valid arbitration agreement,
- (b) whether the tribunal is properly constituted, or
- (c) what matters have been submitted to arbitration in accordance with the arbitration agreement,

by proceedings in the court for a declaration or injunction or other appropriate relief.

(2) He also has the same right as a party to the arbitral proceedings to challenge an award—

- (a) by an application under section 67 on the ground of lack of substantive jurisdiction in relation to him, or
- (b) by an application under section 68 on the ground of serious irregularity (within the meaning of that section) affecting him;

and section 70(2) (duty to exhaust arbitral procedures) does not apply in his case.

73 Loss of right to object

(1) If a party to arbitral proceedings takes part, or continues to take part, in the proceedings without making, either forthwith or within such time as is allowed by the arbitration agreement or the tribunal or by any provision of this Part, any objection—

- (a) that the tribunal lacks substantive jurisdiction,
- (b) that the proceedings have been improperly conducted,
- (c) that there has been a failure to comply with the arbitration agreement or with any provision of this Part, or
- (d) that there has been any other irregularity affecting the tribunal or the proceedings,

he may not raise that objection later, before the tribunal or the court, unless he shows that, at the time he took part or continued to take part in the proceedings, he did not know and could not with reasonable diligence have discovered the grounds for the objection.

(2) Where the arbitral tribunal rules that it has substantive jurisdiction and a party to arbitral proceedings who could have questioned that ruling—

(*a*)   by any available arbitral process of appeal or review, or

(*b*)   by challenging the award,

does not do so, or does not do so within the time allowed by the arbitration agreement or any provision of this Part, he may not object later to the tribunal's substantive jurisdiction on any ground which was the subject of that ruling.

74   Immunity of arbitral institutions, &c

(1) An arbitral or other institution or person designated or requested by the parties to appoint or nominate an arbitrator is not liable for anything done or omitted in the discharge or purported discharge of that function unless the act or omission is shown to have been in bad faith.

(2) An arbitral or other institution or person by whom an arbitrator is appointed or nominated is not liable, by reason of having appointed or nominated him, for anything done or omitted by the arbitrator (or his employees or agents) in the discharge or purported discharge of his functions as arbitrator.

(3) The above provisions apply to an employee or agent of an arbitral or other institution or person as they apply to the institution or person himself.

75   Charge to secure payment of solicitors' costs

The powers of the court to make declarations and orders under section 73 of the Solicitors Act 1974 or Article 71H of the Solicitors (Northern Ireland) Order 1976 (power to charge property recovered in the proceedings with the payment of solicitors' costs) may be exercised in relation to arbitral proceedings as if those proceedings were proceedings in the court.

Supplementary

76   Service of notices, &c

(1) The parties are free to agree on the manner of service of any notice or other document required or authorised to be given or served in pursuance of the arbitration agreement or for the purposes of the arbitral proceedings.

(2) If or to the extent that there is no such agreement the following provisions apply.

(3) A notice or other document may be served on a person by any effective means.

(4) If a notice or other document is addressed, pre-paid and delivered by post—

(a)   to the addressee's last known principal residence or, if he is or has been carrying on a trade, profession or business, his last known principal business address, or

(b)   where the addressee is a body corporate, to the body's registered or principal office,

it shall be treated as effectively served.

(5) This section does not apply to the service of documents for the purposes of legal proceedings, for which provision is made by rules of court.

(6) References in this Part to a notice or other document include any form of communication in writing and references to giving or serving a notice or other document shall be construed accordingly.

77   Powers of court in relation to service of documents

(1) This section applies where service of a document on a person in the manner agreed by the parties, or in accordance with provisions of section 76 having effect in default of agreement, is not reasonably practi cable.

(2) Unless otherwise agreed by the parties, the court may make such order as it thinks fit—

(a)   for service in such manner as the court may direct, or

(b)   dispensing with service of the document.

(3) Any party to the arbitration agreement may apply for an order, but only after exhausting any available arbitral process for resolving the matter.

(4) The leave of the court is required for any appeal from a decision of the court under this section.

78   Reckoning periods of time

(1) The parties are free to agree on the method of reckoning periods of time for the purposes of any provision agreed by them or any provision of this Part having effect in default of such agreement.

(2) If or to the extent there is no such agreement, periods of time shall be reckoned in accordance with the following provisions.

(3) Where the act is required to be done within a specified period after or from a specified date, the period begins immediately after that date.

(4) Where the act is required to be done a specified number of clear days after a specified date, at least that number of days must intervene between the day on which the act is done and that date.

(5) Where the period is a period of seven days or less which would include a Saturday, Sunday or a public holiday in the place where any-thing which has to be done within the period falls to be done, that day shall be excluded.

In relation to England and Wales or Northern Ireland, a 'public holiday'

315

means Christmas Day, Good Friday or a day which under the Banking and Financial Dealings Act 1971 is a bank holiday.

79 Power of court to extend time limits relating to arbitral proceedings

(1) Unless the parties otherwise agree, the court may by order extend any time limit agreed by them in relation to any matter relating to the arbitral proceedings or specified in any provision of this Part having effect in default of such agreement.

This section does not apply to a time limit to which section 12 applies (power of court to extend time for beginning arbitral proceedings, &c).

(2) An application for an order may be made—

(a)   by any party to the arbitral proceedings (upon notice to the other parties and to the tribunal), or

(b)   by the arbitral tribunal (upon notice to the parties).

(3) The court shall not exercise its power to extend a time limit unless it is satisfied—

(a)   that any available recourse to the tribunal, or to any arbitral or other institution or person vested by the parties with power in that regard, has first been exhausted, and

(b)   that a substantial injustice would otherwise be done.

(4) The court's power under this section may be exercised whether or not the time has already expired.

(5) An order under this section may be made on such terms as the court thinks fit.

(6) The leave of the court is required for any appeal from a decision of the court under this section.

80 Notice and other requirements in connection with legal proceedings

(1) References in this Part to an application, appeal or other step in relation to legal proceedings being taken 'upon notice' to the other parties to the arbitral proceedings, or to the tribunal, are to such notice of the originating process as is required by rules of court and do not impose any separate requirement.

(2) Rules of court shall be made—

(a)   requiring such notice to be given as indicated by any provision of this Part, and

(b)   as to the manner, form and content of any such notice.

(3) Subject to any provision made by rules of court, a requirement to give notice to the tribunal of legal proceedings shall be construed—

(a)   if there is more than one arbitrator, as a requirement to give notice to each of them; and

(b)   if the tribunal is not fully constituted, as a requirement to give notice to any arbitrator who has been appointed.

(4) References in this Part to making an application or appeal to the court within a specified period are to the issue within that period of the appropriate originating process in accordance with rules of court.

(5) Where any provision of this Part requires an application or appeal to be made to the court within a specified time, the rules of court relating to the reckoning of periods, the extending or abridging of periods, and the consequences of not taking a step within the period prescribed by the rules, apply in relation to that requirement.

(6) Provision may be made by rules of court amending the provisions of this Part—

(a)   with respect to the time within which any application or appeal to the court must be made,

(b)   so as to keep any provision made by this Part in relation to arbitral proceedings in step with the corresponding provision of rules of court applying in relation to proceedings in the court, or

(c)   so as to keep any provision made by this Part in relation to legal proceedings in step with the corresponding provision of rules of court applying generally in relation to proceedings in the court.

(7) Nothing in this section affects the generality of the power to make rules of court.

81   Saving for certain matters governed by common law

(1) Nothing in this Part shall be construed as excluding the operation of any rule of law consistent with the provisions of this Part, in particular, any rule of law as to—

(a)   matters which are not capable of settlement by arbitration;

(b)   the effect of an oral arbitration agreement; or

(c)   the refusal of recognition or enforcement of an arbitral award on grounds of public policy.

(2) Nothing in this Act shall be construed as reviving any jurisdiction of the court to set aside or remit an award on the ground of errors of fact or law on the face of the award.

82   Minor definitions

(1) In this Part—

'arbitrator', unless the context otherwise requires, includes an umpire;

'available arbitral process', in relation to any matter, includes any process of appeal to or review by an arbitral or other institution or person vested by the parties with powers in relation to that matter;

'claimant', unless the context otherwise requires, includes a counterclaimant, and related expressions shall be construed accordingly;

'dispute' includes any difference;

'enactment' includes an enactment contained in Northern Ireland legislation;

'legal proceedings' means civil proceedings in the High Court or a county court;

'peremptory order' means an order made under section 41(5) or made in exercise of any corresponding power conferred by the parties;

'premises' includes land, buildings, moveable structures, vehicles, vessels, aircraft and hovercraft;

'question of law' means—

(a)   for a court in England and Wales, a question of the law of England and Wales, and

(b)   for a court in Northern Ireland, a question of the law of Northern Ireland;

'substantive jurisdiction', in relation to an arbitral tribunal, refers to the matters specified in section 30(1)(a) to (c), and references to the tribunal exceeding its substantive jurisdiction shall be construed accordingly.

(2) References in this Part to a party to an arbitration agreement include any person claiming under or through a party to the agreement.

83   Index of defined expressions: Part I

In this Part the expressions listed below are defined or otherwise explained by the provisions indicated—

agreement, agree and agreed	section 5(1)
agreement in writing	section 5(2) to (5)
arbitration agreement	sections 6 and 5(1)
arbitrator	section 82(1)
available arbitral process	section 82(1)
claimant	section 82(1)
commencement (in relation to arbitral proceedings)	section 14
costs of the arbitration	section 59
the court	section 105
dispute	section 82(1)
enactment	section 82(1)
legal proceedings	section 82(1)
Limitation Acts	section 13(4)
notice (or other document)	section 76(6)
party—	
—in relation to an arbitration agreement	section 82(2)
—where section 106(2) or (3) applies	section 106(4)
peremptory order	section 82(1) (and see section 41(5))
premises	section 82(1)
question of law	section 82(1)

recoverable costs   sections 63 and 64
seat of the arbitration   section 3
serve and service (of notice   section 76(6)
  or other document)
substantive jurisdiction (in   section 82(1) (and see
  relation to an arbitral tribunal)   section 30(1)(*a*) to (*c*),
upon notice (to the parties or the   section 80
  tribunal)
written and in writing   section 5(6)

84 Transitional provisions

(1) The provisions of this Part do not apply to arbitral proceedings commenced before the date on which this Part comes into force.

(2) They apply to arbitral proceedings commenced on or after that date under an arbitration agreement whenever made.

(3) The above provisions have effect subject to any transitional provision made by an order under section 109(2) (power to include transitional provisions in commencement order).

Part II   Other provisions relating to arbitration

Domestic arbitration agreements

85 Modification of Part I in relation to domestic arbitration agreement

(1) In the case of a domestic arbitration agreement the provisions of Part I are modified in accordance with the following sections.

(2) For this purpose a 'domestic arbitration agreement' means an arbitration agreement to which none of the parties is—

  (*a*) an individual who is a national of, or habitually resident in, a state other than the United Kingdom, or

  (*b*) a body corporate which is incorporated in, or whose central control and management is exercised in, a state other than the United Kingdom,

and under which the seat of the arbitration (if the seat has been designated or determined) is in the United Kingdom.

(3) In subsection (2) 'arbitration agreement' and 'seat of the arbitration' have the same meaning as in Part I (see sections 3, 5(1) and 6).

86 Staying of legal proceedings

(1) In section 9 (stay of legal proceedings), subsection (4) (stay unless the arbitration agreement is null and void, inoperative, or incapable of being performed) does not apply to a domestic arbitration agreement.

(2) On an application under that section in relation to a domestic arbitration agreement the court shall grant a stay unless satisfied—

(a)   that the arbitration agreement is null and void, inoperative, or incapable of being performed, or

(b)   that there are other sufficient grounds for not requiring the parties to abide by the arbitration agreement.

(3) The court may treat as a sufficient ground under subsection (2)(b) the fact that the applicant is or was at any material time not ready and willing to do all things necessary for the proper conduct of the arbitration or of any other dispute resolution procedures required to be exhausted before resorting to arbitration.

(4) For the purposes of this section the question whether an arbitration agreement is a domestic arbitration agreement shall be determined by reference to the facts at the time the legal proceedings are commenced.

87   Effectiveness of agreement to exclude court's jurisdiction

(1) In the case of a domestic arbitration agreement any agreement to exclude the jurisdiction of the court under—

(a)   section 45 (determination of preliminary point of law), or

(b)   section 69 (challenging the award: appeal on point of law),

is not effective unless entered into after the commencement of the arbitral proceedings in which the question arises or the award is made.

(2) For this purpose the commencement of the arbitral proceedings has the same meaning as in Part I (see section 14).

(3) For the purposes of this section the question whether an arbitration agreement is a domestic arbitration agreement shall be determined by reference to the facts at the time the agreement is entered into.

88   Power to repeal or amend sections 85 to 87

(1) The Secretary of State may by order repeal or amend the provisions of sections 85 to 87.

(2) An order under this section may contain such supplementary, incidental and transitional provisions as appear to the Secretary of State to be appropriate.

(3) An order under this section shall be made by statutory instrument and no such order shall be made unless a draft of it has been laid before and approved by a resolution of each House of Parliament.

Consumer arbitration agreements

89   Application of unfair terms regulations to consumer arbitration agreements

(1) The following sections extend the application of the Unfair Terms in Consumer Contracts Regulations 1994 in relation to a term which constitutes an arbitration agreement.

For this purpose 'arbitration agreement' means an agreement to submit to arbitration present or future disputes or differences (whether or not contractual).

(2) In those sections 'the Regulations' means those regulations and includes any regulations amending or replacing those regulations.

(3) Those sections apply whatever the law applicable to the arbitration agreement.

90 Regulations apply where consumer is a legal person

The Regulations apply where the consumer is a legal person as they apply where the consumer is a natural person.

91 Arbitration agreement unfair where modest amount sought

(1) A term which constitutes an arbitration agreement is unfair for the purposes of the Regulations so far as it relates to a claim for a pecuniary remedy which does not exceed the amount specified by order for the purposes of this section.

(2) Orders under this section may make different provision for different cases and for different purposes.

(3) The power to make orders under this section is exercisable—

(a)   for England and Wales, by the Secretary of State with the concurrence of the Lord Chancellor,

(b)   for Scotland, by the Secretary of State with the concurrence of the Lord Advocate, and

(c)   for Northern Ireland, by the Department of Economic Development for Northern Ireland with the concurrence of the Lord Chancellor.

(4) Any such order for England and Wales or Scotland shall be made by statutory instrument which shall be subject to annulment in pursuance of a resolution of either House of Parliament.

(5) Any such order for Northern Ireland shall be a statutory rule for the purposes of the Statutory Rules (Northern Ireland) Order 1979 and shall be subject to negative resolution, within the meaning of section 41(6) of the Interpretation Act (Northern Ireland) 1954.

Small claims arbitration in the county court

92 Exclusion of Part I in relation to small claims arbitration in the county court

Nothing in Part I of this Act applies to arbitration under section 64 of the County Courts Act 1984.

Appointment of judges as arbitrators

93 Appointment of judges as arbitrators

(1) A judge of the Commercial Court or an official referee may, if in all the circumstances he thinks fit, accept appointment as a sole arbitrator or as umpire by or by virtue of an arbitration agreement.

(2) A judge of the Commercial Court shall not do so unless the Lord Chief Justice has informed him that, having regard to the state of business in the High Court and the Crown Court, he can be made available.

(3) An official referee shall not do so unless the Lord Chief Justice has informed him that, having regard to the state of official referees' business, he can be made available.

(4) The fees payable for the services of a judge of the Commercial Court or official referee as arbitrator or umpire shall be taken in the High Court.

(5) In this section—

'arbitration agreement' has the same meaning as in Part I; and

'official referee' means a person nominated under section 68(1)(*a*) of the Supreme Court Act 1981 to deal with official referees' business.

(6) The provisions of Part I of this Act apply to arbitration before a person appointed under this section with the modifications specified in Schedule 2.

Statutory arbitrations

94 Application of Part I to statutory arbitrations

(1) The provisions of Part I apply to every arbitration under an enactment (a 'statutory arbitration'), whether the enactment was passed or made before or after the commencement of this Act, subject to the adaptations and exclusions specified in sections 95 to 98.

(2) The provisions of Part I do not apply to a statutory arbitration if or to the extent that their application—

    (*a*)   is inconsistent with the provisions of the enactment concerned, with any rules or procedure authorised or recognised by it, or

    (*b*)   is excluded by any other enactment.

(3) In this section and the following provisions of this Part 'enactment'—

    (*a*)   in England and Wales, includes an enactment contained in subordinate legislation within the meaning of the Interpretation Act 1978;

    (*b*)   in Northern Ireland, means a statutory provision within the meaning of section 1(*f*) of the Interpretation Act (Northern Ireland) 1954.

95 General adaptation of provisions in relation to statutory arbitrations

(1) The provisions of Part I apply to a statutory arbitration—

    (*a*)   as if the arbitration were pursuant to an arbitration agreement and as if the enactment were that agreement, and

    (*b*)   as if the persons by and against whom a claim subject to arbitration in pursuance of the enactment may be or has been made were parties to that agreement.

(2) Every statutory arbitration shall be taken to have its seat in England and Wales or, as the case may be, in Northern Ireland.

96 Specific adaptations of provisions in relation to statutory arbitrations

(1) The following provisions of Part I apply to a statutory arbitration with the following adaptations.

(2) In section 30(1) (competence of tribunal to rule on its own jurisdiction), the reference in paragraph (*a*) to whether there is a valid arbitration agreement shall be construed as a reference to whether the enactment applies to the dispute or difference in question.

(3) Section 35 (consolidation of proceedings and concurrent hearings) applies only so as to authorise the consolidation of proceedings, or concurrent hearings in proceedings, under the same enactment.

(4) Section 46 (rules applicable to substance of dispute) applies with the omission of subsection (1)(*b*) (determination in accordance with considerations agreed by parties).

97 Provisions excluded from applying to statutory arbitrations

The following provisions of Part I do not apply in relation to a statutory arbitration—

(*a*) section 8 (whether agreement discharged by death of a party);

(*b*) section 12 (power of court to extend agreed time limits);

(*c*) sections 9(5), 10(2) and 71(4) (restrictions on effect of provision that award condition precedent to right to bring legal proceedings).

98 Power to make further provision by regulations

(1) The Secretary of State may make provision by regulations for adapting or excluding any provision of Part I in relation to statutory arbitrations in general or statutory arbitrations of any particular description.

(2) The power is exercisable whether the enactment concerned is passed or made before or after the commencement of this Act.

(3) Regulations under this section shall be made by statutory instrument which shall be subject to annulment in pursuance of a resolution of either House of Parliament.

Part III Recognition and enforcement of certain foreign awards

Enforcement of Geneva Convention awards

99 Continuation of Part II of the Arbitration Act 1950

Part II of the Arbitration Act 1950 (enforcement of certain foreign awards) continues to apply in relation to foreign awards within the meaning of that Part which are not also New York Convention awards.

Recognition and enforcement of New York Convention awards

100　New York Convention awards

(1) In this Part a 'New York Convention award' means an award made, in pursuance of an arbitration agreement, in the territory of a state (other than the United Kingdom) which is a party to the New York Convention.

(2) For the purposes of subsection (1) and of the provisions of this Part relating to such awards—

    (a)　'arbitration agreement' means an arbitration agreement in writing, and

    (b)　an award shall be treated as made at the seat of the arbitration, regardless of where it was signed, despatched or delivered to any of the parties.

In this subsection 'agreement in writing' and 'seat of the arbitration' have the same meaning as in Part I.

(3) If Her Majesty by Order in Council declares that a state specified in the Order is a party to the New York Convention, or is a party in respect of any territory so specified, the Order shall, while in force, be conclusive evidence of that fact.

(4) In this section 'the New York Convention' means the Convention on the Recognition and Enforcement of Foreign Arbitral Awards adopted by the United Nations Conference on International Commercial Arbitration on 10th June 1958.

101　Recognition and enforcement of awards

(1) A New York Convention award shall be recognised as binding on the persons as between whom it was made, and may accordingly be relied on by those persons by way of defence, set-off or otherwise in any legal proceedings in England and Wales or Northern Ireland.

(2) A New York Convention award may, by leave of the court, be enforced in the same manner as a judgment or order of the court to the same effect.

As to the meaning of 'the court' see section 105.

(3) Where leave is so given, judgment may be entered in terms of the award.

102　Evidence to be produced by party seeking recognition or enforcement

(1) A party seeking the recognition or enforcement of a New York Convention award must produce—

    (a)　the duly authenticated original award or a duly certified copy of it, and

    (b)　the original arbitration agreement or a duly certified copy of it.

(2) If the award or agreement is in a foreign language, the party must also produce a translation of it certified by an official or sworn translator

or by a diplomatic or consular agent.

103 Refusal of recognition or enforcement

(1) Recognition or enforcement of a New York Convention award shall not be refused except in the following cases.

(2) Recognition or enforcement of the award may be refused if the person against whom it is invoked proves—

(a) that a party to the arbitration agreement was (under the law applicable to him) under some incapacity;

(b) that the arbitration agreement was not valid under the law to which the parties subjected it or, failing any indication thereon, under the law of the country where the award was made;

(c) that he was not given proper notice of the appointment of the arbitrator or of the arbitration proceedings or was otherwise unable to present his case;

(d) that the award deals with a difference not contemplated by or not falling within the terms of the submission to arbitration or contains decision on matters beyond the scope of the submission to arbitration (but see subsection (4));

(e) that the composition of the arbitral tribunal or the arbitral procedure was not in accordance with the agreement of the parties or, failing such agreement, with the law of the country in which the arbitration took place;

(f) that the award has not yet become binding on the parties, or has been set aside or suspended by a competent authority of the country in which, or under the law of which, it was made.

(3) Recognition or enforcement of the award may also be refused if the award is in respect of a matter which is not capable of settlement by arbitration, or if it would be contrary to public policy to recognise or enforce the award.

(4) An award which contains decisions on matters not submitted to arbitration may be recognised or enforced to the extent that it contains decisions on matters submitted to arbitration which can be separated from those on matters not so submitted.

(5) Where an application for the setting aside or suspension of the award has been made to such a competent authority as is mentioned in subsection (2)(f), the court before which the award is sought to be relied upon may, if it considers it proper, adjourn the decision on the recognition or enforcement of the award.

It may also on the application of the party claiming recognition or enforcement of the award order the other party to give suitable security.

104 Saving for other bases of recognition or enforcement

Nothing in the preceding provisions of this Part affects any right to rely upon or enforce a New York Convention award at common law or under section 66.

Part IV   General provisions

105   Meaning of 'the court': jurisdiction of High Court and county court

(1) In this Act 'the court' means the High Court or a county court, subject to the following provisions.

(2) The Lord Chancellor may by order make provision—

(a)   allocating proceedings under this Act to the High Court or to county courts; or

(b)   specifying proceedings under this Act which may be commenced or taken only in the High Court or in a county court.

(3) The Lord Chancellor may by order make provision requiring proceedings of any specified description under this Act in relation to which a county court has jurisdiction to be commenced or taken in one or more specified county courts.

Any jurisdiction so exercisable by a specified county court is exercisable throughout England and Wales or, as the case may be, Northern Ireland.

(4) An order under this section—

(a)   may differentiate between categories of proceedings by reference to such criteria as the Lord Chancellor sees fit to specify, and

(b)   may make such incidental or transitional provision as the Lord Chancellor considers necessary or expedient.

(5) An order under this section for England and Wales shall be made by statutory instrument which shall be subject to annulment in pursuance of a resolution of either House of Parliament.

(6) An order under this section for Northern Ireland shall be a statutory rule for the purposes of the Statutory Rules (Northern Ireland) Order 1979 which shall be subject to annulment in pursuance of a resolution of either House of Parliament in like manner as a statutory instrument and section 5 of the Statutory Instruments Act 1946 shall apply accordingly.

106   Crown application

(1) Part I of this Act applies to any arbitration agreement to which Her Majesty, either in right of the Crown or of the Duchy of Lancaster or otherwise, or the Duke of Cornwall, is a party.

(2) Where Her Majesty is party to an arbitration agreement otherwise than in right of the Crown, Her Majesty shall be represented for the purposes of any arbitral proceedings—

(a)   where the agreement was entered into by Her Majesty in right of the Duchy of Lancaster, by the Chancellor of the Duchy or such person as he may appoint, and

(b)   in any other case, by such person as Her Majesty may appoint in writing under the Royal Sign Manual.

(3) Where the Duke of Cornwall is party to an arbitration agreement, he shall be represented for the purposes of any arbitral proceedings by such person as he may appoint.

(4) References in Part I to a party or the parties to the arbitration agreement or to arbitral proceedings shall be construed, where subsection (2) or (3) applies, as references to the person representing Her Majesty or the Duke of Cornwall.

107 Consequential amendments and repeals

(1) The enactments specified in Schedule 3 are amended in accordance with that Schedule, the amendments being consequential on the provisions of this Act.

(2) The enactments specified in Schedule 4 are repealed to the extent specified.

108 Extent

(1) The provisions of this Act extend to England and Wales and, except as mentioned below, to Northern Ireland.

(2) The following provisions of Part II do not extend to Northern Ireland—

section 92 (exclusion of Part I in relation to small claims arbitration in the county court), and

section 93 and Schedule 2 (appointment of judges as arbitrators).

(3) Sections 89, 90 and 91 (consumer arbitration agreements) extend to Scotland and the provisions of Schedules 3 and 4 (consequential amendments and repeals) extend to Scotland so far as they relate to enactments which so extend, subject as follows.

(4) The repeal of the Arbitration Act 1975 extends only to England and Wales and Northern Ireland.

109 Commencement

(1) The provisions of this Act come into force on such day as the Secretary of State may appoint by order made by statutory instrument, and different days may be appointed for different purposes.

(2) An order under subsection (1) may contain such transitional provisions as appear to the Secretary of State to be appropriate.

110 Short title

This Act may be cited as the Arbitration Act 1996.

Schedules

Schedule 1 Mandatory Provisions of Part I

Section 4(1)

sections 9 to 11 (stay of legal proceedings);
section 12 (power of court to extend agreed time limits);
section 13 (application of Limitation Acts);

section 24 (power of court to remove arbitrator);

section 26(1) (effect of death of arbitrator);

section 28 (liability of parties for fees and expenses of arbitrators);

section 29 (immunity of arbitrator);

section 31 (objection to substantive jurisdiction of tribunal);

section 32 (determination of preliminary point of jurisdiction);

section 33 (general duty of tribunal);

section 37(2) (items to be treated as expenses of arbitrators);

section 40 (general duty of parties);

section 43 (securing the attendance of witnesses);

section 56 (power to withhold award in case of non-payment);

section 60 (effectiveness of agreement for payment of costs in any event);

section 66 (enforcement of award);

sections 67 and 68 (challenging the award: substantive jurisdiction and serious irregularity), and sections 70 and 71 (supplementary provisions; effect of order of court) so far as relating to those sections;

section 72 (saving for rights of person who takes no part in proceedings);

section 73 (loss of right to object);

section 74 (immunity of arbitral institutions, &c);

section 75 (charge to secure payment of solicitors' costs).

Schedule 2

Section 93(6)

Modifications of Part I in relation to judge-arbitrators

Introductory

1. In this Schedule 'judge-arbitrator' means a judge of the Commercial Court or official referee appointed as arbitrator or umpire under section 93.

General

2.—(1) Subject to the following provisions of this Schedule, references in Part I to the court shall be construed in relation to a judge-arbitrator, or in relation to the appointment of a judge-arbitrator, as references to the Court of Appeal.

(2) The references in sections 32(6), 45(6) and 69(8) to the Court of Appeal shall in such a case be construed as references to the House of Lords.

Arbitrator's fees

3.—(1) The power of the court in section 28(2) to order consideration and adjustment of the liability of a party for the fees of an arbitrator may be exercised by a judge-arbitrator.

(2) Any such exercise of the power is subject to the powers of the Court

of Appeal under sections 24(4) and 25(3)(*b*) (directions as to entitlement to fees or expenses in case of removal or resignation).

Exercise of court powers in support of arbitration

4.—(1) Where the arbitral tribunal consists of or includes a judge-arbitrator the powers of the court under sections 42 to 44 (enforcement of peremptory orders, summoning witnesses, and other court powers) are exercisable by the High Court and also by the judge-arbitrator himself.

(2) Anything done by a judge-arbitrator in the exercise of those powers shall be regarded as done by him in his capacity as judge of the High Court and have effect as if done by that court.

Nothing in this sub-paragraph prejudices any power vested in him as arbitrator or umpire.

Extension of time for making award

5.—(1) The power conferred by section 50 (extension of time for making award) is exercisable by the judge-arbitrator himself.

(2) Any appeal from a decision of a judge-arbitrator under that section lies to the Court of Appeal with the leave of that court.

Withholding award in case of non-payment

6.—(1) The provisions of paragraph 7 apply in place of the provisions of section 56 (power to withhold award in the case of non-payment) in relation to the withholding of an award for non-payment of the fees and expenses of a judge-arbitrator.

(2) This does not affect the application of section 56 in relation to the delivery of such an award by an arbitral or other institution or person vested by the parties with powers in relation to the delivery of the award.

7.—(1) A judge-arbitrator may refuse to deliver an award except upon payment of the fees and expenses mentioned in section 56(1).

(2) The judge-arbitrator may, on an application by a party to the arbitral proceedings, order that if he pays into the High Court the fees and expenses demanded, or such lesser amount as the judge-arbitrator may specify—

(*a*) the award shall be delivered,

(*b*) the amount of the fees and expenses properly payable shall be determined by such means and upon such terms as he may direct, and

(*c*) out of the money paid into court there shall be paid out such fees and expenses as may be found to be properly payable and the balance of the money (if any) shall be paid out to the applicant.

(3) For this purpose the amount of fees and expenses properly payable is the amount the applicant is liable to pay under section 28 or any agreement relating to the payment of the arbitrator.

(4) No application to the judge-arbitrator under this paragraph may

be made where there is any available arbitral process for appeal or review of the amount of the fees or expenses demanded.

(5) Any appeal from a decision of a judge-arbitrator under this paragraph lies to the Court of Appeal with the leave of that court.

(6) Where a party to arbitral proceedings appeals under sub-paragraph (5), an arbitrator is entitled to appear and be heard.

Correction of award or additional award

8. Subsections (4) to (6) of section 57 (correction of award or additional award: time limit for application or exercise of power) do not apply to a judge-arbitrator.

Costs

9. Where the arbitral tribunal consists of or includes a judge-arbitrator the powers of the court under section 63(4) (determination of recoverable costs) shall be exercised by the High Court.

10.—(1) The power of the court under section 64 to determine an arbitrator's reasonable fees and expenses may be exercised by a judge-arbitrator.

(2) Any such exercise of the power is subject to the powers of the Court of Appeal under sections 24(4) and 25(3)(*b*) (directions as to entitlement to fees or expenses in case of removal or resignation).

Enforcement of award

11. The leave of the court required by section 66 (enforcement of award) may in the case of an award of a judge-arbitrator be given by the judge-arbitrator himself.

Solicitors' costs

12. The powers of the court to make declarations and orders under the provisions applied by section 75 (power to charge property recovered in arbitral proceedings with the payment of solicitors' costs) may be exercised by the judge-arbitrator.

Powers of court in relation to service of documents

13.—(1) The power of the court under section 77(2) (powers of court in relation to service of documents) is exercisable by the judge-arbitrator.

(2) Any appeal from a decision of a judge-arbitrator under that section lies to the Court of Appeal with the leave of that court.

Powers of court to extend time limits relating to arbitral proceedings

14.—(1) The power conferred by section 79 (power of court to extend time limits relating to arbitral proceedings) is exercisable by the judge-arbitrator himself.

(2) Any appeal from a decision of a judge-arbitrator under that section lies to the Court of Appeal with the leave of that court.

Schedule 3
Section 107(1)

Consequential amendments

Merchant Shipping Act 1894 (c 60)

1. In section 496 of the Merchant Shipping Act 1894 (provisions as to deposits by owners of goods), after subsection (4) insert—

'(5) In subsection (3) the expression "legal proceedings" includes arbitral proceedings and as respects England and Wales and Northern Ireland the provisions of section 14 of the Arbitration Act 1996 apply to determine when such proceedings are commenced.'.

Stannaries Court (Abolition) Act 1896 (c 45)

2. In section 4(1) of the Stannaries Court (Abolition) Act 1896 (references of certain disputes to arbitration), for the words from 'tried before' to 'any such reference' substitute 'referred to arbitration before himself or before an arbitrator agreed on by the parties or an officer of the court'.

Tithe Act 1936 (c 43)

3. In section 39(1) of the Tithe Act 1936 (proceedings of Tithe Redemption Commission)—

(a) for 'the Arbitration Acts 1889 to 1934' substitute 'Part I of the Arbitration Act 1996';
(b) for paragraph (e) substitute—
   '(e) the making of an application to the court to determine a preliminary point of law and the bringing of an appeal to the court on a point of law;';
(c) for 'the said Acts' substitute 'Part I of the Arbitration Act 1996'.

Education Act 1944 (c 31)

4. In section 75(2) of the Education Act 1944 (proceedings of Independent School Tribunals) for 'the Arbitration Acts 1889 to 1934' substitute 'Part I of the Arbitration Act 1996'.

Commonwealth Telegraphs Act 1949 (c 39)

5. In section 8(2) of the Commonwealth Telegraphs Act 1949 (proceedings of referees under the Act) for 'the Arbitration Acts 1889 to 1934, or the Arbitration Act (Northern Ireland) 1937,' substitute 'Part I of the Arbitration Act 1996'.

Lands Tribunal Act 1949 (c 42)

6. In section 3 of the Lands Tribunal Act 1949 (proceedings before the Lands Tribunal)—

(a) in subsection (6)(c) (procedural rules: power to apply Arbitration Acts), and
(b) in subsection (8) (exclusion of Arbitration Acts except as applied by rules),

for 'the Arbitration Acts 1889 to 1934' substitute 'Part I of the Arbitration Act 1996'.

Wireless Telegraphy Act 1949 (c 54)

7. In the Wireless Telegraphy Act 1949, Schedule 2 (procedure of appeals tribunal), in paragraph 3(1)—

    (a)   for the words 'the Arbitration Acts 1889 to 1934' substitute 'Part I of the Arbitration Act 1996';

    (b)   after the word 'Wales' insert 'or Northern Ireland'; and

    (c)   for 'the said Acts' substitute 'Part I of that Act'.

Patents Act 1949 (c 87)

8. In section 67 of the Patents Act 1949 (proceedings as to infringement of pre-1978 patents referred to comptroller), for 'The Arbitration Acts 1889 to 1934' substitute 'Part I of the Arbitration Act 1996'.

National Health Service (Amendment) Act 1949 (c 93)

9. In section 7(8) of the National Health Service (Amendment) Act 1949 (arbitration in relation to hardship arising from the National Health Service Act 1946 or the Act), for 'the Arbitration Acts 1889 to 1934' substitute 'Part I of the Arbitration Act 1996' and for 'the said Acts' substitute 'Part I of that Act'.

Arbitration Act 1950 (c 27)

10. In section 36(1) of the Arbitration Act 1950 (effect of foreign awards enforceable under Part II of that Act) for 'section 26 of this Act' substitute 'section 66 of the Arbitration Act 1996'.

Interpretation Act (Northern Ireland) 1954 (c 33 (NI))

11. In section 46(2) of the Interpretation Act (Northern Ireland) 1954 (miscellaneous definitions), for the definition of 'arbitrator' substitute—

    ' "arbitrator" has the same meaning as in Part I of the Arbitration Act 1996;'.

Agricultural Marketing Act 1958 (c 47)

12. In section 12(1) of the Agricultural Marketing Act 1958 (application of provisions of Arbitration Act 1950)—

    (a)   for the words from the beginning to 'shall apply' substitute 'Sections 45 and 69 of the Arbitration Act 1996 (which relate to the determination by the court of questions of law) and section 66 of that Act (enforcement of awards) apply'; and

    (b)   for 'an arbitration' substitute 'arbitral proceedings'.

Carriage by Air Act 1961 (c 27)

13.—(1) The Carriage by Air Act 1961 is amended as follows.

(2) In section 5(3) (time for bringing proceedings)—

(*a*)   for 'an arbitration' in the first place where it occurs substitute 'arbitral proceedings'; and

(*b*)   for the words from 'and subsections (3) and (4)' to the end substitute 'and the provisions of section 14 of the Arbitration Act 1996 apply to determine when such proceedings are commenced.'.

(3) In section 11(*c*) (application of section 5 to Scotland)—

(*a*)   for 'subsections (3) and (4)' substitute 'the provisions of section 14 of the Arbitration Act 1996'; and

(*b*)   for 'an arbitration' substitute 'arbitral proceedings'.

Factories Act 1961 (c 34)

14. In the Factories Act 1961, for section 171 (application of Arbitration Act 1950), substitute—

'Application of the Arbitration Act 1996

171. Part I of the Arbitration Act 1996 does not apply to proceedings under this Act except in so far as it may be applied by regulations made under this Act.'.

Clergy Pensions Measure 1961 (No 3)

15. In the Clergy Pensions Measure 1961, section 38(4) (determination of questions), for the words 'The Arbitration Act 1950' substitute 'Part I of the Arbitration Act 1996'.

Transport Act 1962 (c 46)

16.—(1) The Transport Act 1962 is amended as follows.

(2) In section 74(6)(*f*) (proceedings before referees in pension disputes), for the words 'the Arbitration Act 1950' substitute 'Part I of the Arbitration Act 1996'.

(3) In section 81(7) (proceedings before referees in compensation disputes), for the words 'the Arbitration Act 1950' substitute 'Part I of the Arbitration Act 1996'.

(4) In Schedule 7, Part IV (pensions), in paragraph 17(5) for the words 'the Arbitration Act 1950' substitute 'Part I of the Arbitration Act 1996'.

Corn Rents Act 1963 (c 14)

17. In the Corn Rents Act 1963, section 1(5) (schemes for apportioning corn rents, &c), for the words 'the Arbitration Act 1950' substitute 'Part I of the Arbitration Act 1996'.

Plant Varieties and Seeds Act 1964 (c 14)

18. In section 10(6) of the Plant Varieties and Seeds Act 1964 (meaning of 'arbitration agreement'), for 'the meaning given by section 32 of the Arbitration Act 1950' substitute 'the same meaning as in Part I of the Arbitration Act 1996'.

Lands Tribunal and Compensation Act (Northern Ireland) 1964 c 29 (NI))

19. In section 9 of the Lands Tribunal and Compensation Act (Northern

Ireland) 1964 (proceedings of Lands Tribunal), in subsection (3) (where Tribunal acts as arbitrator) for 'the Arbitration Act (Northern Ireland) 1937' substitute 'Part I of the Arbitration Act 1996'.

Industrial and Provident Societies Act 1965 (c 12)

20.—(1) Section 60 of the Industrial and Provident Societies Act 1965 is amended as follows.

(2) In subsection (8) (procedure for hearing disputes between society and member, &c)—

> (a) in paragraph (a) for 'the Arbitration Act 1950' substitute 'Part I of the Arbitration Act 1996'; and
>
> (b) in paragraph (b) omit 'by virtue of section 12 of the said Act of 1950'.

(3) For subsection (9) substitute—

> '(9) The court or registrar to whom any dispute is referred under subsections (2) to (7) may at the request of either party state a case on any question of law arising in the dispute for the opinion of the High Court or, as the case may be, the Court of Session.'.

Carriage of Goods by Road Act 1965 (c 37)

21. In section 7(2) of the Carriage of Goods by Road Act 1965 (arbitrations: time at which deemed to commence), for paragraphs (a) and (b) substitute—

> '(a) as respects England and Wales and Northern Ireland, the provisions of section 14(3) to (5) of the Arbitration Act 1996 (which determine the time at which an arbitration is commenced) apply;'.

Factories Act (Northern Ireland) 1965 (c 20 (NI))

22. In section 171 of the Factories Act (Northern Ireland) 1965 (application of Arbitration Act), for 'The Arbitration Act (Northern Ireland) 1937' substitute 'Part I of the Arbitration Act 1996'.

Commonwealth Secretariat Act 1966 (c 10)

23. In section 1(3) of the Commonwealth Secretariat Act 1966 (contracts with Commonwealth Secretariat to be deemed to contain provision for arbitration), for 'the Arbitration Act 1950 and the Arbitration Act (Northern Ireland) 1937' substitute 'Part I of the Arbitration Act 1996'.

Arbitration (International Investment Disputes) Act 1966 (c 41)

24. In the Arbitration (International Investment Disputes) Act 1966, for section 3 (application of Arbitration Act 1950 and other enactments) substitute—

'Application of provisions of Arbitration Act 1996

3.—(1) The Lord Chancellor may by order direct that any of the provisions contained in sections 36 and 38 to 44 of the Arbitration Act 1996 (provisions concerning the conduct of arbitral proceedings, &c) shall apply to such proceedings pursuant to the Convention as are specified in the order with or without any modifications or exceptions specified in the order.

(2) Subject to subsection (1), the Arbitration Act 1996 shall not apply to proceedings pursuant to the Convention, but this subsection shall not be taken as affecting section 9 of that Act (stay of legal proceedings in respect of matter subject to arbitration).

(3) An order made under this section—

(a)   may be varied or revoked by a subsequent order so made, and

(b)   shall be contained in a statutory instrument.'.

Poultry Improvement Act (Northern Ireland) 1968 (c 12 (NI))

25. In paragraph 10(4) of the Schedule to the Poultry Improvement Act (Northern Ireland) 1968 (reference of disputes), for 'The Arbitration Act (Northern Ireland) 1937' substitute 'Part I of the Arbitration Act 1996'.

Industrial and Provident Societies Act (Northern Ireland) 1969 (c 24 (NI))

26.—(1) Section 69 of the Industrial and Provident Societies Act (Northern Ireland) 1969 (decision of disputes) is amended as follows.

(2) In subsection (7) (decision of disputes)—

(a)   in the opening words, omit the words from 'and without prejudice' to '1937';

(b)   at the beginning of paragraph (a) insert 'without prejudice to any powers exercisable by virtue of Part I of the Arbitration Act 1996,'; and

(c)   in paragraph (b) omit 'the registrar or' and 'registrar or' and for the words from 'as might have been granted by the High Court' to the end substitute 'as might be granted by the registrar'.

(3) For subsection (8) substitute—

'(8) The court or registrar to whom any dispute is referred under subsections (2) to (6) may at the request of either party state a case on any question of law arising in the dispute for the opinion of the High Court.'.

Health and Personal Social Services (Northern Ireland) Order 1972 (NI 14)

27. In Article 105(6) of the Health and Personal Social Services (Northern Ireland) Order 1972 (arbitrations under the Order), for 'the Arbitration Act (Northern Ireland) 1937' substitute 'Part I of the Arbitration Act 1996'.

Consumer Credit Act 1974 (c 39)

28.—(1) Section 146 of the Consumer Credit Act 1974 is amended as follows.

(2) In subsection (2) (solicitor engaged in contentious business), for 'section 86(1) of the Solicitors Act 1957' substitute 'section 87(1) of the Solicitors Act 1974'.

(3) In subsection (4) (solicitor in Northern Ireland engaged in contentious business), for the words from 'business done' to 'Administration of Estates (Northern Ireland) Order 1979' substitute 'contentious business (as defined in Article 3(2) of the Solicitors (Northern Ireland) Order 1976.'.

Friendly Societies Act 1974 (c 46)

29.—(1) The Friendly Societies Act 1974 is amended as follows.

(2) For section 78(1) (statement of case) substitute—

'(1) Any arbitrator, arbiter or umpire to whom a dispute falling within section 76 above is referred under the rules of a registered society or branch may at the request of either party state a case on any question of law arising in the dispute for the opinion of the High Court or, as the case may be, the Court of Session.'.

(3) In section 83(3) (procedure on objections to amalgamations &c of friendly societies), for 'the Arbitration Act 1950 or, in Northern Ireland, the Arbitration Act (Northern Ireland) 1937' substitute 'Part I of the Arbitration Act 1996'.

Industry Act 1975 (c 68)

30. In Schedule 3 to the Industry Act (arbitration of disputes relating to vesting and compensation orders), in paragraph 14 (application of certain provisions of Arbitration Acts)—

> (a) for 'the Arbitration Act 1950 or, in Northern Ireland, the Arbitration Act (Northern Ireland) 1937' substitute 'Part I of the Arbitration Act 1996', and
> (b) for 'that Act' substitute 'that Part'.

Industrial Relations (Northern Ireland) Order 1976 (NI 16)

31. In Article 59(9) of the Industrial Relations (Northern Ireland) Order 1976 (proceedings of industrial tribunal), for 'The Arbitration Act (Northern Ireland) 1937' substitute 'Part I of the Arbitration Act 1996'.

Aircraft and Shipbuilding Industries Act 1977 (c.3)

32. In Schedule 7 to the Aircraft and Shipbuilding Industries Act 1977 (procedure of Arbitration Tribunal), in paragraph 2—

> (a) for 'the Arbitration Act 1950 or, in Northern Ireland, the Arbitration Act (Northern Ireland) 1937' substitute 'Part I of the Arbitration Act 1996', and
> (b) for 'that Act' substitute 'that Part'.

Patents Act 1977 (c 37)

33. In section 130 of the Patents Act 1977 (interpretation), in subsection (8) (exclusion of Arbitration Act) for 'The Arbitration Act 1950' substitute 'Part I of the Arbitration Act 1996'.

Judicature (Northern Ireland) Act 1978 (c 23)

34.—(1) The Judicature (Northern Ireland) Act 1978 is amended as follows.

(2) In section 35(2) (restrictions on appeals to the Court of Appeal), after paragraph (*f*) insert—

'(*fa*) except as provided by Part I of the Arbitration Act 1996, from any decision of the High Court under that Part;'.

(3) In section 55(2) (rules of court) after paragraph (*c*) insert—

'(*cc*) providing for any prescribed part of the jurisdiction of the High Court in relation to the trial of any action involving matters of account to be exercised in the prescribed manner by a person agreed by the parties and for the remuneration of any such person;'.

Health and Safety at Work (Northern Ireland) Order 1978 (NI 9)

35. In Schedule 4 to the Health and Safety at Work (Northern Ireland) Order 1978 (licensing provisions), in paragraph 3, for 'The Arbitration Act (Northern Ireland) 1937' substitute 'Part I of the Arbitration Act 1996'.

County Courts (Northern Ireland) Order 1980 (NI 3)

36.—(1) The County Courts (Northern Ireland) Order 1980 is amended as follows.

(2) In Article 30 (civil jurisdiction exercisable by district judge)—

(*a*) for paragraph (2) substitute—

'(2) Any order, decision or determination made by a district judge under this Article (other than one made in dealing with a claim by way of arbitration under paragraph (3)) shall be embodied in a decree which for all purposes (including the right of appeal under Part VI) shall have the like effect as a decree pronounced by a county court judge.';

(*b*) for paragraphs (4) and (5) substitute—

'(4) Where in any action to which paragraph (1) applies the claim is dealt with by way of arbitration under paragraph (3)—
    (*a*)   any award made by the district judge in dealing with the claim shall be embodied in a decree which for all purposes (except the right of appeal under Part VI) shall have the like effect as a decree pronounced by a county court judge;
    (*b*)   the district judge may, and shall if so required by the High Court, state for the determination of the High Court any question of law arising out of an award so made;
    (*c*)   except as provided by sub-paragraph (*b*), any award so made shall be final; and
    (*d*)   except as otherwise provided by county court rules,

>>> no costs shall be awarded in connection with the action.

>> (5) Subject to paragraph (4), county court rules may—

>>> (*a*) apply any of the provisions of Part I of the Arbitration Act 1996 to arbitrations under paragraph (3) with such modifications as may be prescribed;

>>> (*b*) prescribe the rules of evidence to be followed on any arbitration under paragraph (3) and, in particular, make provision with respect to the manner of taking and questioning evidence.

>> (5A) Except as provided by virtue of paragraph (5)(*a*), Part I of the Arbitration Act 1996 shall not apply to an arbitration under paragraph (3).'.

> (3) After Article 61 insert—

'Appeals from decisions under Part I of Arbitration Act 1996

61A.—(1) Article 61 does not apply to a decision of a county court judge made in the exercise of the jurisdiction conferred by Part I of the Arbitration Act 1996.

(2) Any party dissatisfied with a decision of the county court made in the exercise of the jurisdiction conferred by any of the following provisions of Part I of the Arbitration Act 1996, namely—

>> (*a*) section 32 (question as to substantive jurisdiction of arbitral tribunal);

>> (*b*) section 45 (question of law arising in course of arbitral proceedings);

>> (*c*) section 67 (challenging award of arbitral tribunal: substantive jurisdiction);

>> (*d*) section 68 (challenging award of arbitral tribunal: serious irregularity);

>> (*e*) section 69 (appeal on point of law),

may, subject to the provisions of that Part, appeal from that decision to the Court of Appeal.

(3) Any party dissatisfied with any decision of a county court made in the exercise of the jurisdiction conferred by any other provision of Part I of the Arbitration Act 1996 may, subject to the provisions of that Part, appeal from that decision to the High Court.

(4) The decision of the Court of Appeal on an appeal under paragraph (2) shall be final.'.

Supreme Court Act 1981 (c 54)

37.—(1) The Supreme Court Act 1981 is amended as follows.

(2) In section 18(1) (restrictions on appeals to the Court of Appeal), for paragraph (*g*) substitute—

'(*g*)   except as provided by Part I of the Arbitration Act 1996, from any decision of the High Court under that Part;'.

(3) In section 151 (interpretation, &c), in the definition of 'arbitration agreement', for 'the Arbitration Act 1950 by virtue of section 32 of that Act;' substitute 'Part I of the Arbitration Act 1996;'.

Merchant Shipping (Liner Conferences) Act 1982 (c.37)

38. In section 7(5) of the Merchant Shipping (Liner Conferences) Act 1982 (stay of legal proceedings), for the words from 'section 4(1)' to the end substitute 'section 9 of the Arbitration Act 1996 (which also provides for the staying of legal proceedings).'.

Agricultural Marketing (Northern Ireland) Order 1982 (NI 12)

39. In Article 14 of the Agricultural Marketing (Northern Ireland) Order 1982 (application of provisions of Arbitration Act (Northern Ireland) 1937)—

(*a*)   for the words from the beginning to 'shall apply' substitute 'Section 45 and 69 of the Arbitration Act 1996 (which relate to the determination by the court of questions of law) and section 66 of that Act (enforcement of awards)' apply; and

(*b*)   for 'an arbitration' substitute 'arbitral proceedings'.

Mental Health Act 1983 (c 20)

40. In section 78 of the Mental Health Act 1983 (procedure of Mental Health Review Tribunals), in subsection (9) for 'The Arbitration Act 1950' substitute 'Part I of the Arbitration Act 1996'.

Registered Homes Act 1984 (c 23)

41. In section 43 of the Registered Homes Act 1984 (procedure of Registered Homes Tribunals), in subsection (3) for 'The Arbitration Act 1950' substitute 'Part I of the Arbitration Act 1996'.

Housing Act 1985 (c 68)

42. In section 47(3) of the Housing Act 1985 (agreement as to determination of matters relating to service charges) for 'section 32 of the Arbitration Act 1950' substitute 'Part I of the Arbitration Act 1996'.

Landlord and Tenant Act 1985 (c 70)

43. In section 19(3) of the Landlord and Tenant Act 1985 (agreement as to determination of matters relating to service charges), for 'section 32 of the Arbitration Act 1950' substitute 'Part I of the Arbitration Act 1996'.

Credit Unions (Northern Ireland) Order 1985 (NI 12)

44.—(1) Article 72 of the Credit Unions (Northern Ireland) Order 1985 (decision of disputes) is amended as follows.

(2) In paragraph (7)—

(*a*)   in the opening words, omit the words from 'and without prejudice' to '1937';

(b) at the beginning of sub-paragraph (a) insert 'without prejudice to any powers exercisable by virtue of Part I of the Arbitration Act 1996,'; and

(c) in sub-paragraph (b) omit 'the registrar or' and 'registrar or' and for the words from 'as might have been granted by the High Court' to the end substitute 'as might be granted by the registrar'.

(3) For paragraph (8) substitute—

'(8) The court or registrar to whom any dispute is referred under paragraphs (2) to (6) may at the request of either party state a case on any question of law arising in the dispute for the opinion of the High Court.'.

Agricultural Holdings Act 1986 (c 5)

45. In section 84(1) of the Agricultural Holdings Act 1986 (provisions relating to arbitration), for 'the Arbitration Act 1950' substitute 'Part I of the Arbitration Act 1996'.

Insolvency Act 1986 (c 45)

46. In the Insolvency Act 1986, after section 349 insert—

'Arbitration agreements to which bankrupt is party

349A.—(1) This section applies where a bankrupt had become party to a contract containing an arbitration agreement before the commencement of his bankruptcy.

(2) If the trustee in bankruptcy adopts the contract, the arbitration agreement is enforceable by or against the trustee in relation to matters arising from or connected with the contract.

(3) If the trustee in bankruptcy does not adopt the contract and a matter to which the arbitration agreement applies requires to be determined in connection with or for the purposes of the bankruptcy proceedings—

(a) the trustee with the consent of the creditors' committee, or
(b) any other party to the agreement,

may apply to the court which may, if it thinks fit in all the circumstances of the case, order that the matter be referred to arbitration in accordance with the arbitration agreement.

(4) In this section—

"arbitration agreement" has the same meaning as in Part I of the Arbitration Act 1996; and
"the court" means the court which has jurisdiction in the bankruptcy proceedings.'.

Building Societies Act 1986 (c 53)

47. In Part II of Schedule 14 to the Building Societies Act 1986 (settlement of disputes: arbitration), in paragraph 5(6) for 'the Arbitration

Act 1950 and the Arbitration Act 1979 or, in Northern Ireland, the Arbitration Act (Northern Ireland) 1937' substitute 'Part I of the Arbitration Act 1996'.

Mental Health (Northern Ireland) Order 1986 (NI 4)

48. In Article 83 of the Mental Health (Northern Ireland) Order 1986 (procedure of Mental Health Review Tribunal), in paragraph (8) for 'The Arbitration Act (Northern Ireland) 1937' substitute 'Part I of the Arbitration Act 1996'.

Multilateral Investment Guarantee Agency Act 1988 (c 8)

49. For section 6 of the Multilateral Investment Guarantee Agency Act 1988 (application of Arbitration Act) substitute—

'Application of Arbitration Act

6.—(1) The Lord Chancellor may by order made by statutory instrument direct that any of the provisions of sections 36 and 38 to 44 of the Arbitration Act 1996 (provisions in relation to the conduct of the arbitral proceedings, &c) apply, with such modifications or exceptions as are specified in the order, to such arbitration proceedings pursuant to Annex II to the Convention as are specified in the order.

(2) Except as provided by an order under subsection (1) above, no provision of Part I of the Arbitration Act 1996 other than section 9 (stay of legal proceedings) applies to any such proceedings.'.

Copyright, Designs and Patents Act 1988 (c 48)

50. In section 150 of the Copyright, Designs and Patents Act 1988 (Lord Chancellor's power to make rules for Copyright Tribunal), for subsection (2) substitute—

'(2) The rules may apply in relation to the Tribunal, as respects proceedings in England and Wales or Northern Ireland, any of the provisions of Part I of the Arbitration Act 1996.'.

Fair Employment (Northern Ireland) Act 1989 (c 32)

51. In the Fair Employment (Northern Ireland) Act 1989, section 5(7) (procedure of Fair Employment Tribunal), for 'The Arbitration Act (Northern Ireland) 1937' substitute 'Part I of the Arbitration Act 1996'.

Limitation (Northern Ireland) Order 1989 (NI 11)

52. In Article 2(2) of the Limitation (Northern Ireland) Order 1989 (interpretation), in the definition of 'arbitration agreement', for 'the Arbitration Act (Northern Ireland) 1937' substitute 'Part I of the Arbitration Act 1996'.

Insolvency (Northern Ireland) Order 1989 (NI 9)

53. In the Insolvency (Northern Ireland) Order 1989, after Article 320 insert—

'Arbitration agreements to which bankrupt is party.

320A.—(1) This Article applies where a bankrupt had become party to a contract containing an arbitration agreement before the commencement of his bankruptcy.

(2) If the trustee in bankruptcy adopts the contract, the arbitration agreement is enforceable by or against the trustee in relation to matters arising from or connected with the contract.

(3) If the trustee in bankruptcy does not adopt the contract and a matter to which the arbitration agreement applies requires to be determined in connection with or for the purposes of the bankruptcy proceedings—

(a)   the trustee with the consent of the creditors' committee, or
(b)   any other party to the agreement,

may apply to the court which may, if it thinks fit in all the circumstances of the case, order that the matter be referred to arbitration in accordance with the arbitration agreement.

(4) In this Article—

"arbitration agreement" has the same meaning as in Part I of the Arbitration Act 1996; and
"the court" means the court which has jurisdiction in the bankruptcy proceedings.'

Social Security Administration Act 1992 (c 5)

54. In section 59 of the Social Security Administration Act 1992 (procedure for inquiries, &c), in subsection (7), for 'The Arbitration Act 1950' substitute 'Part I of the Arbitration Act 1996'.

Social Security Administration (Northern Ireland) Act 1992 (c 8)

55. In section 57 of the Social Security Administration (Northern Ireland) Act 1992 (procedure for inquiries, &c), in subsection (6) for 'the Arbitration Act (Northern Ireland) 1937' substitute 'Part I of the Arbitration Act 1996'.

Trade Union and Labour Relations (Consolidation) Act 1992 (c 52)

56. In sections 212(5) and 263(6) of the Trade Union and Labour Relations (Consolidation) Act 1992 (application of Arbitration Act) for 'the Arbitration Act 1950' substitute 'Part I of the Arbitration Act 1996'.

Industrial Relations (Northern Ireland) Order 1992 (NI 5)

57. In Articles 84(9) and 92(5) of the Industrial Relations (Northern Ireland) Order 1992 (application of Arbitration Act) for 'The Arbitration Act (Northern Ireland) 1937' substitute 'Part I of the Arbitration Act 1996'.

Registered Homes (Northern Ireland) Order 1992 (NI 20)

58. In Article 33(3) of the Registered Homes (Northern Ireland) Order

1992 (procedure of Registered Homes Tribunal) for 'The Arbitration Act (Northern Ireland) 1937' substitute 'Part I of the Arbitration Act 1996'.

Education Act 1993 (c 35)

59. In section 180(4) of the Education Act 1993 (procedure of Special Educational Needs Tribunal), for 'The Arbitration Act 1950' substitute 'Part I of the Arbitration Act 1996'.

Roads (Northern Ireland) Order 1993 (NI 15)

60.—(1) The Roads (Northern Ireland) Order 1993 is amended as follows.

(2) In Article 131 (application of Arbitration Act) for 'the Arbitration (Northern Ireland) 1937' substitute 'Part I of the Arbitration Act 1996'.

(3) In Schedule 4 (disputes), in paragraph 3(2) for 'the Arbitration (Northern Ireland) 1937' substitute 'Part I of the Arbitration Act 1996'.

Merchant Shipping Act 1995 (c 21)

61. In Part II of Schedule 6 to the Merchant Shipping Act 1995 (provisions having effect in connection with Convention Relating to the Carriage of Passengers and Their Luggage by Sea), for paragraph 7 substitute—

'7. Article 16 shall apply to arbitral proceedings as it applies to an action; and, as respects England and Wales and Northern Ireland, the provisions of section 14 of the Arbitration Act 1996 apply to determine for the purposes of that Article when an arbitration is commenced.'.

Industrial Tribunals Act 1996 (c 17)

62. In section 6(2) of the Industrial Tribunals Act 1996 (procedure of industrial tribunals), for 'The Arbitration Act 1950' substitute 'Part I of the Arbitration Act 1996'.

Schedule 4   Repeals

Section 107(2)

Chapter	Short title	Extent of repeal
1892 c 43	Military Lands Act 1892	In section 21(*b*), the words 'under the Arbitration Act 1889'.
1922 c 51	Allotments Act 1922	In section 21(3), the words 'under the Arbitration Act 1889'.
1937 c 8 (NI)	Arbitration Act (Northern Ireland) 1937	The whole Act.
1949 c 54	Wireless Telegraphy Act 1949	In Schedule 2, paragraph 3(3).

Chapter	Short title	Extent of repeal
1949 c 97	National Parks and Access to the Countryside Act 1949	In section 18(4), the words from 'Without prejudice' to 'England or Wales'.
1950 c 27	Arbitration Act 1950	Part I. Section 42(3).
1958 c 47	Agricultural Marketing Act 1958	Section 53(8).
1962 c 46	Transport Act 1962	In Schedule 11, Part II, paragraph 7.
1964 c 14	Plant Varieties and Seeds Act 1964	In section 10(4) the words from 'or in section 9' to 'three arbitrators)'. Section 39(3)(*b*)(i).
1964 c 29 (NI)	Lands Tribunal and Compensation Act (Northern Ireland) 1964	In section 9(3) the words from 'so, however, that' to the end.
1965 c 12	Industrial and Provident Societies Act 1965	In section 60(8)(*b*), the words 'by virtue of section 12 of the said Act of 1950'.
1965 c 37	Carriage of Goods by Road Act 1965	Section 7(2)(*b*).
1965 c 13 (NI)	New Towns Act (Northern Ireland) 1965	In section 27(2), the words from 'under and in accordance with' to the end.
1969 c 24 (NI)	Industrial and Provident Societies Act (Northern Ireland) 1969	In section 69(7)— (*a*) in the opening words, the words from 'and without prejudice' to '1937'; (*b*) in paragraph (*b*), the words 'the registrar or' and 'registrar or'.
1970 c 31	Administration of Justice Act 1970	Section 4. Schedule 3.
1973 c 41	Fair Trading Act	Section 33(2)(*d*).

Chapter	Short title	Extent of repeal
1973 NI 1	Drainage (Northern Ireland) Order 1973	In Article 15(4), the words from 'under and in accordance' to the end. Article 40(4) In Schedule 7, in paragraph 9(2), the words from 'under and in accordance' to the end.
1974 c 47	Solicitors Act 1974	In section 87(1), in the definition of 'contentious business', the words 'appointed under the Arbitration Act 1950'.
1975 c 3	Arbitration Act 1975	The whole Act.
1975 c 74	Petroleum and Submarine Pipe-Lines Act 1975	In Part II of Schedule 2— (*a*) in model clause 40(2), the words 'in accordance with the Arbitration Act 1950'; (*b*) in model clause 40(2B), the words 'in accordance with the Arbitration Act (Northern Ireland) 1937'. In Part II of Schedule 3, in model clause 38(2), the words 'in accordance with the Arbitration Act 1950'.
1976 NI 12	Solicitors (Northern Ireland) Order 1976	In Article 3(2), in the entry 'contentious business', the words 'appointed under the Arbitration Act (Northern Ireland)

Chapter	Short title	Extent of repeal
1977 c 37	Patents Act 1977	In section 52(4) the words 'section 21 of the Arbitration Act 1950 or, as the case may be, section 22 of the Arbitration Act (Northern Ireland) 1937 (statement of cases by arbitrators); but'. Section 131(*e*).
1977 c 38	Administration of Justice Act 1977	Section 17(2).
1978 c 23	Judicature (Northern Ireland) Act 1978	In section 35(2), paragraph (*g*)(v). In Schedule 5, the amendment to the Arbitration Act 1950.
1979 c 42	Arbitration Act 1979	The whole Act.
1980 c 58	Limitation Act 1980	Section 34.
1980 NI 3	County Courts (Northern Ireland) Order 1980	Article 31(3).
1981 c 54	Supreme Court Act 1981	Section 148.
1982 c 27	Civil Jurisdiction and Judgments Act 1982	Section 25(3)(*c*) and (5) In section 26 (*a*) in subsection (1), the words 'to arbitration or'; (*b*) in subsection (1)(*a*)(i), the words 'arbitration or'; (*c*) in subsection (2), the words 'arbitration or'.
1982 c 53	Administration of Justice Act 1982	Section 15(6) In Schedule 1, Part IV.
1984 c 5	Merchant Shipping Act 1984	Section 4(8).
1984 c 12	Telecommunications Act 1984	Schedule 2, paragraph 13(8).

Chapter	Short title	Extent of repeal
1984 c 16	Foreign Limitation Periods Act 1984	Section 5.
1984 c 28	County Courts Act 1984	In Schedule 2, paragraph 70.
1985 c 61	Administration of Justice Act 1985	Section 58. In Schedule 9, paragraph 15.
1985 c 68	Housing Act 1985	In Schedule 18, in paragraph 6(2) the words from 'and the Arbitration Act 1950' to the end.
1985 NI 12	Credit Unions (Northern Ireland) Order 1985	In Article 72(7)— (*a*) in the opening words, the words from 'and without prejudice' to '1937'; (*b*) in subparagraph (*b*), the words 'the registrar or' and 'registrar or'.
1986 c 45	Insolvency Act 1986	In Schedule 14, the entry relating to the Arbitration Act 1950.
1988 c 8	Multilateral Investment Guarantee Agency Act 1988	Section 8(3).
1988 c 21	Consumer Arbitration Agreements Act 1988	The whole Act.
1989 NI 11	Limitation (Northern Ireland) Order 1989	Article 72. In Schedule 3, paragraph 1.
1989 NI 19	Insolvency (Northern Ireland) Order 1989	In Part II of Schedule 9, paragraph 66.
1990 c 41	Courts and Legal Services Act 1990	Sections 99 and 101 to 103.
1991 NI 7	Food Safety (Northern Ireland) Order 1991	In Articles 8(8) and 11(10), the words from 'and the provisions' to the end.

Chapter	Short title	Extent of repeal
1992 c 40	Friendly Societies Act 1992	In Schedule 16, paragraph 30(1).
1995 c 8	Agricultural Tenancies Act 1995	Section 28(4).
1995 c 21	Merchant Shipping Act 1995	Section 96(10). Section 264(9).
1995 c 42	Private International Law (Miscellaneous Provisions) Act 1995	Section 3.

Matters on which Parties May Agree

(References are to sections of the Act)

Matters which they are free to *agree* or may agree

3(*a*)   Seat of the arbitration

4(3)   Arrangements for agreement

14(1)   When arbitration proceedings to be regarded as commenced

15(1)   Number of arbitrators and whether chairman or umpire

18(1)   What is to happen in the event of a failure of the procedure for appointment of the tribunal

20(1)   Functions of chairman of tribunal in relation to the making of decisions, orders and awards

21(1)   Functions of an umpire, in particular whether he is to attend the proceedings and when he is to replace the other arbitrators

22(1)   Where two or more arbitrators with no chairman or umpire, how the tribunal is to make decisions, orders and awards

23(1)   In what circumstances the authority of an arbitrator may be revoked

23(4)   Whether to revoke the arbitration agreement

25(1)   (With an arbitrator) the consequences of his resignation

27(1)   Filling of vacancies etc on arbitrator ceasing to hold office

34(1)   Any procedural or evidential matter

35(1)   Consolidation of arbitral proceedings or holding of concurrent hearings

38(1) Powers exercisable by tribunal for the purposes of and in relation to the proceedings

39(1) Power of tribunal to order relief on a provisional basis

41(1) Powers of tribunal in case of a party's default

46(1) Law to be applicable to the substance of the dispute or what other considerations are to apply

48(1) Powers exercisable by tribunal as regards remedies

49(1) Powers of the tribunal to award interest

52(1) Form of an award

55(1) Requirements as to notification of award to the parties

57(1) Powers of the tribunal to correct an award or make an additional award

60 Party is to pay whole or part of the costs of the arbitration provided that the agreement is made after the dispute has arisen

63(1) What costs to be recoverable

76 Manner of service of notices and other documents

78(1) Method of reckoning periods of time

Matters which may be *excluded* by agreement

7 Separability of arbitration agreement

8(1) Agreement not to be discharged by death of a party

17(1) Party may appoint his own arbitrator as sole arbitrator in case of default

26(2) Death of party not to revoke arbitrator's authority

30(1) Tribunal to have power to rule on its own jurisdiction

36(1) Right of party to be represented by a lawyer or other person chosen by him

37(1) Power of tribunal to appoint experts, legal advisers or assessors

42(1) Power of court to make an order requiring a party to comply with a peremptory order of the tribunal

44(1) Power of court to make orders in support of arbitral proceedings

45(1) Power of court, upon application, to determine a question of law arising during the arbitral proceedings (in domestic arbitrations, only where agreement made *after* arbitration commenced. See note on p 243 concerning possible change of law)

47(1) Power of tribunal to make awards on different issues

50(1)   Power of court to extend time for making an award

51(1)   Provisions to apply in the case of settlement of the dispute

53   That, where seat of arbitration is in England and Wales or Northern Ireland, award to be treated as being made there regardless of where signed

54(1)   Power of tribunal to decide date on which award is made

58(1)   That award be final and binding

61(2)   That tribunal awards costs on the general principle that costs follow the event

62   That agreement between parties as to how costs to be borne to extend only to such costs as are recoverable

64   That recoverable costs to include only such fees and expenses of the arbitrators as are reasonable

65   Power of tribunal to direct that recoverable costs be limited to a specified amount

69   Right of party to appeal to the court on a question of law arising out of an award (in domestic arbitrations, only where agreement made after arbitration commenced. See note on p 243 concerning possible change of law)

77(2)   Power of court to make an order in relation to service of documents

79(1)   Power of court to extend time limits generally

Appendix 3

Checklist for Preliminary Meetings

[*Note*: Not all of the following will necessarily be discussed or settled at the preliminary meeting. Many items may be deferred for subsequent meetings after statement of case and/or for pre-hearing review.]

1   General description of issues

2   Whether any issues of jurisdiction arise

3   Whether dispute to be decided in accordance with law or other considerations. What considerations

4   General form of proceedings, eg whether hearing required; languages; translation of documents; any special requirements as to service or delivery of documents

5   Whether arbitrator to have power to make provisional awards

6   Whether arbitrator's default powers to be modified

7   Any matters which may be tried as preliminary issues, or whether issues, and if so what issues, may be heard separately

8   Form of statements of case whether:
   — full narrative statements
   — *Scott* schedules
   — lists of documents relied upon to be annexed
   — copies of all or only principal documents relied upon to be annexed
   — Witness statements/experts' reports to be annexed
   — statements of reply to defence(s) to be allowed?

9   Timing of statements of case:
   — Claim
   — Defence
   — Counterclaim
   — Defence to counterclaim
   — Replies (if allowed)

10 Whether requests for further and better particulars to be allowed; if so time for delivery and reply

11   Whether interlocutories to be allowed; if so times for delivery and reply

12   Any special requirements as to disclosure of documents

13   Time of exchange of witness statements (if not annexed to statements of case). Statements in rebuttal

14   Expert witnesses:
   —   whether limitation of number for each party. Parties to notify each other of identity and disciplines
   —   time for exchange of reports. Timing of meetings of experts of like discipline. Whether joint reports on areas of agreement and disagreement to be prepared

15   Whether experts/legal advisers/technical assessors to be appointed

16   Whether site inspection required; date; who to be present

17   Date of pre-hearing review

18   Date and location of hearing(s); who is to arrange venue

19   Form of hearing; any limitations as to timing of submissions, cross-examination etc; whether witness statements to stand as evidence-in-chief; adversarial or inquisitorial procedure

20   Representation at hearing

21   Preparation of documents for hearing

22   Whether strict rules of evidence to be applied

23   Whether witnesses to be heard on oath/affirmation

24   Whether transcript of hearing required: if so, arrangements

25   Any requirement as to form of award

26   Any limitation on costs

27   Whether parties wish to exclude reference to the court on questions of law/appeal

28   Dates for further meetings/pre-hearing review

29   Costs of meeting and subsequent order

30   Any other business

List of Arbitrator's Powers and Duties

(References are to sections of the Act)

Arbitrators have the following powers *irrespective* of the parties' agreement

61(1) Make an award allocating the costs of the arbitration as between the parties (but any award so made must have regard to any agreement between the parties under s 60)

67(3) Continue the proceedings and make a further award while an application to the court is pending relating to his substantive jurisdiction

Arbitrators have the following powers *unless* the parties agree otherwise

30(1) Rule on his own substantive jurisdiction

34(1) Decide all procedural and evidential matters

34(3) Fix and extend the time within which directions are to be complied with

37(1) Appoint experts or legal advisers and technical assessors

38(3) Order claimant to provide security for the costs of the arbitration

38(4) Give directions in relation to any property which is the subject of the proceedings and as to which any question arises in the proceedings

38(5) Direct that a party or witness shall be examined on oath or affirmation and for that purpose administer any oath or take any affirmation

38(6) Give directions to a party for the preservation of any evidence in its custody or control

41(3) Make an award dismissing a claim if there has been inordinate and inexcusable delay on the part of the claimant

41(4) Continue with the proceedings in the absence of a party if that party fails to attend or be represented at an oral hearing or fails after due notice to submit written evidence or make written submissions

41(5) Make a peremptory order if a party fails to comply with any order or directions issued

41(6) Make an award dismissing the claim if a claimant fails to comply with an order to provide security for costs under section 38(3)

41(7) Take the following action if a party fails to comply with a peremptory order made under section 41(5):

(a) direct that the party in default shall not be entitled to rely upon any allegation or material which was the subject matter of the order;

(b) draw such adverse inferences from the act of non-compliance as the circumstances justify;

(c) proceed to an award on the basis of such materials as have been properly provided;

(d) make such order as he thinks fit as to payment of costs of the arbitration incurred as a consequence of the non-compliance

47(1) Make more than one award at different times on different aspects of the matter to be determined

48(3) Make a declaration as to any matter to be determined

48(4) Order the payment of a sum of money in any currency

48(5) Have the same powers of the court to:

(a) order a party to do or refrain from doing anything;

(b) order specific performance of a contract;

(c) order the rectification, setting aside or cancellation of a deed or other document

49(3) Award simple or compound interest:

(a) on the whole or part of an amount awarded;

(b) on the whole or part of any amount claimed in the arbitration and outstanding at the commencement of the proceedings but paid before the award was made

49(4) Award simple or compound interest on the outstanding amount of any award

54(1) Decide what is to be taken as the date on which the award was made

57(3) On his own initiative or on the application of a party but after affording the other parties a reasonable opportunity to make representations:

    (*a*) correct an award to remove any clerical mistake or error arising from an accidental slip or omission or clarify and remove any ambiguity;

    (*b*) make an additional award in respect of any claim presented but not dealt with in the award

63(3) Determine the recoverable costs of the arbitration

65(1) Direct that the recoverable costs of the arbitration shall not exceed a specified amount

Arbitrators have the following powers if the parties so agree

35(1) (Subject to the terms of the parties' agreement) order consolidation of proceedings or concurrent hearings

39(1) Order on a provisional basis any relief which he would have power to grant in a final award

Arbitrators have the following *duties* irrespective of the parties' agreement

33(1) (*a*) to act fairly and impartially as between the parties, giving each party a reasonable opportunity of putting his case and dealing with that of his opponent;

    (*b*) to adopt procedures suitable to the circumstances of the case, avoiding unnecessary delay or expense so as to provide a fair means for the resolution of the matters to be determined

Arbitrators have the following duty *unless* the parties agree otherwise

61(2) Award costs on the general principle that costs follow the event unless it appears to him that this is not appropriate in the circumstances

Index